AMERICAN MOVIE AUDIENCES

From the Turn of the Century to the
Early Sound Era

Edited by

Melvyn Stokes and Richard Maltby

 Publishing

First published in 1999 by the
British Film Institute
21 Stephen Street, London W1P 2LN

The British Film Institute is the UK national agency with responsibility for encouraging
the arts of film and television and conserving them in the national interest.

Cover design: **ketchup**
Cover image: Crowd at opening of MGM's *The Temptress* at Loew's Warfield Theatre,
New York, October 1926.

Set in Minion by Fakenham Photosetting Limited, Fakenham, Norfolk
Printed in Great Britain by St Edmundsbury Press, Bury St Edmunds

British Library Cataloguing-in-Publication Data
A catalogue record for this book is available from the British Library
ISBN 0–85170–722–X hbk
ISBN 0–85170–721–1 pbk

Contents

List of Contributors

Giorgio Bertellini is currently completing his dissertation on silent film spectatorship at New York University. He is the author of *Emir Kusturica* (Milan, 1996) and of articles published in *Film History, Film Quarterly* and *KINtop*. He has contributed to several anthologies, including *Suburban Discipline, Cinéma: Cent Ans Après*, and *Storia del cinema mondiale*. He has taught film studies at New York University, University of California-Davis and the CUNY-Queen's College.

Leslie Midkiff DeBauche is a professor in the Division of Communication at the University of Wisconsin-Stevens Point. She is the author of *Reel Patriotism: the Movies and World War I* (University of Wisconsin Press, 1997). She is currently working on a study of the films of Mary Pickford.

Thomas Doherty is associate professor of American Studies and chair of the Film Studies Programme at Brandeis University. His most recent book is *Pre-Code Hollywood: Sex, Immorality, and Insurrection in American Cinema, 1930–1934* (Columbia University Press, 1999).

Kathryn Helgesen Fuller is assistant professor of history at Virginia Commonwealth University, where she teaches nineteenth and twentieth century American social history and media studies. She is the author of *At the Picture Show: Small Town Audiences and the Creation of Movie Fan Culture* and co-author, with Garth S. Jowett and Ian C. Jarvie, of *Children and the Movies: Media Influence and the Payne Fund Controversy* (Cambridge University Press, 1996). She is currently completing a study of early film exhibitors Bert and Fannie Cook.

Lee Grieveson is Lecturer in Cinema Studies at the University of Exeter. He has published work in *Screen, New Formations*, and *Cinema Journal*. He is currently completing a study of the regulation of early American cinema.

Alison Griffiths is Assistant Professor in the Department of Speech at Baruch College, CUNY, where she teaches film and media studies. She has published work on early cinema in *Wide Angle, Visual Anthropology Review*, and several anthologies. Her book on the origins of ethnographic film will shortly be published by Columbia University Press.

James Latham is a doctoral candidate in the department of Cinema Studies at New York University. He is completing a dissertation on representation, including depictions of race and ethnicity, in the advertising imagery of early Hollywood. He has taught at New York University and Brooklyn College and has worked as a gallery lecturer at the Museum of Modern Art in New York.

Richard Maltby is Associate Professor of Screen Studies and Head of the School of Humanities at the Flinders University of South Australia. He is the author of *Harmless Entertainment: Hollywood and the Ideology of Consensus* (Scarecrow Press, 1983) and *Hollywood Cinema: An Introduction* (Blackwell, 1995), as well as numerous articles and essays on the cultural history of American cinema. He is currently completing *Reforming the Movies: Politics, Censorship and the Institutions of the American Cinema, 1908–1939*, to be published by Oxford University Press.

Roberta Pearson is senior lecturer in the School of Journalism, Media and Cultural Studies at Cardiff University. She is currently working on a book on historiographic practice and New York City nickelodeons, co-written with William Uricchio. She co-authored, with William Uricchio, *Reframing Culture: The Case of the Vitagraph Quality Films* (Princeton University Press, 1993). Her most recent publication is *Back in the Saddle Again: New Essays on the Western*, co-edited with Edward Buscombe (British Film Institute, 1998).

Steven J. Ross is Professor of History at the University of Southern California, where he teaches courses on American social history and popular culture. He is the author of *Workers on the Edge: Work, Leisure, and Politics in Industrializing Cincinnati: 1788–1890* (Columbia University Press, 1985) and *Working-class Hollywood: Silent Film and the Shaping of Class in America* (Princeton University Press, 1998). He has also published numerous articles on film, labour, and social history.

Melvyn Stokes teaches American and film history at University College London, where he has been principal organiser of the Commonwealth Fund Conference on American History since 1988. His edited books include *Race and Class in the American South since 1890* (Berg, 1994), *The Market Revolution in America: Social, Political, and Religious Expressions, 1800–1880* (University of Virginia Press, 1996), and *The United States and the European Alliance since 1945* (Berg, 1999). He has also published numerous articles on American reform movements, historiography, and film history. He is currently finishing a study of progressive discourse in America before the First World War and researching a book on *The Birth of a Nation*.

Judith Thissen is currently at the Research Institute for History and Culture at Utrecht University in the Netherlands. She has taught film history at Amsterdam and Utrecht universities. She has published an article in *Cinema Journal* and is currently completing her doctoral dissertation, a study of movie-going among Eastern European Jewish immigrants on New York's Lower East Side between 1902 and 1914.

William Uricchio is professor and chair of Film, Television and New Media Studies at Utrecht University. His research focuses on the cultural history of media technology and practice. Forthcoming publications include *The Nickel Madness*, a sequel to his and Roberta Pearson's *Reframing Culture*, and *Blurred Vistas: The Western before 1915*.

Gregory A. Waller teaches film studies at the University of Kentucky. He is the director of *At the Picture Show*, a documentary about small-town movie-going. His recent publications include *Main Street Amusements: Movies and Commercial Entertainment in a Southern City, 1896–1930* (Smithsonian Institution, 1995), which won both the Theatre Library Association Award for 1995 and the Society for Cinema Studies's Katherine Singer Kovacs Award for 1995–97, and several articles on the New Zealand film industry.

Preface

In the past few decades, most work on film history has focused on the background to the production and exhibition of American films. In recent years, however, a number of writers have demonstrated a growing interest in how such films were received by audiences and critics. This prompted the organisation of a conference on the theme of *Hollywood and Its Spectators*, held at University College London in February 1998. The call for papers for this conference produced a truly remarkable international response, revealing the increasing salience of issues of reception in film studies as a whole. In recognition of this growing interest, the British Film Institute proposed a series of four volumes – of which this is the first – to bring together the results of contemporary research into reception.

As editors, we should like to thank Andrew Lockett, Head of Educational Publishing at the BFI, who first conceived the idea of the series. Our thanks also go to Robert C. Allen and Janet Staiger for their warm support for the project from the beginning. Tom Cabot of BFI Publishing has been very helpful in the preparation of this first volume. Amy Davis has worked extremely hard as editorial assistant on the series.

So far as the conference that served as launching-pad for the project is concerned, we should like gratefully to acknowledge financial support from the Commonwealth Fund, Graduate School, and Friends of University College London, the British Academy, the London University Institute of United States Studies, the Royal Historical Society, the History Faculty of Cambridge University, the British Film Institute, W. W. Norton and Company, and Oxford University Press.

Melvyn Stokes and Richard Maltby
February 1999

Introduction: Reconstructing American Cinema's Audiences

Melvyn Stokes

In recent years, as film scholarship has shown an increasing concern with issues surrounding the reception of cinema, one major area of investigation has been the way in which movie-going became part of everyday life in the United States. Who were the cinema's first audiences, and how heterogeneous were they in their social composition? Did the operators of the nickelodeons and converted vaudeville theatres construct their audiences primarily from the new immigrant populations of the major cities, or did they consciously seek to attract a more affluent, bourgeois audience? When, indeed, did movie-going become a common aspect of middle-class, as well as working-class, American experience? Was the American film industry's centralisation and standardisation of its mode of production in Hollywood accompanied by a comparable standardisation of the movie audience's experience and behaviour? Did audiences become more disciplined, less voluble and more passive – and if so, was this a consequence of their social composition, of the architecture of the movie theatres, or of the coming of synchronised sound?

Questions such as these reveal how relatively little we currently know, not only about who actually went to the American cinema during its first decades, but also about the social and cultural functions it performed. The ten essays in this volume all examine aspects of these two issues. With varying emphases, they analyse the nature of cinema audiences from the turn of the century to the 1930s, exploring viewers' often complex and divergent responses to film. They also investigate the ways in which audiences were perceived, both by movie exhibitors and by those who saw themselves as champions of the existing American morality and culture. In addressing these issues, the authors also consider the methodological and historiographical problems involved in seeking to reconstruct the audiences that travelling exhibitors, nickelodeon operators and the managers of picture palaces constructed.

A major problem in the attempt to map historical cinema audiences is, of course, the fact that first-hand evidence (in the form of memoirs, diaries, contemporary letters and surveys of audience opinion) is often hard to come by. Sometimes, it is true, such evidence can be found in newspaper reports or oral histories. For example, we have the testimony of a usually reliable reviewer that, when the white hero in D. W. Griffith's *The Birth of a Nation* (1915) refused to shake the hand of the black leader, audiences (presumably white) 'invariably' applauded.[1] The African-American actor William Walker has recorded the very different response to the film he shared with a black audience viewing it in a seg-regated movie-house in 1916.[2] Such contemporary or recollected accounts offer useful information on audience reactions and also on wider issues such as race relations. At various points in this book, instances of collective or individual audi-ence behaviour are mentioned: for example, the Jewish immigrant who, overcome with excitement, shouted out at the crucial moment in the action of a film. For the most part, however, the authors in this volume have explored a range of other sources in order to make up for the lack of first-hand evidence.

Several contributors have found the newspaper and periodical press of the time to be a fruitful source of material. Giorgio Bertellini, Judith Thissen and joint authors Alison Griffiths and James Latham have consulted the foreign-language or African-American press of New York City. Leslie DeBauche and Gregory Waller have examined the local press in Milwaukee and small-town Kentucky. Steven Ross has explored an array of labour, socialist and radical journals. Other sources used by contributors to illuminate the subject of early audiences include the cor-respondence of exhibitors (Bertellini and Kathryn Fuller), the records of reform, censorship and labour organisations (Lee Grieveson, Roberta Pearson and William Uricchio, Ross, Thissen), Bureau of Investigation files (Ross), city archives (Pearson and Uricchio, Thissen), poster collections (Fuller, Waller), Sears catalogues (Fuller), exhibitors' trade journals (Thomas Doherty) and oral history collections (Ross, Waller).

It seems clear that, for some time after the famous exhibition of moving pic-tures at Koster and Bial's Movie Hall in 1896, the movies did not attract the masses in the United States. Early films were projected in vaudeville theatres, opera houses, cafés, storefronts, summer parks, churches and church halls, YMCAs, department stores and schools.[3] Beginning in 1905, however, the number of store-front movie-theatres – popularly known as 'nickelodeons' – expanded enor-mously. During the next nine years, the nickelodeon, with its cheap seats, one and two reel films, and (usually) musical accompaniments, would demonstrate that there was now a mass audience for the movies.

But who made up that audience? Early writers on American cinema history assumed that audiences at nickelodeons were primarily working class.[4] This view, referred to by Judith Thissen later in this volume as the 'founding myth' of film history, was the prevailing orthodoxy until the 1970s.[5] It was seriously challenged for the first time in an essay published by Russell Merritt in 1976. Merritt argued that film exhibitors did not really approve of the working-class spectators who made up the bulk of early movie-goers. Ambitious and upwardly mobile them-selves, they sought to attract the middle-class family trade. This meant offering special concessions to women and children, showing certain types of film only, and locating nickelodeons not in working-class residential areas, but in commer-cial districts where they might better attract middle-class patrons. Using Boston as a test case, Merritt concluded that by the autumn of 1913 this strategy was pay-ing off. Movies, usually longer and increasingly shown in more luxurious sur-roundings (new motion-picture theatres or formerly legitimate theatres), were attracting more and more middle-class patrons.[6]

Robert C. Allen, in an article first published in 1979, supported Merritt. Allen's own analysis was based on New York City. Using *Trow's Business Directory* for

1908, he managed to locate 123 nickelodeons in Manhattan. Only forty-two of these were in that classic working-class and immigrant district, the Lower East Side. Even more were to be found in four areas of the city that, according to Allen, had an increasingly middle-class residential profile. He also pointed out that a number of primarily working-class, immigrant districts in fact had very few nickelodeons. Examining *Trow's* between 1906 and 1912, Allen found very little alteration in this pattern. What he did discover from other sources, however, was the growing tendency for legitimate theatres to convert to movie-houses appealing to a mainly middle-class clientele by means of a mixture of film and vaudeville. While conceding that it was unclear whether his findings could be applied to other localities besides New York, Allen concluded that, at least in Manhattan, movie-going between 1906 and 1912 'was by no means an exclusive activity of the poor or the immigrant' and that the middle class 'embraced the movies much earlier than is generally believed'.[7]

The arguments of Merritt and Allen did not win universal acceptance. In a 1988 article, Robert Sklar challenged both their methodology and what he saw as their revisionist purpose. Merritt, he noted, had confined his analysis to Boston proper, thus setting aside the 'streetcar suburbs' where many workers and immigrants lived. Allen's count of 123 nickelodeons in Manhattan was almost certainly an underestimate. When the mayor of New York issued an order revoking movie licences across the city in December 1908, contemporary press reports suggested that at least 600 theatres were affected. Moreover, while Roy Rosenzweig's 1983 study of working-class leisure in Worcester, Massachusetts, *Eight Hours For What We Will*, confirmed parts of the Merritt–Allen thesis (for example, the mixing of movies and live entertainment in downtown vaudeville theatres), he also discovered that this was followed by the opening of a series of new, cheap movie-theatres and the creation of a working-class audience which, as late as 1914, still dominated movie-going in the city. Sklar claimed that because Merritt and Allen placed middle-class audiences in movie theatres earlier than traditional accounts had done, their chief aim had been 'to diminish the significance of immigrant and working-class audiences, and the possibility of class struggle, in the formation of early cinema'.[8]

Seven years after Sklar's dissent, *Cinema Journal* published a detailed critique of Allen's New York article. The author, Ben Singer, argued (like Sklar) that Allen had greatly underestimated the number of nickelodeons in Manhattan. A memo from New York's police commissioner to the mayor two weeks before the latter's notorious 1908 order to close all nickelodeons counted a total of 315 movie-theatres in Manhattan. Using a variety of sources, Singer had managed to locate around 70 per cent of these. Although broadly in agreement with Allen on where most Manhattan nickelodeons were located, he challenged Allen's characterisation of these areas as predominantly middle-class. More fundamentally, he questioned whether the social composition of movie audiences necessarily reflected that of the outside neighbourhood. Singer maintained that census data brought into question 'the revisionist argument about the importance of middle-class audiences in the nickelodeon era and early teens'. Acknowledging that traditional histories of the movie industry had been superficial, he nevertheless suggested that 'their emphasis on the immigrant and working-class foundation of early exhibition may not have been as far off the mark as revisionist historians maintain'.[9]

3

The publication of this article stimulated a lively debate. Singer's view was supported by Sumiko Higashi, who considered that the social activities of what she termed the 'genteel middle class' did not correspond to those of workers and immigrants and that any middle-class people who did go to nickelodeons before 1914 'were most likely lower middle class'. Allen himself took issue with Singer's methodology, emphasising that the mapping of any New York nickelodeons found to have existed at some point during a two-year period not only ignored crucial differences between movie-houses in terms of quality, but also created the false impression that they all existed at the same chronological moment. Allen insisted that the clientele of movie-houses varied according to their *location* (there were important social differences between neighbourhoods and even, sometimes, between theatres on the same block) and their *grade* (segments of audiences who attended small-time vaudeville and large-scale picture houses would not also have visited storefront nickelodeons). While noting that there had been a middle-class audience for movies within a year of the first Vitascope screenings, since movies had rapidly come to form part of the standard vaudeville programme, Allen also drew attention to recent work by film historians, who have found evidence that small-town audiences were 'not class segregated', and by social historians, who have questioned in general terms the notion of a clear distinction between classes at this time.[10]

Other criticisms of Singer were advanced by Judith Thissen, and also in a joint response by William Uricchio and Roberta Pearson. Using detailed local sources, Thissen argued that there were fewer closures of Manhattan exhibition venues – as opposed to changes of ownership – than Singer and Allen had believed. The nickelodeon business was, she suggested, more stable than their accounts indicated.[11] Uricchio and Pearson maintained that, as a result of inadequate record-keeping and corruption in New York City departments, the archival evidence was itself too flawed to be a reliable guide to the location of nickelodeons. In any case, they argued, such geographical data was insufficient when it came to establishing how audiences were composed: not only did audiences differ according to the time of day or the day of the week, but some venues also banned particular groups (such as African-Americans or Italians) from attending screenings. Uricchio and Pearson contended that questions such as how audiences were composed, what meanings were given to attendance, and what was the extent of middle-class influence over the cinema in general might more profitably be approached by means of the discursive evidence surrounding them than by the kind of empirical evidence preferred by Singer.[12]

In two essays responding to his critics, Singer insisted that it was sensible to assume that nickelodeon audiences reflected the surrounding neighbourhood, although, he conceded, it was only really useful to make generalisations about audiences on such a basis in neighbourhoods with a relatively high level of social homogeneity. While accepting Uricchio and Pearson's contention about audiences varying even at the same exhibition site, he insisted that he was not aware of any evidence indicating that the ethnic or socio-economic profile of audiences at a typical theatre varied from day to day. Singer criticised Allen's view that small-time vaudeville, with its mixture of vaudeville acts and films, had substantially reconfigured the social circumstances of exhibition in Manhattan. While accepting that some middle-class patrons were indeed attracted to such entertainment, he emphasised that parts of the middle class disapproved of small-time vaudeville nearly as much as they did the nickelodeon itself. He did, however, concede that his first article's definition of the middle class as consisting of 'white-collar professionals and managers' but excluding clerical workers might be revised. In spite of their 'social ambiguity', which often led them to attend the same kind of entertainments as workers, he had now come to perceive clerical workers as 'lower middle class'.[13]

The Singer–Allen controversy has added a good deal to our knowledge of cinema exhibition in New York during the nickelodeon era. While it is still unclear what, if anything, can be generalised from the New York experience, the crucial role of the city in terms of both economics and the entertainment and communications industries is an ample justification for lavishing such attention on it. (The two men who arranged the first Vitascope showings at Koster and Bial's Music Hall noted that they were 'pretty well satisfied that we can do much better and make more money for both parties by exhibiting the machine at the start exclusively in New York City', adding that 'reports through the news-papers go out through the country'.)[14] Yet for all this concentration on New York, there remain considerable gaps in our knowledge of its motion-picture audiences during the nickelodeon era. One of the most glaring of these has been the lack of attention paid to the ethnic and racial composition of those audiences. While Singer himself declared that class and ethnicity were the 'contested issues' in his debate with Allen, as that debate progressed, ethnic groups were rapidly subsumed into the broader category of 'working class'. The first three contributions to this book, which examine aspects of the ethnic and racial movie-going experience in pre-1914 New York, begin to remedy this deficiency. They also suggest that established assumptions about the movies' role in 'Americanising' the immigrant population may need reassessment.

Judith Thissen's essay focuses on the Jews from Eastern Europe who lived on the densely populated Lower East Side, where around 40 per cent of all Manhattan nickelodeons were located.[15] Unusually among ethnic groups in New York, the Jews of the Lower East Side had a thriving ethnic culture, based on Yiddish theatre and music halls, *before* the arrival of the cinema. By the end of 1907, however, almost all the music halls had converted into moving picture palaces. Here, as in the nickelodeons themselves, live variety acts were staged while film reels were changed. To Abraham Cahan (novelist and editor of the *Jewish Daily Forward*) and the Lower East Side Jewish élite, both music-hall entertainment and the movies themselves were emblematic of the 'Americanisation' of Jewish culture.[16] In 1908–9, a strong movement developed to 'Americanise' the American cinema and ensure that it represented more closely the ideals of the native-born middle class. While this was fought by Cahan and others, its most effective opponent, according to Thissen, was the grass-roots Jewish opposition that emerged. Responding to popular demand, Jewish exhibitors diminished the effects of Americanisation by including more 'ethnic' material (in the form of Yiddish live acts) on programmes and by showing more films that were of especial interest to the Jews of the Lower East Side. Although live acts were squeezed out of the cinema over the next few years, the commitment to ethnically-specific programming continued until the

First World War made it virtually impossible to import films from Europe (where nearly all such films originated). By that stage, too, the demise of the Yiddish music hall tradition and the advent of the feature film had changed spectator–film relations, destroying the active, vocal spectatorship that had once characterised the behaviour of movie audiences on the Jewish Lower East Side.

Like Thissen, Giorgio Bertellini also questions the notion of immigrants' easy assimilation and acculturation once they had arrived in the United States. His essay deals with the effects of film-going on Italians who, after the Jews, were the second largest group of so-called 'new' immigrants (from southern and eastern Europe) to arrive in New York in the decades before the First World War. Yet to categorise them as 'Italian', Bertellini points out, is in many respects misleading. Most came from the countryside or isolated communities of southern Italy. They identified themselves more in terms of local or regional, rather than national, origins. Once in New York, however, they were exposed to many Italian-produced films that dealt with classical civilisation, early Christianity and the nineteenth-century struggle for unification.[17] In Italy, these historical re-enactments were helping to develop a new sense of constructed nationhood. In the United States, they presented an idealised view of the Italian past to recent immigrants, forming part of a growing national consciousness that was encouraged by Italian newspapers, festivals, and operatic and theatrical performances. Instead of making New York's Italian immigrants more 'American', therefore, Bertellini contends, the experience of film-going actually played a major role in making them more 'Italian'.

In an essay focusing on another New York ethnic or racial group – African-Americans – Alison Griffiths and James Latham explore how motion pictures gained a stronghold in Harlem, adopting a similar approach to that used by Mary Carbine in her analysis of how film and race intersected in one neighbourhood of Chicago.[18] Griffiths and Latham are primarily concerned with two simultaneous developments: the spread of nickelodeons and other movie exhibition sites in Harlem and the area's increasing identity, as a result of population movements, as a black community. They examine several points at which the rise of cinema and social change in Harlem coincided to create issues over discriminatory exhibition practices at local theatres, the representation of blacks both on screen and in cinematic advertisements, and the ownership and management of nickelodeons. They argue that, so far as the attitude of the black community in Harlem towards films was concerned, its racial unity was imperilled by differences of class and regional origin (large numbers of former rural labourers migrated to Harlem from the South). Like Cahan on the Lower East Side, middle-class blacks, such as film critic Lester Walton, often looked down on the more working-class members of their own community and deplored their movie-going practices.

The coincidence of industrialisation, urbanisation and growing ethnic and racial minorities created tensions and frustrations within American society that were perceived by many members of the native-born middle class as a threat to their own continuing hegemony. They responded to this by attempting to control (or remould) aspects of society itself. This impulse, referred to by contemporaries and later historians alike as 'progressivism' or 'progressive reform', was apparent in a vast number of areas of American life. Its effects were particularly evident in the case of the cinema, which was new, seemingly increasingly influential and patro-nised by significant numbers of workers and immigrants.[19]

In their essay, Roberta Pearson and William Uricchio examine a particular fea-ture of this movement: the attention paid by New York reformers to one large and distinctive minority of cinema-goers – children. For these reformers, children served as a focal point in their attempts to regulate the cinema, since they were considered the section of the audience most susceptible to cinema's mental and physical effects. Pearson and Uricchio deal with the élite's discursive construction of children and with the responses of progressive reformers and the film industry itself to the particular problems posed by children as spectators. They look at the three main strategies used by such reformers: banning children completely from some films or allowing them to attend under certain conditions; the development of special films for children, to be shown at different times and/or places to adult screenings; and regulating the physical conditions (lighting, seating arrangements and fire-proofing) of exhibition venues. The last of these, they find, was probably the most effective. The first largely failed and the second fell foul of the movie industry's inability, in the nickelodeon era, to cater for anything other than an undifferentiated audience.

In November 1907, Chicago established a police censorship board for moving pictures. As Lee Grieveson points out, this symbolised a shift of policy away from the policing of the places in which films were shown to the policing of the films themselves. It was a significant shift in the governance of cinema and would have a major influence on the system of state censorship as it emerged in the next decade. Yet, Grieveson contends, it was itself the result of the conjunction of two distinct but overlapping discourses: the first dealing with concerns over good gov-ernment and citizenship, and the second with what moving pictures were for and how they ought to function in society. The first was a reflection of the anxiety felt by members of the native-born middle class that the working-class, immigrant population of the cities was increasingly ungovernable. It led to attempts to regu-late working-class life that were particularly focused on helping children ('citizens-in-formation') to avoid delinquency. The second involved debates on the role that cinema should play in the wider society. Together, the two provoked numerous investigations into the audiences for motion pictures, followed by regulatory strategies designed to protect children from being led astray as a con-sequence of their movie-going experience.

Steven Ross analyses the consequences of the growing control over American cinema exercised by the middle class from a different angle: the struggle, between 1907 and 1930, to have films about labour relations that showed working-class solidarity and class consciousness in a favourable manner. Ross argues that film historians should expand their perceptions of spectatorship and reception to embrace what he terms 'reactive pressure groups', including businessmen, poli-ticians, reformers, priests, police and censors. For, despite the enthusiasm of mainly working-class audiences for pro-labour films – and the dedication of some workers in producing or exhibiting them – conservative reactive pressure groups eventually succeeded in suppressing almost all films of this type. After 1918–19, Ross maintains, such groups increased their power. In the wake of post-war labour militancy and the 'Red Scare', government officials investigated and persecuted the makers of such films. At the same time, changes within the cinema industry itself increased the impact of such pressure groups. As the centralised film industry of Hollywood emerged in the 20s, it showed itself more amenable to censorship pressures against commercially-produced liberal/radical films on the class struggle. Its own attempt to build a cross-class audience involved the rejection of such films in favour of 'society' films. Meanwhile, as studios and theatre chains tightened their monopolies over distribution and exhibition, it became progressively harder for independently-produced pro-labour films to reach a mass audience.

While Thissen, Bertellini and Griffths and Latham all to some extent challenge the idea of standardised or disciplined audiences in the period before 1914, they all assume that this was the case afterwards. Ross sees standardisation as occurring later. But several crucial questions remain. How standardised were audiences outside major urban centres like New York? Does the record document a progressive standardisation happening over time? Did some audiences – at various times and places – resist standardisation? The following four essays address these issues in a variety of ways.

Kathryn Fuller examines images of enthralled audiences watching movie shows in early cinema advertising. Such images, she argues, were vital in selling the movie-going experience to its first audiences. They appeared in – among other places – Sears, Roebuck catalogues and the promotional literature of travelling exhibitors such as Lyman Howe and Bert Cook. By 1900, however, most people involved with the cinema had ceased to use them. Cook, who showed his films in the small towns of upstate New York, was an exception, continuing to use audience images on his advertising until 1907. Modern cinema historians, including Charles Musser, have perceived the period 1895 to 1907 as one of dramatic change, with itinerant exhibition giving way to the nickelodeon boom and what Tom Gunning has called the 'cinema of attractions' succeeded by the rise of the narrative film. Fuller argues that Cook's enduring use of illustrations relating to his audiences may suggest that the movie-going experience, at least for provincial townsfolk, actually had major elements of continuity throughout these years. Cook's continuing success, she believes, may indicate that the kind of audiences he was familiar with did not reject the 'cinema of attractions' as rapidly as their big-city counterparts.

On the other hand, Leslie DeBauche's essay on cinema audiences in Milwaukee during the First World War indicates the extent to which going to the movies had become an increasingly standardised experience by 1918. She points out that Milwaukee differed from other American centres of population of the time in ways that might have influenced and inflected the experience of movie-going. It was in the Midwest, an area noted for its isolationism in foreign policy; it had a large German population; it had a strong local socialist tradition; and it was represented in the Senate by Robert M. La Follette, who had spoken and voted against war in April 1917. If any city in the country could have resisted the wartime torrent of patriotism and anti-German feeling, that city was Milwaukee. What actually happened, DeBauche shows, was that Milwaukee played a full part in the war effort, and that the city's movie theatres joined in. Consequently, movie-goers in the most German city in the country found themselves watching anti-German films, singing patriotic songs in advance of screenings, and, urged on by visiting movie stars, participating in drives to sell Liberty Bonds.

If DeBauche's essay emphasises elements of homogeneity in the movie-going experience at the start of Hollywood's classic period, Thomas Doherty's essay on the early 30s explores the varieties of behaviour still available to audiences after the coming of sound. Doherty dissents from the ideas of a number of scholars, including Miriam Hansen and Lawrence Levine, on the disciplining of audiences, and also resists the view that movies offered increasingly standardised entertainment. Audiences of the depression era, he argues, were audible rather than silent, active rather than passive. They applauded showcase performers and celebrities featured on the bill, responded audibly to opening and closing credits and comments and speeches they approved or disapproved of in the film, and attacked the partisanship evident in some newsreels. In emphasising the importance of the 'balanced programme', Doherty draws attention to the usually neglected role of short subjects in attracting an audience. He also points out that most theatres did not advertise their programmes' starting times, and that it was quite normal viewing practice for members of the audience to enter the theatre halfway through the main feature, and leave at the point 'where we came in'. Doherty's account of such audience behaviour not only suggests a continuing level of at least passive spectatorial resistance to the disciplinary effects of Hollywood's standardisation, it also provides a useful corrective to the tendency in textual studies of cinema to overemphasise the centrality of narrative at the expense of other pleasures offered by the cinematic experience.

Gregory Waller's essay returns to the question of locality by demonstrating how movie theatres in small-town, south-central Kentucky were embedded in the everyday life of the local community during the Depression. These theatres were managed by businessmen who maintained good relations with local organisations, allowing many of them to use the local theatre for their meetings, so that the movie theatre came to take over many of the social functions fulfilled in the previous century by the municipal opera house. Locally-made newsreels and advertisements for local merchants and products were also often included on programmes, and managers could sometimes gear their offerings to local tastes by booking or holding over films with regional associations. They also arranged live performances of country and western music, using regional talent, to go with their regular film programmes, although – as Waller points out – the fact that the radio was broadcasting such music all over the United States undercuts the idea of it as a distinctively regional product.

Collectively, these essays emphasise the diversity of movie-going experience in the first decades of the century, suggesting that however much the movies themselves became standardised in production, distribution and even exhibition, their audiences remained far from unified, either in terms of their composition or responses. The history of the audience remains the most elusive aspect of cinema history, since audiences form only the most temporary of communities, and leave few traces of their presence. But the historical significance of film (as of most of popular culture) is to be found more in its reception than its production – in the meanings, often not clearly articulated, that audiences read into it and the uses to which they put it. As these essays show, reconstructing histories of audiences requires a wide range of empirical and interpretative skills in their interrogation of a multiplicity of source materials. None of them, of course, claims to provide the last word on their subject. Rather, it is hoped, they will stimulate others to join in the exploration of a complex and constantly shifting set of relationships and illuminate avenues for future research.

Notes

1 Francis Hackett, 'The Birth of a Nation', The New Republic (20 March 1915), reprinted in Stanley Kauffman with Bruce Henstell (eds), American Film Criticism: From the Beginnings to 'Citizen Kane' (New York: Liveright, 1972), p. 92.
2 William Walker, interviewed in D. W. Griffith: Father of Film, documentary, directed by Kevin Brownlow and David Gill, 1993.
3 See Charles Musser, The Emergence of Cinema: The American Screen to 1907 (Berkeley: University of California Press, 1994), pp. 122–8, 139, 140, 150, 183, 218, 223, 252, 263, 303, 366, 374.
4 Terry Ramsaye, A Million and One Nights: A History of the Motion Picture Through 1925 (New York: Simon and Schuster, 1926); Benjamin Hampton, A History of the Movies (New York: Civici, Friede, 1931), pp. 44–8; Lewis Jacobs, The Rise of the American Film (New York: Harcourt, Brace, 1939), pp. 55–7.
5 See Joseph H. North, The Early Development of the Motion Picture: 1887–1909 (New York: Arno, 1973), p. 239; Robert Sklar, Movie-Made America (New York: Random House, 1975), pp. 3, 14–20.
6 Russell Merritt, 'Nickelodeon Theatres, 1905–1914: Building an Audience for the Movies', in Tino Balio (ed.), The American Film Industry (Madison: University of Wisconsin Press, 1976), pp. 59–79.
7 Robert C. Allen, 'Motion Picture Exhibition in Manhattan, 1906–1912: Beyond the Nickelodeon', Cinema Journal, 19, no. 2 (Spring 1979), reprinted in John Fell (ed.), Film Before Griffith (Berkeley: University of California Press, 1983), pp. 162–75.
8 Robert Sklar, 'Oh! Althusser!: Historiography and the Rise of Cinema Studies', Radical History Review, 41 (Spring 1988), reprinted in Robert Sklar and Charles Musser (eds), Resisting Images: Essays in Cinema and History (Philadelphia: Temple University Press, 1990), pp. 12–35.
9 Ben Singer, 'Manhattan Nickelodeons: New Data on Audiences and Exhibitors', Cinema Journal, 35, no. 3 (Spring 1996), pp. 3–35.
10 Sumiko Higashi, 'Dialogue: Manhattan's Nickelodeons', Cinema Journal, 35, no. 3 (Spring 1996), pp. 72–3; Robert C. Allen, 'Manhattan Myopia: or, Oh! Iowa!', ibid., pp. 75–103. Allen cites, among other works, Gregory A. Waller, 'Situating Motion Pictures in the Pre-nickelodeon Period: Lexington, Kentucky, 1897–1906', Velvet Light Trap, 25 (1990), pp. 12–28; Stuart M. Blumin, The Emergence of the Middle Class: The Process of Growth in Boston, 1870–1900 (Cambridge, MA: Harvard University Press, 1989); Steven J. Ross, Workers on the Edge: Work, Leisure, and Politics in Industrializing Cincinnati: 1788–1890 (New York: Columbia University Press, 1985).
11 Judith Thissen, 'Oy, Myopia! A Reaction from Judith Thissen on the Singer–Allen Controversy', Cinema Journal, 36, no. 4 (Summer 1997), pp. 102–7.
12 William Uricchio and Roberta E. Pearson, 'Dialogue: Manhattan's Nickelodeons New York! New York!', Cinema Journal, 36, no. 4 (Summer 1997), pp. 98–102.
13 Ben Singer, 'New York, Just Like I Pictured It ...', Cinema Journal, 35, no. 3 (Spring 1996), pp. 104–28; Singer, 'Manhattan Melodrama – A Response from Ben Singer', Cinema Journal, 36, no. 4 (Summer 1997), pp. 107–12.
14 Norman C. Raff and Frank R. Gammon to T. Cushing Daniel and Thomas Armat, n.d. (c. 26 December 1895), quoted in Charles Musser, The Emergence of Cinema: The American Screen to 1907, p. 115.

15 By 1910, the Jewish population of the Lower East Side had reached a peak of 542,000. Frederick M. Binder and David M. Reimers, *All the Nations Under Heaven: An Ethnic and Racial History of New York City* (New York: Columbia University Press, 1995), p. 117.

16 This claim, with regard to movies at least, Thissen points out, should be regarded with suspicion. Between 1905 and 1909, many of the films screened in New York were actually of French, rather than American, origin.

17 Bertellini, like Thissen, emphasises the importance of 'foreign' (i.e. non-American) films to ethnic spectators during the nickelodeon era.

18 Mary Carbine, ' "The Finest Outside the Loop": Motion Picture Exhibition in Chicago's Black Metropolis, 1905–1928', *Camera Obscura*, vol. 23 (May 1990), pp. 9–41.

19 On this point generally, see Anthony M. Platt, *The Child Savers: The Invention of Delinquency* (Chicago: University of Chicago Press, 1969); Paul Boyer, *Urban Masses and Moral Order in America, 1820–1920* (Cambridge, MA: Harvard University Press, 1978); and Elizabeth J. Clapp, *Mothers of All Children: Women Reformers and the Rise of Juvenile Courts in Progressive Era America* (University Park: Pennsylvania State University Press, 1998). On progressives and the film industry, see Robert Fischer, 'Film Censorship and Progressive Reform: The National Board of Censorship of Motion Pictures, 1909–1922', *Journal of Popular Film*, 4 (1975), pp. 143–50; Kathleen D. McCarthy, 'Nickel Vice and Virtue: Movie Censorship in Chicago, 1907–1915', *Journal of Popular Film*, 5 (1976), pp. 37–55.

PART ONE
The Social Formulation of Audiences

1 Jewish Immigrant Audiences in New York City, 1905–14

Judith Thissen

Between 1880 and 1914 nearly two million East European Jews emigrated to the United States in search of a better life. The majority of them disembarked in New York, where first-generation Jewish immigrants and their children became the largest ethnic group in the city.[1] Their integration into American society took place for the most part in the decades during which American cinema was becoming a dominant mass medium.

On the Lower East Side of Manhattan, the East European Jews formed a dynamic, Yiddish-speaking community supporting a wide range of amusement venues, including saloons, dancing halls, nickelodeons, Yiddish variety houses and 'legitimate' theatres.[2] Theatre-going played a prominent role in the social and cultural life of many Jewish immigrants – intellectuals as well as uneducated workers. The popularity of the Yiddish stage and its famous actors, such as Jacob Adler, Boris Thomashevsky and David Kessler, has been impressed upon us by Jewish-American memoir literature. Few authors, however, seem to remember the presence of the nickel-and-dime theatres that were spread all over the Lower East Side. An exception is the autobiography of the playwright Bella Cohen Spewack.[3] In *Streets: A Memoir of the Lower East Side*, written in 1922 when Spewack was twenty-three, she recalled how much going to the movies was part of her youth in the ghetto. As a little girl, Bella was taken to 'the Victoria Music Hall where moving pictures and Yiddish and English sketches were presented'. A few years later, on the day her mother remarried, she was packed off with fifteen cents for a pair of new silk stockings and ten cents more to take a friend to the 'nickel show'.[4]

It is significant that memoirs of Jewish immigrant life in New York rarely mention the nickelodeons. In retrospect, moving pictures seem to have been exclusively associated with American culture and hence ignored, while the 'legitimate' Yiddish theatre became the quintessence of the Old World-flavoured immigrant culture of the turn of the century and the object of nostalgic reminiscence. In reality, however, both the 'legitimate' Yiddish theatres and the East Side nickelodeons stood at the crossroad of two worlds. On the one hand, their commercial and heterosocial character represented a fundamental break with traditional Jewish culture; on the other, East Side nickelodeon exhibitors and patrons alike sought to preserve their cultural heritage just as much as did the Yiddish theatre stars and their audiences.

American Films, American Identities

Whereas, in Jewish-American autobiographies, the memories of *muving piktshur pletser* have been repressed almost entirely, the same movie houses have generated in American film and social history the founding myth of Hollywood's democratic nature. From Lewis Jacobs' *The Rise of the American Film* (1939) through Garth Jowett's *Film: The Democratic Art* (1976) to the social history survey text *Who Built America?* (1992), the ghetto nickelodeon stands as a symbol for the close affinity between the 'melting pot' ideology of early American cinema and the upwardly-mobile aspirations of its working-class and immigrant audiences.[5] Especially by historians on the left, American cinema has been hailed as a fundamentally progressive institution, a thoroughly popular art, and a powerful Americanising agency.[6] Jacobs, for instance, emphasised in his influential study that from the outset:

> The movies gave the newcomers, particularly, a respect for American law and order, an understanding of civic organisation, pride in citizenship and in the American commonwealth. Movies acquainted them with current happenings at home and abroad. Because the uncritical movie-goers were deeply impressed by what they saw in the photographs and accepted it as the real thing, the movies were powerful and persuasive. More vividly than any other single agency they revealed the social topography of America to the immigrant, to the poor, and to the country folk.[7]

How accurate *is* this historical picture? To what extent did early American cinema shape the values of Jewish immigrants who lived in Manhattan's Lower East Side? During the first part of the so-called nickelodeon era (1905–9), the French firm Pathé Frères dominated the American market. According to the 1907 figures of Eastman Kodak, Pathé was selling twice as much positive film stock as all the American film producers combined.[8] It appears that nickelodeons relied heavily on the French company's products. Hence, at least until 1909, Jewish immigrants were more likely to 'roar at French buffoonery', as *Harpers Weekly* put it, than to learn American values and virtues from American films.[9] When, around 1907, social workers and Progressive reformers began to realise that cinema had become an important factor in city life, the popularity of the Pathé films with immigrant audiences became an issue of moral concern. Pathé's dominance in the US film market was especially undesirable at a time when hundreds of thousands of new immigrants from Eastern and Southern Europe had to be Americanised. As Richard Abel points out:

> At issue was whether or not, as a 'foreign' company selling 'foreign' commodities – specifically its trademark 'red rooster films' – Pathé could be 'assimilated' within the developing American cinema industry, and whether or not it should take part in circulating ever more significant representations of social life and behaviour.[10]

Pathé was not only embroiled in heated discussions about the construction of American identity, but its activities in the United States were also increasingly frustrated by the more powerful elements of the American film industry, headed by the Edison and Vitagraph studios. It has been argued that these American manufacturers not only intended to gain control over the domestic market, but also tried to reposition American cinema as a middle-class entertainment rather than a cheap amusement for immigrants and workers.[11] Abel argues persuasively that as economic interests and the demands for social regulation converged, 'Pathé found itself more and more circumscribed in public discourse as representative of much that was "low" and "illegitimate" about the cinema'.[12] By 1913, the red rooster had been almost entirely pushed out of the mainstream US film market. I very much doubt, however, that Pathé had also lost the favour of the Jewish film exhibitors and audience on the Lower East Side – and that American cinema, for its part, had managed to secure their blessing.

This chapter explores the history of exhibition practices in nickel-and-dime theatres on the Lower East Side between 1905 and 1914, and attempts to answer the question: what was the impact of the 'Americanisation of American cinema' on movie-going in Jewish neighbourhood theatres? The main source used in my analysis is the *Jewish Daily Forward* (*Forvertz*), at the time the leading Yiddish-language newspaper in America.[13] Under the editorship of Abraham Cahan, a socialist intellectual, the *Forward* helped to shape the image and aspirations of many East European Jewish immigrants. It built bridges between the Old World and the New, between Jewish traditions and modern American culture. The greatest quality of Cahan's *Forward* was its relentless curiosity about the life of its own people. From their headquarters on the Lower East Side, the *Forward* staff frequently reported on the Jewish immigrant life that surrounded them. More than anyone else, they wrote about moving picture entertainment and other cheap amusements in New York's largest Jewish neighbourhood.

The Beginnings of Film Exhibition in the Jewish Quarter

Around 1906, Jews who wanted to watch moving pictures could go to the vaudeville theatres on Union Square and East Fourteenth Street, or visit the much cheaper penny arcades on the nearby Bowery. During the summer, like other New Yorkers, they could enjoy 'free' moving picture shows in Coney Island saloons. It was also possible to see films in a specifically Jewish setting, namely in the Yiddish music halls. Nearly every important street on the Lower East Side had a *myuzik hol* or vaudeville house. At least ten of them offered variety programmes that combined live acts with moving pictures for an admission price of ten to thirty-five cents.[14]

The history of the Yiddish music hall business goes back to 1902, when East Side saloonkeepers started offering Yiddish vaudeville shows in the backrooms of their saloons.[15] Initially, no admission was charged, but clients were required to order a glass of beer for five cents. Unlike their English-language counterparts, these Yiddish concert saloons accommodated both men and women, and even families with children.[16] Sometime around 1905, the more successful saloonkeepers turned nearby dance halls into auditoria with wooden galleries and facilities for the projection of moving pictures, and began to charge admission (ten to twenty-five cents).[17] Their business flourished, but, starting in mid-1906, the Yiddish music halls experienced competition from the five-cent *muving piktshur pletser* that opened up in the neighbourhood. At first, there were only a few of these specialised moving picture theatres in the heart of the Jewish quarter, although *Films and Views Index*, the tradepaper for nickelodeon managers, was emphasising as early as October 1906 that this could be a very profitable venture:

> At the beginning of the past summer two slot machine arcades were established on Grand Street, and having done business, one moving picture man determined to take the chance. He built a very attractive little theatre and advertised that moving pictures could be seen for five cents. The result was very gratifying. The place commenced to do a rushing business and is doing it yet. The films are changed frequently and the East Siders are willing to be kept interested. This knocked to pieces the theory that the Bowery is the only place where moving pictures would pay, yet exhibitors seem to be slow taking the hint.[18]

The next season, however, more and more Jewish entrepreneurs tried their luck in the booming nickelodeon business by opening storefront theatres in the tenement district east of the Bowery. Soon, the Lower East Side had the highest density of nickelodeons in Manhattan.[19] On many blocks, stores were turned into nickel theatres with a seating capacity of 300 people. The managers of the Yiddish music halls also became increasingly interested in film exhibition. A bill of moving pictures, illustrated songs, and perhaps a sketch or a dance cost less to put on than a variety show, with movies as a sideline. The high turnover of the audience would largely compensate for the lower admission price of five to ten cents. Furthermore, the shift would settle once and for all the never-ending conflicts with the Hebrew Variety Actors' Union. By the end of 1907, nearly all Yiddish music halls on the East Side had been turned into moving picture theatres.[20]

Despite the severe economic depression of 1907–8, the moving picture business continued to flourish. In May 1908, the *Forward* reported, 'when you go through the streets of our neighbourhood you will be amazed by the mass of moving picture houses. Four or more "shows" can be found on one street. In some streets, there are even two "shows" on one block, facing each other'.[21] This was certainly the case in the most congested part of the Lower East Side, the Tenth Ward, where many blocks had over 3,000 inhabitants.[22] On the corner of Essex and Rivington Streets, for example, three nickel theatres offered moving picture entertainment only a stone's throw from one another. The Golden Rule Vaudeville House, a former saloon and meeting hall, located at 125 Rivington Street, had offered motion pictures in combination with live entertainment since 1905–6. Inspired by the success of the Golden Rule, Charles Steiner convinced his father that they should turn their livery stable on 133 Essex Street into a moving picture house. In March 1908, Steiner's Essex Street Theatre opened its doors.[23] Two months later, yet another competitor appeared on the scene. This time the newcomer was located right in front of the Golden Rule Hall. Arthur Alexander leased two stores for his World Amusement Company Theatre, commonly referred to as 'the WACO'.[24] In 1910, yet a fourth nickelodeon, the Metropolitan, opened in a tenement building on 134 Essex Street.[25]

The Show

What did these storefront theatres offer for five or ten cents? A half-hour show that consisted primarily of moving pictures, with 'a song and a dance, as an extra'.[26] Most members of the Hebrew Variety Actors' Union lost their well-paid jobs when the Yiddish music halls switched to moving pictures as their main attraction. Forced by circumstance, many variety actors continued to work – but now for low wages in the former music halls and in other nickel theatres. In between the films, while the reels were changed, they entertained the Jewish audiences with skits, jokes, dances or songs.[27] For instance, in December 1908, the Golden Rule Hall treated its patrons to sketches by Mister Tuchband and Miss Kaplan, a popular Yiddish variety duo.[28] According to the Yiddish press, the moral quality of these live acts was usually low. For a few dollars a week, the professional variety actors rivalled amateurs and each other with ever lewder songs and dirtier jokes. Low-life topics and coarse language had always been a feature of Yiddish vaudeville entertainment. However, in the eyes of certain observers, the situation now went from bad to worse. In March 1909, Abraham Cahan complained in a *Forward* editorial that, in some moving picture houses, Yiddish variety actors were using 'words that three years ago even a manager of an indecent music hall would not have accepted on the stage'.[29] Of course, his descriptions of Yiddish vaudeville should be read with some scepticism, for they reflected Cahan's own moralistic bias rather than his readers' measurable response to this form of entertainment.[30]

By mid-1908, movie-going had become a part of everyday life on the Lower East Side, as common as soda fountains and ice-cream parlours, and certainly more common than going to one of the three 'legitimate' Yiddish theatres. As a reporter put it, 'the moving pictures have totally revolutionised the Jewish quarter: it is heaven and earth and moving pictures'.[31]

Unfortunately, during the course of my research, I have found little information about the films that were shown in the East Side nickelodeons. Film exhibitors did not advertise in the Yiddish press until the early 1910s and, even then, advertisements for specific films were an exception. Although precise evidence is currently unavailable, Jewish neighbourhood nickelodeons appear to have been an important market for Pathé films.[32] The nickel theatres on the Lower East Side programmed comedies as well as tragedies, but, according to the *Forward*, the Eastern European Jews (female viewers in particular) favoured tearjerking tragedies based on novels or historical events such as 'the life of the Roman emperor Nero, the French Revolution or the war between Russia and Japan'.[33] Hence, while the desirability of having Pathé's gruesome sensational melodramas and *film d'art* productions in the American market was extensively debated in the American trade press, such films certainly matched the taste of the Jewish immigrants who patronised the nickelodeons of the Lower East Side.

Jewish versus American Tastes

In the 'legitimate' Yiddish theatres, Jewish audiences also preferred 'tragedy and serious drama with sad endings' to comedy.[34] It is likely that this penchant came

19

from the nineteenth-century Russian theatrical tradition, in which plays almost always ended in tragedy (as did a large number of early Russian films).[35] Light operettas and comedies, on the other hand, were perceived as typically American. While, in the critical discourse, the European realist drama was highly esteemed and held up as an example for Yiddish dramatists, the American theatre was often regarded with contempt. According to Jacob Gordin, the prominent Yiddish playwright, Americans considered that:

> Theatre[s], just as sports, races, fistic contests, 'rooster fights', and beer saloons, must be visited merely for amusement – and for the reason that after supper, to get good digestion and to avoid dyspepsia, it is advisable to do some 'giggling'.[36]

Jews, on the other hand, it was remarked, visited the Yiddish theatre 'to think, to sigh and to cry'.[37] The belief that Jewish immigrants visited the Yiddish theatre to reflect on what they saw should probably be considered wishful thinking on the part of an intellectual élite which aspired to enlighten the 'uneducated' masses. Nevertheless, unlike Broadway hits, most successful Yiddish plays of this period, *shund* (trash) as well as literary drama, included numerous heartbreaking and horrifying scenes. The *Forward* cynically remarked that even

> When a manager of a Yiddish theatre decides to produce a comedy, he adds a couple of pogroms, some suicides, a few poor orphans, and a deserted woman – of course – to make sure that the people will weep more than they will laugh.[38]

In the discussions over the differences in American and Jewish tastes in terms of subject matter and dramatisation, as well as in the broader intellectual debate about 'highbrow' versus 'lowbrow' entertainment, the *Forward* frequently played on a conception of American culture as 'low' and 'other', against which to construct a Jewish difference.

Thus, when the first Yiddish music halls emerged on the East Side, a heated discussion broke out in the Yiddish press over their function in the Jewish immigrant community. In the eyes of intellectuals like Cahan and Gordin, Yiddish variety entertainment was an appropriation of the 'low' expressions of American culture and a 'wrong' kind of Americanisation.[39] As Nina Warnke points out, due to the 'relative weakness of community structures and social control on the Lower East Side', these prominent figures could regard themselves 'as the immigrants' cultural and political educators, as guardians of immigrant morality and as guides on the road to a cautious Americanisation'.[40] It is not surprising, then, that again and again Cahan urged his readers to boycott the Yiddish musical halls.[41]

When the 'moving picture craze' hit the Lower East Side at the beginning of 1908, the *Forward* described the movies as 'a popular amusement' and a novelty which 'just like the music halls, comes from uptown, from the Christians'.[42] In sharp contrast with the *Forward*'s initial reception of the Yiddish music halls, cinema did not become a contested site of Americanisation until late 1909. What made cinema's position in immigrant culture an issue in the Yiddish press at that particular moment was the increasing awareness of the growing power of film exhibitors. This, in turn, raised the question of who would ultimately exercise control over the Jewish immigrant entertainment business, and educate and direct Jewish immigrants on the threshold of Americanisation: the American film industry or the cultural élite of the Lower East Side.

The Grand Scandal

In December 1909, Nathan Fleissig, the manager of the Grand Street Music Hall, announced triumphantly that the moving pictures had been defeated and that his theatre would be devoted again to 'first-class Yiddish variety'.[43] By presenting the shift in exhibition practice in terms of a cultural war with the moving pictures, Fleissig shrewdly linked the reopening of the Grand Music Hall with the 'Grand scandal' that had roused the emotions of the Yiddish press a few weeks earlier. In September 1909 Yiddish theatre's star and impresario Jacob Adler had sold the lease of the 2,000-seat Grand Theatre to Marcus Loew and Adolph Zukor, who turned the home of Yiddish literary drama into an English-language, small-time vaudeville house in which moving pictures were also shown. In the opinion of the *Forward*, that fact that Adler had given the Grand Theatre to a 'million-dollar trust of American theatre managers' was a dishonour for the whole East Side.[44] Cahan and his staff never mentioned that the new lessees were Jews too. Instead, they emphasised, again and again, that the Grand had been turned into a *goyish* (gentile) moving picture theatre and, as such, it began to symbolise the loss of *Yiddishkayt* in the New World.

In the aftermath of the 'Grand scandal', the staff of the *Forward* began to redefine the cultural positions within the field of Jewish immigrant entertainment. In schematic terms, cinema was constructed as the new 'low Other' and relegated to the bottom end of the cultural hierarchy, the position previously occupied by Yiddish vaudeville. The latter was legitimised as a Yiddish theatrical tradition and structurally promoted to a middlebrow position, while the 'legitimate' Yiddish stage maintained its status as a 'highbrow' institution. In fact, the redefinition of the cultural position of Yiddish vaudeville involved a set of complex and ambiguous discursive strategies that were intended to control the leisure activities of the Jewish immigrants.[45]

The Appeal of Yiddish Vaudeville

The rationality at work in the *Forward*'s critical discourse on Jewish immigrant entertainment should not be confused with the logic that dictated the cultural practices in the moving picture theatres on the East Side. As a matter of fact, the *Forward* was overtaken by the latest developments in film exhibition. At the beginning of the 1909–10 season, there had been a remarkable revival of Yiddish vaudeville in the nickel-and-dime theatres in the Jewish quarter. Film exhibitors had added more and longer Yiddish vaudeville acts to their bills, and most former Yiddish music halls had switched back to full-fledged Yiddish vaudeville shows.[46]

Why did Jewish exhibitors decide to invest in an old-fashioned form of ethnic entertainment? How did it come about that Yiddish vaudeville was no longer programmed in the moving picture theatres out of sheer necessity to amuse the audience while the reels were changed, but that it became a substantial part of the show?

Perhaps we should consider the revival of the Yiddish music halls as the local equivalent of the emerging small-time vaudeville trend. Robert C. Allen found that the rise of small-time vaudeville had been stimulated by a number of factors, which included cut-throat competition among nickelodeons, a shortage of new films, the involvement of vaudeville managers with motion picture exhibition and the desire among certain moving picture exhibitors to attract a more middle-class audience.[47] The first two factors also played a role in the film exhibition business on the East Side. However, there appears to be no evidence suggesting that there was any financial backing for the small-scale Yiddish entertainment business other than by Jewish real estate investors. Finally, the exhibitors certainly did not programme Yiddish vaudeville to attract a better class of patrons because they knew only too well that it had a long-established reputation for vulgarity and indecency. Ever since the opening of the first concert saloons on the East Side, the Yiddish newspapers had strongly condemned the variety actors, their shows, their bosses, and even their union. Zukor and Loew might have set the trend with the opening of the Grand Theatre as a small-time vaudeville house, but, in the meantime, there was something else at stake.

According to the *Forward*, the main impetus behind the 'resurrection of the Yiddish music halls' came from the fact that, once the novelty of the movies had gone, youngsters formed the bulk of the audiences in the nickel-and-dime theatres in the Jewish quarter.[48] It was reported that film exhibitors had reintroduced 'old-time' Yiddish vaudeville – single turns, sketches, one-acters, and even three-act melodramas – to lure adults back to their theatres. Since the majority of the adult population on the East Side was foreign born, this implies that the live part of the bill was aimed specifically at first-generation Jewish immigrants. The analysis of the *Forward* was, of course, too simplistic. Movie houses were certainly among the favourite meeting places for young people, not least because the theatre's darkness encouraged opportunities for romance and sexual expression.[49] However, the *Forward*'s claim that adults rarely patronised the nickel theatres is untenable, even if we take into account the fact that fewer 'greenhorns' (recently arrived immigrants who had yet to discover the excitement of moving pictures) poured into the East Side nickel theatres because immigration into the United States declined by nearly 50 per cent between mid-1908 and mid-1909.[50]

Yet the link which the *Forward* made between the revival of Yiddish vaudeville and movie-going among first-generation immigrants does turn out to be revealing when we consider what modern film historians believe to have been occurring at this point. The managers of the East Side nickel theatres began to include more ethnic entertainment in their shows in order to attract first-generation immigrants at a crucial moment in the history of American cinema – that is, when it was becoming 'Americanised' and transformed into a vehicle for middle-class ideals of respectability, upward mobility and assimilation into mainstream culture.[51] In the process of creating a mass-cultural audience that submerged all

22

social and cultural distinctions under the banner of middle-class values, non-filmic activities which aimed at building audiences on the basis of a shared ethnic or class identity were largely eliminated. The 'real' social, cultural and physical space of the movie theatre became increasingly subordinated to the fictional world on the screen and the film text became the prime site of meaning.[52] Initially, however, exactly the opposite happened in the Jewish nickel-and-dime theatres houses on the Lower East Side, where early film–viewer relations, determined less by the film itself than by the context of reception, were preserved by the integration of more Yiddish vaudeville acts into the moving picture shows.

The revival of Yiddish vaudeville can therefore also be explained as a grass-roots resistance to the increasing influence of mainstream American culture, which threatened the cohesiveness of Jewish immigrants as a community. Yiddish vaudeville jeopardised the part cinema might have played in the process of assimilation on the part of Jewish immigrants. For one thing, it reinforced feelings of belonging to an ethnic community with shared values and pleasures, based on a communal language and history. For another, Yiddish vaudeville shaped the reception of the films that were shown, thus reducing the Americanising tendency of the silver screen.

By allotting more time to live acts, exhibitors could continue to offer a product that corresponded with the sensibilities, values and expectations of the Jews who lived on the Lower East Side. If they did so, it was not because these exhibitors, who shared their customers' ethnic and social background, believed in defending Jewish culture against Americanisation, but because they expected to make more money with the music hall format. In this respect, it would be very useful to know whether the exhibition practices also changed in moving picture theatres which were located in the more middle-class Jewish neighbourhoods of greater New York. Did the upwardly-mobile Eastern European Jews, especially the American-born second generation, demand more *Yiddishkayt* too in their neighbourhood theatres?

On the Lower East Side, the bulwark of Yiddish culture in New York City audiences and exhibitors alike sought to preserve the conditions that encouraged manifestations of ethnicity, not only at the level of content, but also in terms of spectatorial behaviour. The Yiddish music hall format authorised a 'participatory, sound intensive form of response' and 'active sociability' similar to that of the early nickelodeons.[53] This convivial mode of reception, which deviated from that of the American middle classes, had been a feature of Jewish immigrant entertainment since the beginnings of Yiddish theatre in America in the 1880s. For three decades, the intellectual élite of the East Side had tried to domesticate *Moishe*, the peanut-cracking and boisterous Jewish immigrant audience of the Yiddish theatres, but without success. As it turned out, only the feature film was finally capable of imposing the 'discipline of silence' on the Jewish immigrant audiences of the East Side nickelodeons.

Feature Films and Ethnic Experience

Although the introduction of feature-length films (around 1912–13) meant that there would be less time available for Yiddish vaudeville in a programme, the trend towards longer films was received with enthusiasm by many motion picture exhibitors on the East Side, and for good reasons.

As early as 1910, the Yiddish music halls had sought to differentiate their product from that of the mixed-bill nickelodeons by programming three-act melodramas and short operettas. They thus hoped to secure a competitive position in the entertainment market, but the managers of the nickel shows followed the latest developments in the music hall business without much delay.[54] Within a year, most 'vaud-pic' nickel theatres were presenting two new three-act productions a week, in addition to their regular bill of moving pictures and vaudeville acts.[55] During the 1911–12 season, the managers of the Yiddish music halls turned to four-act plays (the standard of the 'legitimate' stage), even though the cut-throat competition with the nickel-and-dime theatres had forced them to reduce their prices. Although business was thriving, exhibitors were hard pressed to keep their houses profitable – especially after the Hebrew Variety Actors' Union managed to impose better working conditions for its members, including a maximum workload of five turns a day (instead of ten to twelve).[56] With costs up, box-office takings down and additional competition from three new 1,000-seat houses (Loew's Delancey Street Theatre, the Odeon Theatre and the National Winter Garden), some managers began to view the feature film as a welcome alternative to long plays. In February 1912, just a few weeks after the deal with the Hebrew Variety Actors' Union, the Grand Music Hall began to programme feature films. For ten cents, the audience could watch 'the biggest sensation of the century, the $100,000 production of *Dante's Inferno*'.[57] After this, the entertainment business on the Lower East Side changed rapidly.

In 1913, Loew curtailed his activities on the Lower East Side in order to concentrate on the operation of his Delancey Street and Avenue B theatres. The Grand Theatre was turned into a Yiddish-language vaudeville house which offered feature films as its main attraction. Many Yiddish music halls, especially the smaller ones, closed their doors for good. Others became playhouses, presenting programmes which were almost entirely devoted to four-act plays, just as in the 'legitimate' theatres. In fact, in terms of repertoire, the distinction between these vaudeville houses and the 'legitimate' theatres became increasingly blurred during the early 1910s since both favoured light comedies and operettas for their staple entertainment.[58] Apparently, Jewish immigrant audiences no longer cultivated a 'Russian' preference for tragedies.

Most managers of mixed-bill nickelodeons cut out vaudeville altogether. The city's new building code for moving picture theatres gave them the opportunity to enlarge their seating capacity from 300 to 600, if they invested in new buildings. The ordinance caused a genuine construction fever among the more enterprising film exhibitors on the Lower East Side. The new nickel-and-dime theatres that they opened were generally equipped with two projection machines.[59] This not only facilitated the showing of multi-reel films, but it also meant that vaudeville acts and songs were no longer needed to divert the audience while the reels were changed.[60] In short, this time Yiddish vaudeville had lost the battle on nearly all fronts.

Had the Jewish cultural heritage also been defeated? Let me use the case of the

American Movies, a 600-seat cinema that opened in April 1914 on East Third Street, as a historical shorthand for the condition of film exhibition on the Lower East Side at the eve of the First World War. Considering the name Charles Steiner gave to his new theatre, we could expect that he offered his patrons American films. So he did, but he also showed foreign films and, more importantly, his selection of films was rather biased. Between 11 April and 24 July 1914, Steiner advertised in the *Forward* for the following features: *Esther and Mordechai* (Gaumont, 1910?), 'a wonderful Biograph production: the biblical story of *Judith and Holophernes*' (*Judith of Bethulia*, Biograph, 1914), *Samson the Hero* (*Samson*, Universal, 1914), *Joseph's Trials in Egypt* (Eclectic Film Co/Pathé, 1914), *Mendel Beilis*,[61] 'Jacob Gordin's greatest drama *Di shkhite* made in Russia with the greatest Jewish actors, such as Ester Rochel Kaminski and Sam Adler' (*The Slaughter*, Kosmofilm, 1914), *Bar Kochba* (*Bar Kochba – The Hero of a Nation*, Supreme, 1913), '*Should a woman tell?*, performed by the Imperial Russian Company of St. Petersburg with the beautiful Olga Tshernova' (Apex, 1914), and '*Uriel Acosta* performed in moving pictures by the best actors of the Yiddish stage' (Great Players, 1914).

Of course, this overkill of Jewishness is to a large extent the result of a carefully planned marketing strategy. On the one hand, Steiner only promoted titles dealing with Jewish subject matter and films that had strong ties with Eastern Europe. On the other hand, he provided no information whatsoever about the single and double reels which were offered in addition to the special feature films and which might have shown more American subjects.[62] Advertisements from other movie theatres on the East Side confirm that local exhibitors continued to build audiences on the basis of ethnic identity. The ethnic experience of movie-going was no longer organised around Yiddish vaudeville, but embedded in a specific selection of films. This shift marked the end of the first-generation film exhibitors, those who had started out as saloonkeepers and whose vernacular had been Yiddish. The lead was taken up by a second generation of exhibitors, American-born Jews like Charles Steiner, who had started out during the nickelodeon boom and who were certainly more assimilated than the previous generation. Yet, the programmes of their moving picture theatres kept an ethnic flavour.

The First World War brought immigration from Eastern Europe to the United States almost entirely to a halt. During the war, only a few thousand Eastern European Jews arrived each year at Ellis Island. The export of European films to America also declined drastically. Hence, for the managers of the movie theatres in the Jewish quarter, it became difficult to maintain their ethnically specific programming practices. However, Yiddish vaudeville did not revive a second time. It appears that Jewish immigrants who went to the movies no longer appreciated active sociability and vocal familiarity in their neighbourhood theatres. On 28 July 1914, a few days before the outbreak of war, the *Forward* depicted how the Jewish audience amused itself at the moving pictures on the East Side. The audience was 'totally absorbed by the show', a feature film about a young man who had abducted his sweetheart from her father's house. Followed by the father and the police, dogs and cars, the lovers tried to escape over mountains, fields, roads and rivers. At the most critical moment of the film, when the couple fell from a mountain into a river, the 'strenuous silence' in the auditorium was suddenly interrupted by an 'excited man' screaming: 'Oy, vey, she has fallen into the water'. In other words, a viewer who was not yet used to the middle-class standard of reception brought back the 'real' space of the theatre to an audience that was completely absorbed by the story on the screen, and his cry caused a blunt interruption of the classic film-spectator relationship. Was the man a greenhorn, a newcomer recently–arrived from Russia? Perhaps, but, in any case, it is more relevant to know what the reaction of the audience was: '*sharop!*'[63]

Notes

I wish to thank Peter Kramer and Derek Rubin for their extensive comments and helpful suggestions. All translations from the Yiddish are my own.

1 By 1910, 1.2 million Jews from different backgrounds lived in New York, where they accounted for almost a quarter of the city's population. This essay focuses exclusively on the Jews of East European descent, who made up the bulk of the city's Jewish population.
2 By 1910, just over half a million Jews lived on the Lower East Side. Gerard Sorin, *A Time for Building: The Third Migration, 1880–1920* (Baltimore: Johns Hopkins University Press, 1992), pp. 70–1.
3 Bella Cohen Spewack, *Streets: A Memoir of the Lower East Side* (New York: Feminist Press at the City University of New York, 1995).
4 *Ibid.*, pp. 51, 70.
5 Lewis Jacobs, *The Rise of the American Film: A Critical History* (New York: Harcourt, Brace and Company, 1939); Garth Jowett, *Film: The Democratic Art* (Boston: Little Brown, 1976); American Social History Project, The City University of New York, *Who Built America?* (New York: Pantheon Books, 1992), vol. 2, pp. 182–3, 283–4.
6 Miriam Hansen, *Babel and Babylon: Spectatorship in American Silent Film* (Cambridge, Mass.: Harvard University Press, 1991), pp. 67–8.
7 Jacobs, *The Rise of the American Film*, p. 12.
8 Richard Abel, 'The Perils of Pathé, or the Americanization of Early American Cinema', in Leo Charney and Vanessa R. Schwartz (eds), *Cinema and the Invention of Modern Life* (Berkeley: University of California Press, 1995), p. 190.
9 Barton W. Currie, 'The Nickel Madness', *Harpers Weekly*, 24 August 1907, quoted in Abel, 'The Perils of Pathé', p. 188.
10 Abel, 'The Perils of Pathé', p. 184.
11 See, for example, William Uricchio and Roberta E. Pearson, *Reframing Culture: The Case of the Vitagraph Quality Films* (Princeton: Princeton University Press, 1993), pp. 41–64.
12 Abel, 'The Perils of Pathé', p. 199.
13 During the teens, the *Forward* became America's largest-selling foreign-language newspaper. Its circulation increased from 72,000 in 1908 to around 140,000 at the beginning of 1914.
14 For contemporary descriptions of the Yiddish music halls see, for example, Paul Klapper, 'The Yiddish Music Hall', *University Settlement Studies Quarterly*, vol. 2, no. 4 (1906), pp. 19–23; Khayim Malits, 'Yidishe myuzik hols in nyu york', *Der amerikaner*, 30 November 1906, p. 13; Abraham Cahan, 'A shpatsir iber di yidishe myuzik hols', *Tsaytgayst*, 13 October 1905, p. 24. See also Nina Warnke, 'Immigrant Popular Culture as Contested Sphere: Yiddish Music Halls, the Yiddish Press, and the Processes of Americanization, 1900–1910', *Theatre Journal*, 48 (1996), pp. 321–5.
15 Jacob M. Gordin, 'The Yiddish Stage', *Yearbook of the University Settlement Society of*

New York (1901), pp. 29–30; 'Di yidishe muzik hols zaynen a skandal ohn an "ober"', *Forward*, 17 March 1902.

16 Warnke, 'Immigrant Popular Culture as Contested Sphere', p. 326.

17 Klapper, 'The Yiddish Music Hall', p. 20.

18 'An Unexploited Field and Its Possibilities', *Views and Films Index*, 6 October 1906. The two mentioned moving picture venues are most likely Adolph Zukor's Automatic Vaudeville on 263 Grand Street and Morris Boom's Fycent on number 265. I would like to thank Richard Abel for drawing my attention to this article.

19 For exact figures, see Ben Singer, 'Manhattan Nickelodeons: New Data on Audiences and Exhibitors', *Cinema Journal*, 34; no. 3 (Spring 1995), pp. 5–35; and Judith Thissen, 'Oy, Myopia!: A Reaction from Judith Thissen on the Singer–Allen Controversy', *Cinema Journal*, 36, no. 4 (Summer 1997), pp. 104–6.

20 'Vo zaynen ahingekumen di yidishe myuzik hols?', *Forward*, 24 May 1908.

21 *Ibid.*

22 Moses Rischin, *The Promised City: New York's Jews, 1870–1914* (Cambridge, Mass.: Harvard University Press, 1962), p. 79. For the residential block density in the Rivington–Essex Street neighbourhood, see *Fifteenth Annual Report of the College Settlement*, 1903–1904, plate no. 1 (based on the *First Report of the Tenement House Department of the City of New York*).

23 Pre-1917 Conveyances Section II, liber 137 cp 269, Office of the City Register. Alteration Docket for Manhattan 1908, application no. 83, Bureau of Buildings (at the New York City Municipal Archives). See also Judith Thissen, 'Oy, Myopia!', p. 103.

24 Pre-1917 Conveyances Section II, liber 179 cp 43 and liber 180 cp 25, Office of the City Register.

25 Pre-1917 Conveyances Section II, liber 196 cp 322, liber 199 cp 266, Office of the City Register.

26 'Vo zaynen ahingekumen di yidishe myuzik hols?', *Forward*, 24 May 1908.

27 'Vo zaynen ahingekumen di myuzik-hol "stars"?', *Forward*, 26 November 1908.

28 *Forward*, 13 December 1908, p. 1; *Dos yidishes tageblatt*, 13 December 1908, p. 1.

29 'Di ekelhafte shmuts fun gevise muving-piktshur pletzer', *Forward*, 15 March 1909.

30 In previous years Cahan had led several moral crusades against the *shmuts* (filth) in the Yiddish music hals. See Warnke, 'Immigrant Popular Culture as Contested Sphere'.

31 'Vo zaynen ahingekumen di yidishe myuzik hols?', *Forward*, 24 May 1908.

32 Abel, 'The Perils of Pathé', p. 201.

33 *Ibid.*

34 'Farvos hoben di amerikaner lieb komedyes un yiden nit', *Forward*, 13 May 1908.

35 Yuri Tsivian, 'Some Preparatory Remarks on Russian Cinema', in Paolo Cherchi Usai and Yuri Tsivian (eds), *Silent Witnesses: Russian Films 1908–1919* (Pordenone: Edizioni Biblioteca dell'Immagine and London: British Film Institute, 1989), pp. 24–5.

36 Gordin, 'The Yiddish Stage', p. 29.

37 'Farvos hoben di amerikaner lieb komedyes un yiden nit?' *Forward*, 13 May 1908.

38 *Ibid.*

39 Gordin, 'The Yiddish Stage', pp. 29–30; Warnke, 'Immigrant Popular Culture as Contested Sphere', pp. 324–8.

40 Warnke, 'Immigrant Popular Culture as Contested Sphere', p. 323.

41 See, for example, Cahan's editorials in *Forward* 17, 18, 20 and 28 March 1902, as well as 4 April 1902; Cahan, 'A shpatsir iber di yidishe myuzik hols', *Tsaytgayst*, 13 October 1905, and 'Di klipe fun di myuzik hols in yidishe kwartal', *Tsaytgayst*, 20 October 1905. See also Fanny Reinhardt, 'Wegen di unanshtendige lieder in di muyzik hols', *Forward*, 21 December 1905 (a letter to the editor, written by a variety actress in reaction to Cahan's negative campaigns in the *Forward* and *Tsaytgayst*).

42 'Di muving piktshur geleris', *Forward*, 4 March 1908 and 'Vo zaynen ahingekumen di yidishe myuzik hols?', *Forward*, 24 May 1908.

43 Advertisement, *Forward*, 13 December 1909.

44 *Forward*, 3 September 1909, p. 1.

45 For instance, prostitution, white slavery and loose sexual behaviour – vices of urban America that had been associated with the Yiddish music halls – were now regularly linked with the moving picture houses on the East Side. See '2 yidishe boys fershikt in Sing-Sing als kadeten', *Forward*, 31 January 1910, p. 1; 'Vider di gefahr fun di muving piktshurs', *Forward*, 2 February 1911. Also see Janet Staiger, *Bad Women: Regulating Sexuality in Early American Cinema* (Minneapolis: University of Minnesota Press, 1995), pp. 44–52, 99–103, 120–8.

46 These variety shows lasted a whole matinee or evening, for an admission price of ten to thirty cents. Admission remained continuous and moving pictures were still part of the programme. See, for example, advertisements of Atlantic Garden, Grand Street Music Hall and Houston Hippodrome in the *Forward*. Also see 'Tkhies-hame'ysim fun di myuzik hols', *Forward*, 25 December 1909 and 'Vos hert zich in di muzik hols?', *Forward*, 26 August 1910.

47 Robert C. Allen, 'Motion Picture Exhibition in Manhattan, 1906–1912: Beyond the Nickelodeon', *Cinema Journal*, 18, no. 2 (spring 1979), reprinted in John Fell (ed.), *Film Before Griffith* (Berkeley: University of California Press, 1983), p. 171; *idem*, *Vaudeville and Film 1895–1915: A Study in Media Interaction* (New York: Arno Press, 1980), pp. 230–50; *idem.*, 'Manhattan Myopia; or, Oh! Iowa!', *Cinema Journal*, 35, no. 3 (Spring 1996), pp. 84–95.

48 'Tkhies-ham'ysim fun di myuzik hols', *Forward*, 25 December 1909.

49 Kathy Peiss, *Cheap Amusements: Working Women and Leisure in Turn-of-the-Century New York* (Philadelphia: Temple University Press, 1986), p. 151.

50 Eastern European Jewish immigration to the US declined by nearly 50 per cent from 103,387 to 57,551. Immigration figures from Commissioner General's reports, in *American Jewish Yearbook* (Philadelphia: Jewish Publication Society of America, 1913), p. 429.

51 Abel, 'The Perils of Pathé'; Uricchio and Pearson, *Reframing Culture*, pp. 41–64.

52 Hansen, *Babel and Babylon*, pp. 76–89.

53 Hansen, *Babel and Babylon*, p. 95.

54 For a detailed analysis, see Judith Thissen, 'Charles Steiner's Houston Hippodrome', in Gregg Bachman and Tom Slater (eds), *A Slightly Different Light: Exploring Marginalized Issues and Forces in American Silent Film* (Southern Illinois University Press, forthcoming).

55 For example, advertisements of Steiner's Theatre, the Metropolitan, Monroe Theatre, Rutgers Theatre, Suffolk Theatre and Thalia Music Hall, *Forward*, 16 January 1911.

56 'An erklehrung tsu alle rekhtdenkende menshen!, di hibru verayeti ektors yunion lok. 5', *Forward*, 16 January 1912.

57 Advertisement, *Forward*, 17 February 1912.

58 Warnke, 'Immigrant Popular Culture as Contested Sphere', p. 331.

59 See, for example, the clause regarding the erection of a projection booth for the operation of two machines in the lease of the New Law Theatre, 23 Second Avenue, built in 1913. Pre-1917 Conveyances Section II, liber 225 cp 2, Office of the City Register.

60 Eileen Bowser, *The Transformation of Cinema: 1907–1915* (Berkeley: University of California Press, 1990), p. 199.

61 Three films were made about the Mendel Beilis case: *The Black 107* (Ruby, 1913), *Terrors of Russia* (Italian American Film Co, 1913) and *The Mystery of the Mendel Beilis Case* (Germany, 1914). Patricia Ehrens, *The Jew in American Cinema* (Bloomington: Indiana University Press, 1984), pp. 59–60; Jim Hoberman, *Bridge of Light: Yiddish Film Between Two Worlds* (New York: Schocken Books/MoMa, 1991), pp. 28–9.

62 In 1914, the bulk of the films released on the American market still consisted of single and double reels. Bowser, *Transformation of Cinema*, p. 213.

63 'Vi azoi der yidishe oylem amuzirt zikh in muving piktshurs', *Forward*, 28 July 1914.

2 Italian Imageries, Historical Feature Films, and the Fabrication of Italy's Spectators in Early 1900s New York
Giorgio Bertellini

The traditional historiography of early cinema has long claimed that the small, storefront movie theatres, crammed into pockets of Manhattan between 1905 and the early 1910s, typified cinema's general emergence in America at the beginning of the twentieth century. Those dark and cramped 'nickelodeons' embodied the movies' widely-acclaimed power to generate – from the bottom up – mass urban recreation through amalgamation and standardisation. According to these accounts, the practice of movie-going was an unmistakable index of the mass co-option of the working class and immigrants into the leisure-time offerings and lifestyles of the modern metropolis. New York's movie theatres fostered the cultural and social communion of mass entertainment and mass society.

More recently, lively debates have challenged the overall picture of early cinema as a mainly working-class medium. Film historians have argued that from its very inception, cinema was a widespread form of entertainment shared by the middle class, and that moving pictures were deeply embedded with bourgeois ideologies of respectability, decorum and edification. The concern over cinema's ultimate social constituency has proved to be a crucial one, for this discussion has entailed outlining the social and aesthetic patternings of the most important mass medium of the twentieth century. Several territories of film history have been involved: the historical dynamics of film form, including its narrative, stylistic, communicative and ideological characteristics; movies' exhibition sites and contexts, including censorship and patrons' movie-going habits. This speculative framework has expanded the traditional modes of film history, obliging it to accommodate not only the requirements of film theory and criticism, but also those of sociology, cultural studies, urban and intellectual history, and religion.

The controversies over the social composition and cultural experience of early cinema's audiences have, however, consistently displayed a remarkable disregard for non-American factors. In particular, immigrants have been subsumed into the category of 'working class members', thereby discounting their cultural and historical specificities. Immigrants did not, of course, arrive alone or live in solitude in America. Agencies such as mutual-aid societies, local churches and especially ethnic newspapers helped shape the daily lives of the newcomers and, at the same time, heavily influenced their perception of domestic and international events. When it came to Italian immigrants, for example, an examination of the newspapers they read in their own language reveals the extent to which they showed deep ties with the economic, political and cultural forces then active in Italy.

It is also important to emphasise the international character of early film exhibition. Between 1908 and 1915, roughly 1,600 Italian films circulated among American exchanges, a fact almost completely ignored by film historians. These movies inevitably complicate the usual historical perception of working-class spectators watching American-produced film in American nickelodeons.[1] Such crucial foreign components of early cinema's consumption have at times been acknowledged, but they have nevertheless been marginalised in most discussions of the period.[2]

In this chapter, I shall explore ethnic film reception by means of an analysis of a unique and uncharted encounter between a specific group of immigrants, those coming from Italy (mainly from the South), and a particular genre of Italian film, the historical re-enactments produced after 1908/1909 and widely distributed in the US between 1908 and 1915. The sources used in this study include Italian filmographies, American distributors' business records, the New York City Italian-American press and American trade periodicals. These shed considerable light on literary and performative narratives centred on antiquity and Christian virtue, a rising nationalism in Italian culture and politics, and the problematics of Italian immigrant popular culture. They also indicate the degree to which this encounter with a particular genre of film influenced Italian immigrants' self-conception. Until coming to the US, in fact, Southern Italians had mainly established their identity by means of their local or municipal origins, and had viewed Italy's political unification as one more form of 'colonial subjugation'.[3] Once in America, they experienced two distinctive but convergent sets of cultural imageries which contributed to the construction of a national affiliation and a patriotism that had previously been for the most part precarious, undefined, or non-existent.

One such imagery, prominent both in Europe and America, related to the touristic and aesthetic normalisation of Italy as the shrine of artistic culture and civilisation. Called the 'touristic-aesthetic conception' by Richard H. Brodhead, it grew out of the quasi-sacred ground of art works associated with 'classic Italy'.[4] The second imagery, distinctively Italian, brought together Roman antiquity, classic humanism and imperial rule with the modern practice of nationalism. The former had flourished in America in the second half of the nineteenth century when an emerging gentry class found legitimation of its superior status in the leisure-time attractions of high culture, opera, classic art and the Grand Tour. The latter had a more recent origin, relating to the long struggles for Italian political unification, the *Risorgimento*, although its more pedagogic emphasis on the incomparable past of *Romanità* was timed to an early twentieth-century ambition to have (or mystically 'maintain') an imperialistic share of Northern Africa.[5]

These two constructed traditions met or overlapped most blatantly in the public spheres of exported Italian entertainments: opera, circus shows and, in particular, historical films. Eager to gain exclusive rights to the international allure of antiquity, Italian film companies quickly capitalised on such internal resources and assets as architectural settings, staging traditions and cheap extras. These historical dramas soon reached New York's upscale movie theatres and vaudeville houses, since they were originally intended to attract middle-class patrons and marketed as closer in style to the city's most elevated entertainment, opera. These films' subsequent runs in venues frequented by working-class patrons and immigrants have, however, been left so far uncharted by ethnic history.[6] On America's movie screens, films like *The Last Days of Pompeii* (1908 and 1913), *Nero, or the Burning of Rome* (1909), *Spartacus* (1909 and 1913), *Quo Vadis?* (1913) or *Antony and Cleopatra* (1913) promoted the immigrants' encounter, exploration, and construction of their nation's conflicted past, which juxtaposed Roman and Christian civilisations, Pagan and Catholic laws, civic and religious values. As Benedict Anderson has noted, 'new-emerging nations imagined themselves antique. [Thus] "antiquity" [was], at a certain historical juncture, the *necessary consequence* of "novelty"'.[7]

A closer look at urban immigrant movie-going communities reveals not a fast and consensual process of Americanisation so much as a unique phenomenon of discontinuity. The glorious antiquity depicted on screen, together with its educational and religious highlights, brought to Italy's immigrants the modernist novelty of national identity. That identity also constituted a basic requirement for adaptation as a singular ethnic group within American society.[8]

One of the most recurring obsessions of American turn-of-the-century urban society was the forceful gentrification and Americanisation of public life, including health, work, politics and entertainment. This followed a cultural crisis on the part of native-born Americans worried over the threat to their hegemony posed by the arrival of millions of immigrants and changing social conditions. Anxious over the spread of new crimes and diseases, along with the rise of leftist activism, several constituencies of American society reacted with aggressive attempts to strengthen traditional values and re-establish bourgeois economic, cultural and moral leadership. One could speak of such processes as forms of 'domestication', understanding it either as an introduction to and training in particular habits and rules, or as a move toward Americanisation. It is important to keep the two separated, since the adoption of modern leisure-time habits in the country's largest metropolis did not imply *ipso facto* the embracing of an American identity.

The tendency to classify early film audiences by social class makes a basic assumption that, because of their unfamiliarity with and subjection to modern life, immigrants were innocent viewers. This discursive practice reproduces contemporary regulatory and rhetorical procedures of education and control of leisure time in general, and of the movie-going phenomenon in particular. The hegemonic rhetorics of urban and health policies, political language, reformers' and religious groups' protests, and censorship commissions have largely dominated the historical debate until now.[9] Such historians as William Uricchio and Roberta Pearson have legitimately avowed their methodological predilection for the 'constructed perception' and 'melodramatic discursive emplotment' of early film audiences in place of loosely essentialist and hardly definitive investigations of the 'real entities'.[10] Their work must be singled out for showing a fairly rare interest in the discursive and ideological pressures of the Progressive Era, but their inquiry has deliberately left out the specific responses of ethnic communities to dominant cultural gentrifications. While it remains undeniable that, between 1907 and 1913, middle-class social and cultural anxiety led to a 'bourgeoisification' of the American film industry and film exhibition practices in New York, the scrutiny of middle-class ideology alone fails to account for other non-American constituencies. This appears to be a particularly problematic approach for a city in which immigrants made up more than 40 per cent of the total population between 1910 and 1920, while 80 per cent of its population were the children of foreign-born parents.

As a result, several questions have not even been posed, let alone answered: who were these immigrant spectators? How should one write about them – as individuals and/or as a community? In addition, which films did they watch? And what kind of experience might those immigrants have had? Before saying anything about Italian audiences' reception of Italian films, it is necessary to discuss briefly their self-conception, the problematic state of national bonding among 'Italians' in the early twentieth century, and the American reverberations of the image of Italy disseminated in European novels, tourist guides and art catalogues throughout the eighteenth and nineteenth centuries.

I do not claim to be able to assess real people's experiences in front of Italian historical films. 'Direct evidence' is hard to find when dealing with a population that was, for the most part, illiterate. My intention, therefore, is to emphasise the problematics of this film audience's ethnic singularity, their 'Italianness' so to speak, all too often misunderstood as a ready-made status. I argue that the consumption of Italian films, in particular of Italian historical films, contributed to the construction of Italy's immigrants' ethnic and national identity. While still remaining within the boundaries of an evidential paradigm, my endeavour aims to point to a real and uncharted dimension of early film spectatorship in America.

As already noted, I resist calling Italy's immigrants 'Italians' since before the advent of the First World War, the geographical and cultural self-conception of these migrants, predominantly peasants from the South, mainly insisted on a local or municipal origin, not a national one.[11] If one regards the process of Italy's political unification in 1860–1 as a colonial annexation by Northern interests, concerned with gaining position and status within Europe, then Southern populations constitute an example of what historian Pasquale Verdicchio has termed 'colonized peoples' or 'dissonant national subjects'.[12] Their economic backwardness, social subalternity to local ruling élites and cultural resistance to the ideals and policies of nationhood, were all elements composing that troublesome scenario termed by Gramsci 'the Southern question'.

At the end of the nineteenth century, 'Italian' society had remained a largely agrarian one, and although political unification had been achieved almost half a century earlier, linguistic, cultural and civic unity had yet to be brought about.

The origins of a nationalist impetus in Italy should not be read as a political response to cultural needs, as happened in most countries, but as quite the opposite: 'cultural responses to rising economic and political needs'.[13] Immediately after political unification, the government attempted to manufacture a sacred sense of nation, a form of lay religion capable of competing with the established Catholic doctrine. In such efforts to sacralise the State, its monarchic institutions and its history, monuments were erected around the burial sites of the Wars of Independence, and attempts were made to imbue the State's army services and newly mandatory schools with ideals of national destiny and memories of ancient glories. The endeavours to create a shared civic doctrine, however, failed miserably throughout the second half of the nineteenth century because of the lack of any lay spirit of regeneration among the masses – not by chance had the *Risorgimento* been called an 'incomplete national revolution' by bitter anti-monarchists and democrats – and because of the utter inadequacy of the ruling class to commit itself seriously to mass politics.

The new century brought fresh incentives for the creation of a national liturgy and, although not of political design, the new impetus would in the long run overthrow the political groups in power. The most astonishing transformative factor in Italian life during the early 1900s was the growth of industrial production. Economic factors, however, fail to explain the extension and make-up of the semiotic output that the myths of *Romanità* and antiquity were able to provide, with their religious and mystical solicitations mixed with utopianism and nativism. Other forces were at work, in a better position to help forge a popular imagery. A small group of middle-class integralists, the Nationalists, composed of radical intellectuals, journalists and educated outsiders, first expressed their anti-bourgeois and anti-parliamentary views in élite literary journals. Soon, however, they capitalised on the conflicts between liberals, socialists and the prime minister, Giolitti, and became an active pressure group in parliament. Backed by industrialists, especially after the economic crisis of 1907, the Nationalists quickly organised themselves. If 1910 marked the birth of the Nationalist Association (*Associazione Nazionalistica Italiana*), 1911 marked Italy's surprise invasion of Libya as a result of the government's unexpected concession to the Nationalists' war requests. Although the Nationalists were still a political minority, their influence was heavily supported by those industrial groups who feared that their North African business was threatened by France's potential expansion in the region. The Nationalists' recreation of a new Italy incorporated the Futurists' aesthetics of modern war, which they also viewed as an ideological embellishment to strengthen or, as they put it, to save the nation's pride and honour.

The year of the Libyan war was a crucial one, for it also marked the fiftieth anniversary of the Statute and Unification of Italy. Nationwide meetings and commemorations were held, characterised by intense patriotism and nostalgia for Italy's glorious past. By the early years of the new century, the Universal Exposition in Turin and festivities around and about Rome had become a unique opportunity to strengthen the delicate relationships between the Vatican and the State. The artistic and cultural magnificence of the Roman Empire could somehow blend its grandiosity with the matchless spirituality of the capital of Christianity.

Around the 1870s, a particular theatrical production had begun exploring the shared fascination for antiquity and *Romanità*. Pietro Cossa, a prolific tragedy writer, became extremely popular for his capacity to bring ancient historical figures to life in dramatic stagings that featured grand sets and large 'plebeian' crowds. Between 1871 and 1881, Cossa staged such plays as *Nero*, *Plauto*, *Cleopatra*, *Messalina* and *Giuliano L'Apostata*, in which the main attraction lay in realistic renderings of the private lives of historical characters, facing daily, banal dilemmas between instinct and virtues, dissolution and restraint. To describe Cossa's work, critic and philosopher Benedetto Croce coined the expression 'historical realism' (*verismo storico*).[14]

Similarly, the newly fuelled patriotism bestowed a remarkable influence on the Italian literature of emigration.[15] Abandoned were the 'necrophilic and pietist tones' of nostalgia, misery and death recurrent in earlier diaries, personal accounts and novels (e.g. De Amicis' novel, *Sull'Oceano*, 1889). The new productions displayed a self-confident nationalistic pride which turned the migrants' daily struggles (and the public perception of their experiences) into remarkable manifestations of cultural and economic opportunity. The most remarkable contribution was from Giovanni Pascoli, still regarded today as one of Italy's greatest poets. Through his short and delicate lyrics in which he evoked his sad childhood or celebrated nature and family life, Pascoli contributed to easing the cultural and ideological antinomy between the historical problem of emigration and a dehistoricised and mythical pageant of patriotism. Distant from the aggressive elaborations of such politicised writers as Gabriele D'Annunzio or Enrico Corradini, Pascoli focused his lyrics on the moral virtues of *italianità* (Italianness), centred around the master trope of ruralism and familial relationships. In his poems, Italy's natural beauty and wealth become an unforgotten 'ancient mother' (*antica madre*), whose sons are dispersed but united by a brotherly love and a common destiny as exiles. Pascoli's metahistorical, ethno-rural and anti-cosmopolitan profile of the Italian *émigré* was widely used as a glorification of the peasant-soldier during the First World War and in the ruralist and romantic ideology of the Fascist provincial *squadristi* in the 1920s. His pastoral portraits also had a deep impact among Italian-Americans thanks to the circulation of his ideas in the ethnic press.[16]

Italian cinema was relatively responsive to the patriotic impulses and mannerisms of anniversaries, public ceremonies and contemporary literary, theatrical or artistic productions. From its beginning in 1905 to the rise of feature films in the early 1910s, it always displayed special care in its historical re-enactments and high-class literary adaptations. The very first Italian fiction film was an edifying exaltation of *Risorgimento*, titled *La presa di Roma: 20 settembre 1870* (*The Taking of Rome: 20 September 1870*, Alberini-Santoni, 1905), which in seven scenes visualised a crucial event of Italian history: the seizing of Rome by the newly formed Italian army and the selection of the city as the nation's capital. The film's plotline literally paraphrased the lay and monarchic historiography of Italy's ruling bourgeoisie.

From its inception, cinema had emerged as an international industrial and aesthetic commodity, and Italian film-makers quickly learned to combine the growing domestic taste for historical re-enactments with the widespread ideal conception of Italy as the cradle of civic humanism, antiquity, classical art and architecture. The use of Roman and Greek artistic icons, together with Latin literacy and pillared architectures had been widely adopted in America as an ideological and pedagogical practice since the late seventeenth century, used in order to attain political and cultural legitimacy and then developed into a well-rehearsed mixture of instruction, discipline and hegemony.[17] A blend of *Romanità* and Christianity, medieval cruelties and Renaissance splendours contributed to the construction of a stereotypical and pervasive image of Italy, that of a *paesaggio* (landscape), rigidly lodged in its own history and geography.[18]

The Rome-based film company, Cines, which had opened a New York office as early as August 1907, exploited the association of its productions with Italian

Moving Picture World, *11 April 1908.*

art and culture at an early stage in its American advertising strategies. On 11
April 1908, the front page of *Moving Picture World* was almost entirely covered
by Cines' promotion of fourteen of its films, introduced by a symptomatic
paragraph:

> We have delved into the classics and there found material for Comedy and Drama, and
> garbing our stories in the matchless splendor of Italian Art, we are going to give you a
> product which will be lauded from ocean to ocean. [...] The past is full with evidence
> of the glory and greatness of the Italian masters – Raphael, Michael Angelo, Leonardo

Da Vinci, Del Sarto, Correggio, and others. The achievements of that age are truthfully reflected in the present. Films in white and black, tones, tints and colors, with blendings indicative of these masters, will be our offering.[19]

Italian film companies were often able to market the national product as 'Italian'. Apart from the historical and mythological costume dramas, there were numerous actualities, 'views' and melodramas that highlighted Italy's natural and cultural landscape but also, in the case of Neopolitan films, a sense of Plebeian realism. The connotation of 'Italianness' was, however, less blatant for comedies, which were often paired with French productions.

It was, however, the unprecedented international success of the first large-scale Italian spectacle film, Ambrosio's *The Last Days of Pompeii* (an adaptation of the famous 1835 novel by Edward G. Bulwer-Lytton, screened just three years after the widely reported Vesuvius's eruption) that exemplified what the Italian national film industry could do best. Produced in 1908, the film was first shown in the US in April 1909, and became a paradigm for the artful re-enactments of ancient daily life and death. This film was followed, in November 1909, by *Nero, or the Burning of Rome*, another Ambrosio film (the first in the so-called 'Golden Series'), which was highly praised for its choreographic accuracy, its enticing realism and its red-toned sequences.[20] The story (not the film), with a slightly different title (*Nero, or the Destruction of Rome*), had already been a sensational and widely exported circus show, produced by Imre Kiralfy (associated with P. T. Barnum's *The Greatest Show on Earth*) and premièring at the Olympia Theatre in London in 1889.

For the Italian film industry, the success of Ambrosio's films opened the way to similarly grandiose productions, which reproduced the most distinctive features of Italian films: historical settings, large-scale and lavish production values and, by comparison to the stage flatness of most contemporary American films, a three-dimensionality in their use of settings. By 1909, this pattern can be immediately recognised in several Italian-exported films: Pineschi's *Spartacus*, Itala's *Julius Caesar*, Cines' *Macbeth*, and *Othello*, produced by Film d'Arte Italiana in 1909 and released in the US in early 1910. The great achievements of these films in the world's largest movie market were of much commercial and cultural importance because they combined the internationally shared necessity for the cinema to gain censors' approval, social respectability, industrial rationalisation and commercial stability with established visual and stage traditions from both sides of the Atlantic, and also with Italy's rising nationalistic spirit.[21] Within the next four years, several films followed in the successful footsteps of those predecessors: *Dante's Inferno* (Milano Films, 1911), *The Fall of Troy* (Itala, 1911), two versions of *The Last Days of Pompeii* (Ambrosio and Pasquali, 1913), *Spartacus* (Pasquali, 1913), *Quo Vadis?* (Cines, 1913) and *Cabiria* (1914). Their exhibition venues ranged from high-class theatrical houses to movie theatres that were competing fiercely not only for the respectable American patron, but the Italian one as well.

Between 1908–9 and 1915–16, Italian films in the American market succeeded quite well overall, although the actual exporting records of each film company appear fairly discontinuous throughout the period.[22] In common with many Vitagraph films and Pathé's Film d'Art, these historical films were quickly singled

36

out for their meritorious educational status and for their artistic adaptation of major works in the western cultural and religious canon. Furthermore, the praise for the realism of Italian films was quite unmatched. Different from the *tableaux vivants* of French religious subjects or American passion plays, the historical dramas of Ambrosio, Cines and Milano Films were often recognised as merging a fascination for celebrated histories with a startling visual authenticity in their re-creation. Not only were their realism and naturalness conveyed through the exploitation of real settings (Roman buildings, Renaissance palaces, Napoleonic façades, or authentic Shakespearian locations), but also through the visual and narrative inclusion of large open-air spaces and the spectacular employment of crowds of thousand of extras, as never seen before. As an effect, the spatial and human plenitude appeared to underline the truth and accuracy of the representation.

What sort of 'truth' can one refer to when examining the film experience of Italy's immigrants in New York? As Antonio Gramsci described it, the Italian bourgeoisie – unlike the French – had been unable and unwilling to 'unite the common people' through a political and cultural sense of nationhood. Southern masses were hardly affected in their material and social lives by nationalistic traditions – at least, until they emigrated.[23] It was only in New York that Italy's Southern population experienced an intense, albeit idealised image of their nation, as it was mediated by Italian movies. And yet, the expensive costume-drama productions were neither made for nor marketed to the ethnic working man on the Bowery, a stereotypical figure quite different from the bourgeois *flâneur* sampling highbrow entertainments in the theatre district. But, as we shall see, the film competition among historical super-spectacles and celebrated dramatisations allowed Italy's 'cosmopolitan' films to develop in somewhat eccentric directions.

When dealing with an investigation of film spectatorship, the main challenge relates, of course, to the question of evidence. As already observed, such film historians as Uricchio and Pearson have been quite careful not to define their work as the examination of 'real people's response' to specific films, preferring instead to focus on 'conditions of reception', 'class-bound discursive formations', or 'reading positions'.[24] Their analysis has focused on 'cultivated folks' or the circles of educated spectators longing for edifying amusement. A reasonable hypothesis relating to Italian immigrants' viewing engagement cannot be developed out of evidence connected solely to their experience in New York. Any local evidence must be read with reference to how Southern Italians conceptualised their identity *before* coming to the US.

As a concrete instance of the question at issue, I shall examine the ideological discourse of two Italian newspapers printed in New York, *Il Progresso Italo-Americano* (1880–1988), with an average circulation for the period 1909–15 of more than 90,000 copies; and *L'Araldo Italiano* (1889–1921, consolidated with *Il Telegrafo* from 1913), less successful, but still among the city's best-selling papers with an average of 35,000 copies.[25] What is most indicative about them is their constant emphasis on a metahistorical Italianness in their coverage of various events, from the war in Libya and Italy's economic growth to Italian achievements in the arts, sciences and in terms of producing film spectacles.

37

A close examination of newspaper highlights, editorials, columns and regular sections (especially those announcing new spectacles such as opera, theatre, or moving pictures) suggests that nationalistic discourse was a commonly established practice. The Italian community was constantly referred to as *la colonia*, or the colony, which emphasised both its apparently temporary character – trips to the homeland were much more frequent among Italians than among other ethnic groups – but also its close-knit fabric, reproducing familiar settlements in foreign territory.[26]

Newspapers rehearsed a sense of patriotism mainly with reference to the 'Past'. Daily and weekly space was devoted to the mention or praise of countless Italian figures (navigators, politicians, emperors, scientists, inventors, poets, singers, artists, musical composers, even strong men) and Italian anniversaries (e.g. Columbus Day and 20 September, the celebration of national unity). *Romanità* and the display of Italian ingeniuousness shaped the aesthetics of several discourses, ranging from health advertisements, articles on ancient daily habits, patriotic editorials, and the frequently partisan reports on the war in Libya through advertisements for the sale of illustrated books and pictures of victorious battles in the midst of the barbarious wilderness of the African continent.

In terms of popular culture, both *L'Araldo* and, especially, *Il Progresso* regularly reported on the three sources of Italian pride: patron saints' *feste*, opera performances and theatrical plays. But they also extensively covered international and Italian developments in film. Such coverage ranged from cinema's competing relationship with theatre to its pedagogic virtues and flaws; from the increasing size of the film industry and the scale of movie-going throughout the world to the various attempts to create the talking picture; or the inevitability of cinema's world success. However, Italian papers did not address the explosion of film-going in New York while it was actually happening, around 1905 and 1906. Before 1910, indeed, there was no such thing as a film review in the Italian papers published in New York. The most important mention of the cinema was a column titled *Cinematografando* (literally, 'shooting'), first published in *Il Progresso Italo-Americano*, on 17 September 1907.[27] *Cinematografando* collected short stories, foreign anecdotes and curious jokes, apparently edited according to no particular criteria and without overall comment by a columnist. The column reproduced in writing the 'attractions and effects' of film watching. No specific mention was made of Italian films or characters. Film coverage, however, radically changed in the early 1910s with the circulation of feature films such as *The Fall of Troy* (Itala Film, 1911), *Dante's Inferno* (Milano Films, 1911), *Jerusalem Delivered* (Cines, 1911) and *Odyssey* (Milano Films, 1911).

From December 1911 onwards, the most important Italian films, the costly historical re-enactments, were consistently advertised and promoted as 'Italian productions' both in *L'Araldo* and in *Il Progresso,* although endorsements were hardly longer than the headlines and never matched the lengthy examinations of them in *Moving Picture World, The New York Dramatic Mirror* or *Motography*.[28] Still, what Italian-American papers' coverage of Italian films does most surprisingly show us relates to movies' patterns of exhibition. If, at first, these upscale moving pictures played at mid-town theatres and large vaudeville houses, their subsequent runs brought them closer to the ethnic spectator, both in terms of location and price.

The construction site of George Kleine's PhotoDrama Theatre DeLuxe at 226 West 42nd Street, New York City. Construction was financed by Sam H. Harris, Sal Bloom and George Kleine, for George Kleine Film Productions. The photograph was taken in January 1914 – the theatre opened as a motion picture house on 14 May that same year.

Dante's Inferno, for example, was playing in mid-December 1911 at the Gane's Manhattan Theatre (31st Street and Broadway) for fifteen and twenty-five cents, but, by 20 January 1912, it was also playing at the Fair Theatre (122 East 14th Street) for ten and fifteen cents.[29] George Kleine's distributing decisions about the feature films he imported – in particular *Quo Vadis?* and *The Last Days of Pompeii* (Ambrosio, 1913) – are particularly interesting in terms of the accessibility and marketability of such productions for working-class Italian immigrants. For example, in mid-October 1913, *The Last Days of Pompeii* was playing both at the

86th Street Theatre and at the Bijou (1243 Broadway at 30th Street), with a minimum admission of twenty-five cents.[30] During the same period, the Kleine–Ambrosio film's rival version, produced by Pasquali (also from Turin), opened next door to the Bijou, at the Wallack Theatre (northwest corner of Broadway and 30th Street), for prices as low as fifteen cents. While at the Bijou, *The Last Days of Pompeii* was advertised as a 'Kleine accomplishment' ('George Kleine dà lo squisito dramma cinematografico'), whereas Pasquali's version was explicitly publicised as an Italian production ('The greatest triumph of Italian cinematography'), enriched by an Italian-American twist ('Produced by Pasquali American Co. New York President, Alberto Amato').[31] Interestingly, Pasquali's production was also presented as 'such a wonderful spectacle that [,] being the victorious rival over *Quo Vadis?*, no Italian could miss it'.[32]

The distribution of the Pasquali production successfully attracted the urban middle-class consumer as well as the patriotic ethnic spectator. In November 1913, Pasquali's film, advertised using nationalistic slogans, was playing uptown at the Park Theatre (59th Street and Columbus Circle) for fifty, twenty-five, *and* fifteen cents.[33] The same film, retitled *La distruzione di Pompeii* (*The Destruction of Pompeii*), probably for fear of copyright infringement, opened on Saturday 20 December 1913 at the West Village Bella Sorrento (180 Thompson Street), where owner L. T. Calderone charged a flat fifteen cents for entrance. The ad insisted: 'Spectacular production of Pasquali Company, in 8 acts and with a length of 10,000 feet!'[34]

Kleine understood the lesson. At a price of fifty cents, or even twenty-five cents, and at a forty-block distance, a photoplay proudly announced and reviewed in the Italian press was still not easily affordable. Once it reached the downtown commercial hubs around Union Square and with a price tag of only fifteen cents, the 'talk of the town' was within reach of everybody's pocket. Although Kleine's Italian 'classics' had not been produced for such a general consumption, their closer marketability to ethnic enclaves was going to greatly further their commercial achievement.

The issue of how to exploit *Quo Vadis* – the longest film ever produced – created a major headache for Kleine. At first, he thought to exploit Cines' masterpiece by turning the Special Feature – once it had exhausted its upscale marketability – into a Multiple Release, to be screened in parts at cheaper outlets.[35] But what occurred with the versions of *The Last Days of Pompeii* forced him to rethink his strategy. In September 1913, *Quo Vadis?* was still running at the Astor (where it had opened almost six months before), advertised as a 'Grand Cinematographic production designed by great Italian artists'. Still, the admission price was quite high: twenty-five and fifty cents. By mid-February 1914, however, the film had finally opened at the Union Square Theatre (56 East 14th Street) with tickets as low as fifteen cents.[36]

Meanwhile, shorter Italian films were shown daily on the Bowery. At the Maiori Theatre, Italian titles were never mentioned but, on a couple of occasions, the newspaper advertisements for the theatre specified that out of the six new films per week, one was from Italy.[37] The theatre was among the cheapest in the area, with prices ranging from five to fifteen cents. From October 1913, other theatres in and around Little Italy started advertising the exhibition of moving pictures for five cents, such as Teatro Cassese on Grand Street, Bowery's Thalia Theatre (owned by Feliciano Acierno), Bella Sorrento, Jefferson Theatre on the corner of 14th Street and 3rd Avenue and Teatro Garibaldi on East 4th Street. The latter differentiated its performances by showing moving pictures for five cents and opera performances, without moving pictures, for a minimum of thirty cents.[38]

An overview of film exhibition among Italy's immigrants, as it appears from newspaper evidence, would emphasise several features: the presence of Italian exhibitors, owners either of nickelodeons or large theatres (offering variety shows, including moving pictures), both charging as little as five cents; the frequent attendance at film shows of Italian children, either accompanied or not by their parents; the lively and boisterous atmosphere of movie-going among Italy's immigrants; and the regular correlation of the Italian films shown (although hardly being singled out by title) with the advertising strategies' patriotic tone.[39]

Film's influence in defining and fabricating a proud nationalistic discourse is further evidenced by the appearance of extended articles on the art of film-making and reviews following an Italian film première. On 27 November 1913, *Il Progresso* published a lengthy interview with Cines director Enrico Guazzoni on the new historical feature film *Antony and Cleopatra* (*Marcantonio e Cleopatra*). The tone of the interview was enthusiastic and constant nationalistic allusions made their way into the article: ancient figures and atmosphere were said to have been perfectly recreated through the mixture of 'high patriotic ideals and sensual pleasures typical of the life of those past times'.[40] After detailing the colossal scale of the production (1,500 extras, hundreds of horses and wild beasts), the discourse shifted to the unfair competition of 'some foreign companies' which had been marketing outdated movies with similar historical subjects, both in Italy and abroad. Fortunately, the article concluded, the uniqueness of this Cines production would persuade spectators to applaud the 'glories of Roman eagles everywhere triumphant'.

At the beginning of the twentieth century, New York was the main hub for the circulation of American and European movies, theatrical plays, circus attractions and music throughout the United States. In the city itself, established cosmopolitan archetypes reproduced and expanded themselves through the rise of mass entertainment and an industry of urban leisure. For members of the American middle class, Italy had its own *topos* as the birthplace of western humanistic values and as a nation ideally unified by its enduring cultural tradition. Art, opera and, lastly, historical films appeared to best embody such an archetype.

During the same period, New York was also one of the main centres for international migration, especially from Southern and Eastern Europe. Here, too, Italy held a *topos*, although quite a different one. As a dislocated, largely illiterate, and subaltern people, Italy's Southern immigrants appeared far removed from the bourgeois and high-class idealisation of their country of origin as the land of artistic supremacy and poetic inspiration. Italian film companies, especially those connected to Northern and central areas such as Turin and Rome, participated in the cultural consolidation of Italy's historic and artistic image through the production of costume dramas set in remote historical periods, especially during the times of the Roman Empire. Meanwhile, Italy's economic and political atmosphere called for a radicalisation of old-time patriotism. An emerging and more aggressive nationalism insisted on the *continuity* of the nation's past greatness with the present. Such nationalism spread its influence throughout politics, literature and the cinema.

In the South of Italy, national acculturation and pedagogy were a forceful process of colonisation, performed by élite political and intellectual groups in search of power and representation. There, nationalism was an invention with the blatant stamp of fiction. For Italy's immigrants in the US, however, the association with a national identity was a requirement to adapt to the American multinational society and the 'imaginary reverberation' – as Benedict Anderson put it – of a newly perceived ethnic communality.

Notes

Valerie Walsh was most precious for her readings of earlier versions of the essay and for her unfailing support. This is for Guido Lavagnini (1943–95).

Frequent abbreviations used are *Moving Picture World* (*MPW*), the most important film-trade periodical of the silent period; *Il Progresso Italo-Americano* (*PIA*) and *L'Araldo Italiano* (*AI*), the most successful Italian-language dailies published in New York City during this period. I will simply mention the 'Kleine Papers' when referring to the Kleine Collection, Manuscript Division, Library of Congress. Unless otherwise noted, all translations are my own.

1 Italian film historian Aldo Bernardini, in his detailed filmography of Italian cinema, *Archivio del cinema muto italiano* (Rome: ANICA, 1991), has accounted for 1,580 Italian films distributed in the US between 1908 and 1915. They were: 105 in 1908; 191 in 1909; 255 in 1910; 254 in 1911; 277 in 1912; 293 in 1913; 173 in 1914 and 32 in 1915. More detailed statistics would show how many of these films were historical mythological re-enactments, although this particular genre was doubtless the most distinct and remarkable.

2 Some exceptions are Richard Abel, 'Booming the Film Business: The Historical Specificity of Early French Cinema', *French Cultural Studies* 1, no. 1 (1990), now in R. Abel, *Silent Film* (New Brunswick, NJ: Rutgers University Press, 1996), pp. 109–24; Abel's 'The Perils of Pathé, or the Americanization of Early American Cinema', in Leo Charney and Vanessa R. Schwartz (eds), *Cinema and the Invention of Modern Life* (Berkeley and Los Angeles: University of California Press, 1995), pp. 183–223; Roland Cosandey and François Albèra (eds), *Cinéma sans frontières/Images Across Borders* (Montréal: Nuit Blanche Éditeur, 1995), in particular William Uricchio and Roberta E. Pearson's essay, 'Italian Spectacle and the US Market', pp. 95–105.

3 This expression is used by Pasquale Verdicchio in his *Bound by Distance: Rethinking Nationalism through the Italian Diaspora* (London: Associated University Presses, 1997), p. 22.

4 Richard H. Brodhead, 'Strangers on a Train: The Double Dream of Italy in American Gilded Age', *Modernism/Modernity*,1, no. 2 (1994), pp. 1–19.

5 On the genealogy of the cult of *Romanità* in Italian culture throughout the nineteenth century, see Piero Treves, *L'idea di Roma e la cultura italiana del secolo* XIX (Milan–Napoli: Ricciardi Editore, 1962).

6 When dealing with popular entertainments, ethnic history has traditionally correlated the formation of an Italian-American identity with theatrical plays, opera, and religious parades (*feste*), disregarding any discussion of the role of films and movie-going. See Anna Maria Martellone, 'La "rappresentazione" dell'identità italo-americana: teatro e feste nelle Little Italy statunitensi', in Sergio Bertelli (ed.), *La chioma della Vittoria*

(Florence: Ponte delle Grazie, 1997), pp. 357–91; and Emelise Aleandri and Maxine Schwartz Seller, 'Italian-American Theatre', in M. Schwartz Seller (ed.), *Ethnic Theatre in the United States* (London: Greenwood Press, 1983), pp. 237–76.

7 Benedict Anderson, *Imagined Communities: Reflections on the Origin and Spread of Nationalism* (London: Verso, [1983] 1991), p. xiv (emphasis in the text).

8 I discuss some of the methodological challenges of this research in 'Shipwrecked Spectators: Italy's Immigrants at the Movies in New York, 1906–1916', *The Velvet Light Trap*, 44 (Fall, 1999). A French translation of this essay has been included in Germain Lacasse and André Gaudreault (eds), *Cinéma, cent ans après* (Québec, Canada: Éditions Nota Bene, forthcoming).

9 This evidence, however, has shown remarkable flaws in relation to the New York situation. Numerous uncertainties remain about the social status of selected urban areas (i.e. along 125th Street or 3rd Avenue) or about class mixings related to patrons' habits of leaving their own neighbourhoods to watch a movie.

10 Among their essays, see William Uricchio and Roberta E. Pearson, 'Constructing the Audience: Competing Discourses of Morality and Rationalization During the Nickelodeon Period', *Iris* 17 (Autumn, 1994, Special Issue on 'Movie Spectators and Audiences'), pp. 43–54; 'Dante's Inferno and Caesar's Ghost: Intertextuality and Conditions of Reception in Early American Cinema', *Journal of Communication Inquiry* (1990), now in Richard Abel (ed.), *Silent Film*, pp. 217–33. See also their forthcoming book: *The Nickel Madness: The Struggle Over New York City's Nickelodeons, 1906–1913* (Washington, DC: Smithsonian Institution Press). Among other work analysing melodramatic polarisations of the period, see Richard Maltby, 'The Social Evil, the Moral Order and the Melodramatic Imagination, 1890–1915', in Jacky Bratton, Jim Cook and Christine Gledhill (eds), *Melodrama: Stage, Picture, Screen* (London: BFI, 1994), pp. 214–30.

11 For data and statistics about immigrants' geographical origin, see Ercole Sori, *L'emigrazione italiana dall'Unita' alla seconda guerra mondiale* (Bologna: Il Mulino, 1979).

12 See P. Verdicchio, *Bound by Distance*, Chapters 1 and 3.

13 See V. Maher, 'Gerarchie del nazionalismo', in *Quaderni Storici* 21, no. 63 (1986), p. 223.

14 On Cossa, see Benedetto Croce, 'Pietro Cossa', an essay originally published in 1904, now in *La letteratura della Nuova Italia. Saggi critici.* (Bari: Laterza, [1914] 1943), pp. 150–72; and Giovanni Calendoli, *Materiali per una storia del cinema italiano* (Parma: Maccari Editore, 1967), pp. 67–74.

15 On literary productions about emigration throughout the nineteenth and twentieth centuries, see Emilio Franzina, *Dall'Arcadia in America. Attività letteraria ed emigrazione transoceanica in Italia (1850–1940)* (Turin: Fondazione Giovanni Agnelli, 1996).

16 Franzina, *Dall'Arcadia in America*, pp. 136–48.

17 Marcello Pacini (ed.), *La virtù e la libertà. Ideali e civiltà italiana nella formazione degli Stati Uniti* (Turin: Fondazione Giovanni Agnelli, 1995).

18 These stereotypes worked synecdochically: the entire territory of Italy was reduced to a few canonical places (an extended *locus mirabilis*, a site of famous cathedrals or Roman ruins); or it was metamorphosed into a stage of history or a condition of the artist's spirit. Consequently, the entire territories south of Naples (where most of the immigrants came from) were dismissed as not worth mentioning.

19 *Moving Picture World* (*MPW*) 11 April 1908, p. 309. By the same token, a half-reeler like *Judith and Holopherne* (Cines, 1907) was defined as 'A classic done in the noblest Roman Art'.

20 On 6 November 1909, *MPW* reviewed *Nero* in a long editorial titled 'The Qualities of Imported Film': p. 636.

21 For an overview of the presence of Italian companies in the American film market, see Kristin Thompson, *Exporting Entertainment. America in the World Film Market, 1907–1934* (London: BFI, 1985), Chapters 1 and 2, and Appendix 1. For an overview of economic and cultural strategies adopted by the Italian film industry during the gener-

ally difficult period of 1907–8, see Aldo Bernardini, 'An Industry in Recession. The Italian Film Industry 1908–1909', *Film History* 3, no. 4 (1989), pp. 341–68. On the general emergence of public interest in antiquarian subjects and their de-exoticisation in the first decades of the twentieth century, see Stefania Parigi, 'La rievocazione dell'antico', in Riccardo Redi (ed.), *Gli ultimi giorni di Pompei* (Naples: Electa Napoli, 1994), pp. 67–84.

22 Apart from Cines and Ambrosio, which were MPPC licensees (respectively through Biograph/Kleine and Raleigh & Robert/Kleine), most film companies had precarious business relationships with the equally unstable conglomerates of independent exchanges. Itala, Milano Films, Pasquali and Gloria, but also Ambrosio oscillated between having their regular agent, establishing their own distribution company (Itala Film of America, Ambrosio American Co., Pasquali American Co.), or distributing through existing companies (i.e. Monopol, Universal).

23 Antonio Gramsci, 'Notebook 3, § 90', in Antonio Gramsci, *Prison Notebooks Volume II* (Joseph A. Buttigieg, trans. and ed., New York: Columbia University Press, 1996), pp. 91–2. See also, A. Gramsci, *Selections from Cultural Writings* (David Forgacs and Geoffrey Nowell-Smith eds, Cambridge, Mass.: Harvard University Press, 1985), pp. 196–257.

24 Uricchio and Pearson, 'Dante's Inferno and Caesar's Ghost', p. 218.

25 For a general overview of Italian papers in the US, see Lubomyr R. Wynar and Anna T. Wynar, *Encyclopedia Directory of Ethnic Newspapers and Periodicals in the US* (Littlejohn, CO, 1976), especially pp. 100–8. The best account of the Italian-American press is Rudolph J. Vecoli, 'The Italian Immigrant Press and the Construction of Social Reality, 1850–1920', in James P. Danky and Wayne A. Wiegand (eds), *Print Culture in a Diverse America* (Urbana: University of Illinois Press, 1998), pp. 17–33.

26 In *Il Progresso Italo-Americano* (*PIA*) the name of the column devoted to the life of New York Italian immigrants was called *Su e giù per la colonia* ('Up and Down the Colony').

27 *PIA*, 17 September 1907, p. 5. In his linguistic research on film terms, Sergio Raffaelli has noted that the verb 'cinematografare' has two principal meanings. The first one denotes the mere photographic reproduction and registration, the second one involves issues of new spectacles and representation: it nominates the playful and colourful *tableaux* that comprise the column. See Sergio Raffaelli, *Cinema, Film, Regia* (Rome: Bulzoni, 1978), pp. 34ff. 'Cinematografando', later renamed 'Cinematografo', became a place for instantaneous flashes of comic energy, micro-narratives of exotic attractions, or irreverent parodies of common sense and morals.

28 An early but still fundamental discussion on the critical reception of Italian films in the US is Davide Turconi, 'I film storici italiani e la critica americana dal 1910 alla fine del muto', in *Il film storico italiano e la sua influenza sugli altri paesi*, (Rome: Edizioni di Bianco e Nero, 1963), pp. 40–55.

29 *L'Araldo Italiano* (*AI*), 14 December 1911, p. 4; *AI*, 20 January 1912, p. 2.

30 *AI*, 20 October 1913, p. 4. Kleine Papers, Box 32, '*The Last Days of Pompeii* and *Quo Vadis?*, distribution in the US, 1912; 1926', and Box 69, 'Schedule of Releases, 1913–1918'.

31 *PIA*, 19 October 1913, p. 3.

32 'Nessun italiano può mancare di vedere questo meraviglioso spettacolo vittorioso rivale del *Quo Vadis?*', *PIA*, 19 October 1913, p. 3.

33 *Il Telegrafo*, 9 November 1913, p. 3, and 12 November 1913, p. 3. See also *PIA*, 9 November 1913, p. 4, which advertised both Kleine's and Pasquali's versions.

34 *Il Telegrafo*, 20 December 1913, p. 3. 'La Spettacolosa produzione della casa Pasquali in 8 atti e lunga 10,000 piedi'.

35 Kleine Papers, Box 49, '*Quo Vadis?* Contracts 1912–1921'. See also George Kleine to A. H. Woods, Eltinge Theatre, 17 February 1913, Kleine Papers, Box 7, 'Cines, 1913. January–June'.

36 As it was announced in *PIA*, 12 February 1914, p. 4.

37 For announcements of the weekly Italian film in the programme, see *Il Telegrafo*, 21 October 1913, p. 2 or *Il Telegrafo*, 2 November 1913, p. 2, also *PIA*, 31 March 1914, p. 4,

where the film screening at the Maiori is publicised as 'of Italian interest'. Antonio Maiori, the stage director and impresario, had moved (presumably that summer) from another theatre on the Bowery, the former Miner's (Bowery and Broome Street) to the former London and Lipzin Theatre (235–7 Bowery), where not only did he perform such shows as 'Cristoforo Colombo ovvero la scoperta dell'America', but also hosted circus numbers, exotic dances and songs, and Fregoli's famous shows of *transformism*.

38 *Il Telegrafo*, 26 November 1913, p. 3.
39 Unspecified 'Weekly Entertainments for Italians' took place in the Big Hall (9 Second Avenue) after January 1913. The programme of these free gatherings included music, instructive lectures and a film, possibly a comedy. See, *PIA*, 18 January 1913, p. 2. At the Florence Theatre (331 Bowery), a publicity announcement reminded possible patrons that, thanks to the return of manager Salvatore Calderone, either Italian films or films 'of great Italian interest' were shown: 'Tutti i giorni vengono esibite pellicole lunghissime, capolavori delle migliori case europee, specie italiane'. *PIA*, 5 April 1913, p. 2.
40 *PIA*, 27 November 1913, p. 7.

3 Film and Ethnic Identity in Harlem, 1896–1915
Alison Griffiths and James Latham

Introduction

New York's Harlem district has long been a bustling centre of African-American culture, politics and commerce. This identity, however, took time to develop. Less than a century ago, it was a profoundly different place, a white middle-class neighbourhood undergoing dramatic social change. By the late 1870s, Harlem had developed an ethnic and cultural identity associated with a prosperous community of first- and second-generation Irish-, British- and German-Americans. In the early 1890s, this genteel middle-class identity began to alter as working-class Italian immigrants moved into the area, followed by East European Jews and African-Americans. Black people had lived and worked in Harlem in small numbers as early as the seventeenth century, initially as slaves on local farms and estates in a Dutch area then known as *Nieuw Haarlem*.[1] In 1900, both the small African-American community and the new medium of cinema remained marginal in Harlem, but this situation changed rapidly between 1905 and 1910, when black people began to move into the 135th Street area in increasing numbers and nickelodeons proliferated all over New York City. By the mid-teens, both the movies and the African-American community were firmly established in an area of the city which would become strongly identified with African-American arts and culture during the Harlem Renaissance of the 20s.

Our aim in this chapter is to analyse the transformation of Harlem between the 1890s and the mid-1910s in terms of two wider socio-economic and cultural changes: the rapid growth of nickelodeons in New York City and the migration of African-Americans uptown. We focus primarily on local film exhibition and reception, rather than on the content of specific films (although filmic content is addressed when it was singled out for commentary by black critics), examining early cinema in the 125th Street commercial and entertainment district and the area surrounding 135th Street, the earliest centre of African-American settlement. Drawing on trade papers and local publications, most notably the writings of *New York Age* arts critic Lester A. Walton, we examine several aspects of race relations in Harlem, including theatre ownership and desegregation, as related indicators of increasing black involvement in Harlem film-going.

As the city's foremost black newspaper, *The New York Age* informed its mostly middle-class readers about a range of subjects affecting black political and cultural life. From about 1906, arts critic Lester Walton included motion pictures alongside his discussions of vaudeville, minstrel shows and legitimate black theatre. Almost all of Walton's writings on cinema in *The New York Age* addressed two themes: the representations of African-Americans in films and the discriminatory practices of local theatres. Walton encouraged local African-Americans to fight both problems by acquiring and programming motion picture theatres themselves. His sustained interest in how motion pictures related to the political, social and economic lives of African-Americans makes Walton a key commentator on early African-American film reception. His impassioned responses to moving pictures suggest how film-going quickly became linked to diverse community issues, including real estate development, demographic shifts and black entrepreneurship.[2] Before addressing Walton's contribution, however, we trace the simultaneous emergence of cinema in Harlem and African-American migration in the pre-nickelodeon period.

Popular Culture in Harlem Before the Nickelodeon

Motion pictures arrived in Harlem by 27 October 1896, when Thomas Edison's Vitascope previewed at the Trinity ME Church on 118th Street between First and Second Avenues.[3] By this time Harlem was already host to a range of cultural entertainments that were to influence the local exhibition and reception of cinema. While Harlem's élite mingled at the luxurious Harlem Opera House, which offered Broadway-quality opera, drama and, on occasion, 'high-class' vaudeville, working-class audiences enjoyed sensationalist attractions, including fake decapitations, at dime museums located along Third Avenue. Other early Harlem theatres presented popular vaudeville programmes, while the local YMCA and several churches offered magic lantern shows and illustrated lectures designed to inspire and inform as well as entertain. Audiences for these entertainments were almost exclusively white, since relatively few African-Americans lived or worked in Harlem and even fewer attended the local theatres. Black people were commonly excluded from theatres, if not segregated within them, a practice commonly known as 'drawing the colour line'.

In the late 1880s, theatre impresario and real estate speculator Oscar Hammerstein began building imposing theatres along 125th Street in anticipation of an influx of middle- and upper middle-class white residents: the Harlem Opera House (1889), the Columbus Theatre (1890) and the Harlem Music Hall (1897) (see Figures 1 and 2).[4] The Harlem Opera House was the first Manhattan theatre built north of Central Park and for years served as 125th Street's most prestigious theatrical venue, charging the highest prices to its white middle-class audiences. Featuring legitimate opera and drama, the Harlem Opera House distinguished itself from other local venues that offered more populist forms of entertainment, including vaudeville and the later moving pictures. Except for a special appearance by the Biograph in 1897 and a winter holiday screening of Edison's popular film *The Great Train Robbery* in 1903, the Harlem Opera House resisted film exhibition until 1906. The management's resistance was motivated by the theatre's success with traditional prestige attractions. There were few compelling reasons to add attractions like motion pictures so long as Broadway-quality opera and

Figure 1: The Columbus Theatre, pre-1900. This theatre was located close to Third Avenue – a working-class area. Although this theatre had a small storefront, its auditorium seated 1,700 and had two balconies (The Museum of the City of New York).

theatre were profitable and were expected to remain so, in line with the antici-pated continuing middle-class migration uptown.

As in other middle-class communities, some of the cultural stigma attached to early moving pictures in Harlem was due to their association with cheap dime museums and similar sites of popular amusement. In such places, spectators could find entertainments very different from those available at the Harlem Opera House, including Punch and Judy shows, tattooed ladies, burlesque dances and juggling acts. Like the later nickelodeons, Harlem's dime museums were at times vilified in the local press for their exploitative fare, morally dubious environments

Figure 2: Hurtig and Seamon's Music Hall, formerly the Harlem Music Hall, in the early 1900s (The Museum of the City of New York).

and, implicitly, for the economic threat they posed to more respectable local theatres with whom they competed.[5] But, despite the low cultural position of dime museums, public disdain for them was not constant or universal, even among Harlem's middle class. Specific documentation of the patronage of Harlem dime museums is scarce, but it is at least plausible that curiosity, proximity, and a desire for novelty brought some middle-class Harlem residents to these establishments.

Motion pictures inserted themselves quickly, if unevenly, into the cultural landscape of Harlem. Between 1896 and 1900, films were occasionally shown by travelling exhibitors in local theatres, dime museums and churches, as well as the YMCA and the Harlem River Park and Casino. Each of these venues had its own complex and changing identity, performing different functions for different audiences at different times. In the churches and YMCA, film often served educational or moral purposes, while in theatres and dime museums the emphasis was very much on entertainment. Each screening site had frequent changes in staff and physical facilities and unique programmes, hours and admission prices that shifted according to local trends in theatre competition.

Between 1900 and 1905, the line between legitimate and popular entertainments in Harlem increasingly blurred as new audiences entered the neighbourhood and large vaudeville theatres were constructed, mostly on 125th Street: the Orpheum (1901), the West End and the New Star (both 1902), the Gotham (1904) and the Family and the Alhambra theatres (both 1905). Audiences for these theatres were probably more ethnically and economically diverse than those for the Harlem Opera House, since their entertainment offerings and lower admission

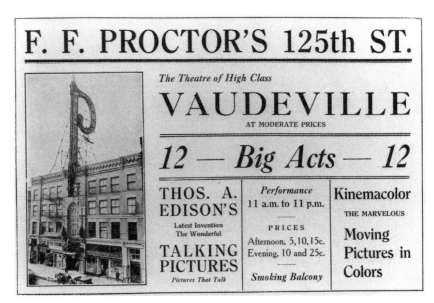

F. F. PROCTOR'S 125th ST.

The Theatre of High Class

VAUDEVILLE
AT MODERATE PRICES

12 — Big Acts — 12

THOS. A. EDISON'S	Performance	Kinemacolor
Latest Invention The Wonderful	11 a.m. to 11 p.m.	THE MARVELOUS
	PRICES	Moving
TALKING	Afternoon, 5,10,15c.	
PICTURES	Evening, 10 and 25c.	Pictures in
Pictures That Talk	*Smoking Balcony*	Colors

Figure 3: Proctor's 125th Street Theater in 1913 (formerly the Columbus Theater). The sound and Kinemacolor processes are early attempts at film sound and colour. The 86-foot tall letter 'P' was the largest electric sign in Harlem at this time and one of the largest in the city (The New York Historical Society, from Harlem Magazine, *July 1913).*

prices would have attracted more working-class residents, including many Italian and Eastern European Jewish immigrants.

Harlem's increasing ethnic variety paralleled a growing diversity in popular theatrical entertainments, including performances by African-Americans. During the 1890s and early 1900s, African-Americans increasingly entertained white audiences in Harlem as 'coon' singers and other theatrical stereotypes in popular vaudeville shows such as *A Trip to Coontown* and *In Old Kentucky.* Historian David Nasaw has argued that the racist stereotypes in American theatres during this time offered a sense of racial identity for an ethnically diverse white audience:

> [T]he comedic 'darkies' and 'coons' remained an integral part of the vaudeville and musical-comedy show because they served a vital purpose. They provided a heterogeneous 'white' audience with a symbol of a racial 'other' and, in so doing, helped to cement it into a sort of 'herrenvolk' democracy. Everyone in the audience, whether rich or poor, new immigrant, old immigrant, or native-born of native parents, was redefined as 'white' by participating in a collective, derisive laughter at the superstitions, the stupidities, the misuse of language and logic, the sentimentality and inherent childishness of the 'blacks' cavorting on the stage before them.[6]

Such 'coon' acts may have resonated among Harlem's white population at a time when the local class and ethnic compositions were undergoing rapid change. By identifying with an 'imaginary community' across class, linguistic and ethnic divides, white vaudeville audiences could momentarily relieve the pressures on traditional bonds of identity and community brought about by migration and urban industrial life. The largely visual form of the spectacle of 'otherness' paraded on stage and screen ensured that even the newest immigrant could experience a sense of affiliation constituted along racial lines.

Film exhibition was sporadic in Harlem before 1900, when Proctor's 125th Street Theatre became the only theatre in Harlem to show moving pictures regularly prior to the nickelodeon 'boom' of 1905–10 (see Figures 3).[7] William Paley's opening night kalatechnoscope programme of 20 August 1900 made 'a distinct hit' and included views of the recent Paris Exposition and 'other timely subjects'; admission prices for this première varied from fifteen to fifty cents, indicating an economically diverse audience.[8] Despite this initial success and Paley's continuing use of films, they were never highlighted in the theatre's programmes, instead appearing at the end or as fillers between acts. Harlem's other large theatrical houses showed motion pictures less frequently between 1900 and 1905, with Hurtig & Seamon's Music Hall probably showing the most. Local dime museums continued to exhibit films throughout this period, although, as in other neighbourhoods, such venues began to feel competition from the larger theatres.[9] Beyond such competitive features of the young motion picture trade in Harlem, the opening of the New York City subway was to have the greatest impact on Harlem's ethnic composition and entertainment culture.

The Opening of the Subways and the Growth of Nickelodeons

Although Harlem had a high degree of economic self-sufficiency in the 1880s and 1890s, with its own department stores, yacht clubs, fraternal organisations, beer gardens, banks, newspapers, churches and opulent legitimate theatres, its status as a suburban middle-class enclave ultimately relied on its accessibility to the population and financial centres of lower Manhattan. By the early 1880s, the elevated railroad had reached Harlem, running along Second, Third, Eighth and Ninth Avenues, and ushering in the prosperous Irish- and German-Americans who quickly came to dominate the area. The elevated railroad was, however, slow and vulnerable to the weather, so for some twenty years Harlem's middle-class leaders and real estate interests lobbied in the local press for more efficient underground mass transit. The announcement in 1898 that the new subway system would extend up to Harlem created feverish real estate development and speculation. During the construction of the subways over the next six years, Harlem real estate speculators built luxurious homes for the wealthier white people who were expected to move into the neighbourhood. This development led to years of artificially high real estate prices, with a crash in prices coming in 1904–5, ironically just as the subways finally opened.

The years following Harlem's real estate bust saw the rapid growth of film exhibition in the community and the rest of the city. Between 1905 and 1910, nickelodeons took over many small storefronts, while motion pictures were added to the bills of more legitimate theatres, including the stately Harlem Opera House, which was taken over by the Keith–Proctor vaudeville chain in 1906 and showed movies regularly during the nickelodeon period.[10] This nickelodeon boom stimulated local tensions similar to those provoked by the earlier dime museums. While

51

the nickelodeons brought profits to Harlem's white theatre owners, they were also seen by some in the community as potentially threatening to safety, public decency and the jobs of white stage entertainers. Harlem's community leaders, like those of other New York City neighbourhoods, sought to restrict film exhibition through censorship, fines, enforced Sunday closings and other legal tactics. During the winter holiday season of 1907, for example, a police magistrate publicly denounced the owner of a Harlem nickelodeon for showing a film depicting the inside of an opium den.[11] These exhibition restrictions were defied by some exhibitors, including the Comedy Theatre (68 West 125th Street), which was closed by the police in 1907 for being the only theatre in Manhattan to violate a Sunday closing ordinance.[12] Other exhibitors adopted marketing techniques that portrayed films as educational and movie theatres as respectable, as in the case of a theatre at 114th Street and Fifth Avenue, which offered local schoolchildren a free afternoon lecture and screening of the film *Hiawatha*.[13] Some theatres also boasted respectable sounding names, like the 'Family Theater' and the 'Ideas Theater'.

Despite the efforts of community leaders hostile to nickelodeons, by October 1907 *Moving Picture World* reported that on one unspecified street in Harlem (probably 125th Street) there were 'as many as five' nickelodeons to a block, each showing films to as many as 'one thousand people an hour'.[14] Another report that same month in *Views and Films Index* expressed concern over the effects of nickelodeons on women and children, pointing out that the entrances of nickelodeons in Harlem were regularly 'encumbered' with 'go-carts and perambulators'.[15] The proliferation of nickelodeons was so great that by May 1908, the *New York Clipper* reported that the film business had 'secured a stronghold in Harlem and the Bronx', and was making 'serious inroads into the vaudeville business'.[16] In the years to come, Harlem's theatre managers offered audiences more film and less vaudeville, gradually eliminating the latter form of entertainment altogether. Motion pictures had arrived in Harlem and permanently changed the nature of the local leisure culture. At the same time, African-Americans brought changes to the community that would be even more profound.

Redrawing the Colour Line: Harlem's Early Black Neighbourhood and the Reception of Film

When African-Americans migrated into Harlem after 1904, most settled in the residential area around 135th Street and Seventh Avenue. This Harlem migration was part of a larger national migration from poverty and racism in the rural South and Caribbean to the northern cities of New York and Chicago, and also part of an internal New York City migration of African-Americans fleeing the squalor of Manhattan's West Side and San Juan Hill sections, where race riots had erupted in 1900 and 1905. African-Americans from all backgrounds saw in the newly affordable neighbourhood of Harlem an opportunity for better housing, a safer, more attractive environment and the promise of less racial tension.[17]

In the early years of the migration, the black press informed potential migrants of the opportunities and problems Harlem offered. *The New York Age*, which has been described as 'one of the main forces behind the growth of a black community in Harlem', informed African-Americans about a wide range of national and local issues, including real estate, politics, religion, hygiene, education, sports and entertainment.[18] During the nickelodeon period, *The New York Age* covered a spirited debate within the African-American church between those who considered nickelodeons to be dens of iniquity competing with churches for Sunday audiences and others who were more sympathetic to motion pictures. In 1910, some black clergymen called for a crusade against all films, arguing that their church attendances had been dropping off since 1906 due to the nickelodeon boom. However, Rev. Adam Clayton Powell, Sr. and other clergy advocated 'purification' of the emerging film industry rather than its 'annihilation', arguing that people's leisure time would be better spent in movie theatres than saloons, gambling houses or on street corners.[19] Rev. Powell favoured protests against certain offensive films and theatres, but not against cinema *per se*, arguing that the former strategy would be more popular and effective with the public.[20]

Lester Walton apparently shared Powell's attitude towards motion pictures when he became the arts critic for *The New York Age* in 1905. Walton used this forum to advocate social change on behalf of 'the race' and his writings on film in the *Age* constitute a valuable record of the early African-American response to moving pictures in New York and a barometer of the euphoria, frustration and anger occasioned by cinema.[21] Moreover, his criticism of the complicity of black performers and audiences with racist representations suggests some of the historiographic and theoretical challenges involved in studying film exhibition and reception. Like any other demographic group, early twentieth-century African-American communities were not monolithic. Nor did the Harlem community consist of individuals with simple, discrete ethnic or racial identities. Instead, groups and whole communities were composed of individuals whose identities were formed by intersections of race, class, age, gender, religion, regional background, language and ideology. Just as white people varied in their beliefs, values and life experiences, so did African-Americans, perhaps even more so, given the conflicts shaping African-American consciousness that were explored by W. E. B. Du Bois in *The Souls of Black Folk* (1903). The almost schizophrenic valences of being black in a white world, free yet not free, and often a stranger in one's own house must have been felt by many of the African-Americans who struggled to establish a home in Harlem.[22] Walton's writings, then, constitute a telling example of how affiliations emerged along class as well as racial lines on the subject of popular entertainments.

As a musician and member of the black middle class, writing for a middle-class readership, Walton probably preferred more 'respectable' artistic forms, such as legitimate theatre and classical music, to the more popular medium of film.[23] He also feared that the conversion of legitimate theatres to cinemas was shrinking career opportunities for black performers, who at the time competed with moving pictures for limited engagements in and around the city. In 1911, he criticised the 'craze for motion pictures' for almost putting 'the popular-priced theatres out of business' because 'colored shows were not generally considered Broadway attractions'.[24] Nevertheless, Walton also took the social power of film seriously, addressing a range of issues involving cinematic representations of race and the treatment of African-Americans in local theatres.

Walton devoted considerable space to criticising the racist representations of African-Americans playing in cinemas in Harlem and elsewhere in the city. In a 1909 column titled 'Degeneracy of the Moving Picture Theatre', he objected to an advertisement posted outside a Sixth Avenue theatre which promoted a film about a lynching; the poster depicted a 'crudely painted' image of a black man being burned at the stake with text reading: 'John Smith of Paris, Texas, Burned at the Stake. Hear his Moans and Groans. Price, One Cent!'[25] Expressing outrage at the film's content and promotion, Walton denounced the hypocrisy of those who claimed cinema was educational: 'We would like to know where do the elements of education come in so far as the picture in question is concerned'. He warned readers that 'if we do not start now to put an end to this insult to the race, expect to see more shocking pictures with the Negro as the subject in the near future'. Walton, who had formerly considered that films could educate both whites and blacks about the true nature of the black experience in America, condemned this film unreservedly, maintaining that it was effectively planting 'the seeds of savagery in the breasts of those whites who even in this enlightened day and time are not any too far from barbarism and to whom such acts of inhumanity would appeal'.[26]

Walton frequently urged the black community to organise itself against racist representations in films. In 1913, he called on African-American movie theatre managers to scrutinise all films produced by a film company in Atlanta, Georgia, because one of its releases, titled *Slim the Cowpuncher*, portrayed black men drinking gin, shooting dice and stealing watermelons.[27] Walton advocated boycotts of other racially denigrating films such as the comedy *One Last Evening* (1914; released as *A Night in Coontown* for white audiences), in which a black preacher tries to seduce a doctor's wife. *The New York Age* also launched a scathing attack on D. W. Griffith's 'vicious' film *The Birth of a Nation* (1915), informing its readership of public protests during the film's first six months of release. Contributing editor James W. Johnson criticised Griffith's film for depicting black people as 'degraded brutes' and 'objects of prejudice and hatred' and Walton vented his anger on the Liberty Theatre in New York for continuing to exhibit the film despite an ongoing legal battle to have it withdrawn from distribution.[28] As late as 1917, Walton spoke out against such films as *The Bar Sinister*, in which a white woman's confession that she may have a 'taint of Negro blood' causes her white fiancé to abandon her, only to return when he is reassured that she is a 'pure' white (see Figure 4). Walton labelled this form of prejudice '*dementia Americana*', citing actual cases of white employees losing their jobs on discovery of their mixed-race parentage.[29]

While Walton's polemics were usually directed towards racist white films, he also criticised African-American audiences for their lack of support for black independent production companies and their complicity with institutions that perpetuated black oppression. In 1917, he blamed black audiences for the difficulties facing the Frederick Douglass Film Company, a black-owned, independent production company. Walton quoted Dr W. S. Smith, the company's co-founder, on his unsuccessful efforts to persuade an Eighth Avenue theatre manager to book the company's latest release, *The Scapegoat*. According to Smith, the white manager of this mostly black theatre defended not showing the film on grounds that 'colored people did not want such a Negro play [since they] liked the pictures with

BROADWAY THEATRE

NEW YORK
COMMENCING SUNDAY, MAY 27th
The REMARKABLE EDGAR LEWIS PHOTODRAMA *of*
RACE PREJUDICE

THE BAR SINISTER

" I AM A NEGRESS !"

NOT — *Greatest, Enormous Spectacle, Most Stupendous, Marvelous, Magnificent, Awe Inspiring, Staggering, etc., etc., etc.*

BUT — one of those rare theatrical hits—those powerful human interest dramas that play upon the heart strings of audiences and do a big box-office business because every man, woman and child talks about them and wants to see them again and again. **"THE BAR SINISTER"** will live long as a photodrama classic because it contains that mysterious something which stirs the soul and appeals to the masses.

Prices for territorial rights now available

FRANK HALL PRODUCTIONS, Inc.
LONGACRE BLDG.   **NEW YORK**

Figure 4: Advertisement for The Bar Sinister *(Moving Picture World, 2 June 1917).*

slap-stick Negro characters'. If audiences continued to crowd this theatre 'to see obnoxious Negro types', Smith wrote, the manager alone could not be blamed.[30] The commercial success of racist popular films among black audiences is here linked to the economic marginality of black independent film, although white theatre managers' estimates of the tastes of their African-American audiences are difficult to verify and probably biased.

While Walton generally wrote more about music and legitimate theatre than about motion pictures in his newspaper column, and devoted much of his film commentary to attacks on racist representations of African-Americans, he also actively promoted films which portrayed black people positively. One such film

THERE'S A REASON

Figure 5: Moving Picture World, *20 August 1910.*

was *A Trip to Tuskegee*, a documentary about Booker T. Washington's industrial school in Alabama, featuring students at work 'in the fields, planting, plowing, milking, working in the dairy, [and] building roads'.[31] This film was exhibited in black churches around the country. In New York, it was shown at Mother Zion AME. Church on West Eighty-Ninth Street and at a public meeting at Carnegie Hall.[32] Other non-fiction films Walton singled out for praise included some 'splendid moving pictures' of the Clef Club boys performing musical concerts and the controversial *Johnson–Jeffries Fight* (filmed in Las Vegas on 4 July 1910), in which African-American pugilist Jack Johnson defeated Jim Jeffries, who was known as 'The Great White Hope'.[33]

Beyond commenting on specific films in *The New York Age*, Walton also addressed more general issues concerning the reception of films, including theatre desegregation and campaigns for black management and ownership. A cartoon in an August 1910 issue of *Moving Picture World*, depicting the outcome of the Johnson–Jeffries fight, also illustrates the situation Walton confronted regarding theatre desegregation (see Figure 5). The image depicts an audience of middle-class black and white movie-goers sitting in a large theatre, possibly a converted vaudeville house; the better seats on the floor of the theatre are racially integrated, while the balcony is all-black. Despite the boxing match context of the cartoon, the image functions as a metacommentary on the issue of theatre integration because, in addition to being irritated at the outcome of the fight, the white spectators are depicted as unhappy because they must sit among African-Americans. Although the cartoon appeared without commentary and the 'There's a Reason' caption is somewhat ambiguous, Miriam Hansen has identified the creator as H. F. Hoffman, an exhibitor with 'strong views on the need to recuperate "the most desirable class"' of white film-goers.[34] While Hoffman realised that integrated theatres would attract new black audiences, he also knew that integration would alienate middle-class whites, especially if potentially inflammatory films such as the Johnson–Jeffries fight were shown. The issue of desegregating movie theatres was controversial for a growing film industry seeking middle-class audiences in neighbourhoods like Harlem that were experiencing their own demographic changes.

Although Hoffman's cartoon depicts African-Americans as a monolithic group, and black people in Harlem faced a common experience of racial discrimination, the growing African-American community had its own internal divisions. As in Chicago's South Side and other emerging urban black communities across the country, African-American racial solidarity in Harlem was tempered by differences of class and regional origin. The small African-American middle class was torn between the desire for acceptance by the local white leadership and the imperative to resist overt white racism, and middle-class black people tended to be ambivalent about popular entertainments and the boisterous audience behaviour they encouraged among many working-class African-Americans.[35] Such class-based tensions frequently played out on the pages of the culturally conservative *New York Age*, which often criticised the 'unwelcome' elements among the black community.[36] These tensions within the black community arose partly from differences in regional backgrounds between the more established and prosperous Northern urban blacks and the poorer rural folk migrating from the South. Gilbert Osofsky writes that the established prosperous black people had 'railed against the lower-class southern Negro with the virulence' of some white racists, and were, as one black clergyman described it, 'embarrassed by the raucousness, vulgarity, and violence' of these southern migrants.[37] The established African-Americans in Harlem used such terms as 'riff-raff', 'illiterate', 'lazy', 'uncouth' and 'dirty' to describe the Southern migrants, and blamed them for recent increases in racist white behaviour.[38] According to Osofsky, similar tensions were also common among Jews, Italians, Greeks and other New York immigrant groups, as 'earlier generations seemed overwhelmed by the problems of later arrivals from their countries'.[39]

Although Hoffman's cartoon alludes most directly to theatre conditions in the southern United States, it also has echoes for Harlem at this time, in so far as the partial integration of the theatre in the cartoon was analogous to the racial settlement of Harlem itself. Some of Harlem's white leadership expressed fears that African-Americans were moving not only into the peripheral 135th Street area, but that black settlement might also expand into and take over Harlem's main commercial and residential areas. As the local black population increased, these fears became more widely expressed.

As a direct consequence of increasing African-American settlement around 135th Street, theatres and movie houses in this area were the first to cater to black audiences, although African-Americans were still subject to segregationist seating policies and excluded altogether from some theatres. From its opening in 1905, the Alhambra Theatre on 126th Street and Seventh Avenue reportedly required all black people to sit in its second balcony, 'in spite of the fact that many of the top acts on the stage were colored stars', including Bert Williams and Bill 'Bojangles' Robinson.[40] In 1915, a theatre operator was refused a license to build a theatre at the corner of Lenox Avenue and 129th Street because a group of white ministers, lawyers and businessmen argued that it would bring 'the Negroes in large numbers to that section' (for many of these anti-black campaigners, 130th Street was seen as the dividing line between black and white Harlem).[41] The Family Theatre, on 125th Street, seems an exception to such racist practices, as it advertised briefly in *The New York Age* in 1909, just before being taken over by William Fox. Like other landowners a few blocks uptown on 135th Street, the owners of this theatre may have been in financial straits and therefore willing to break with discriminatory seating policies.[42] In most theatres, however, white audience members tended to resist being seated alongside African-Americans, regardless of their socio-economic status, education or comportment.

For Walton, however, it was imperative that white-owned theatres be integrated, especially in black neighbourhoods. Thus, in 1909, he proudly announced the opening of Harlem's first racially integrated theatre as a watershed in African-American community development. The Crescent Theatre opened in December 1909 in the heart of the growing black community, offering programmes of moving pictures and vaudeville, and was advertised as 'beautifully decorated' and 'first-class and up-to-date in every respect'.[43] In an article titled 'Mission of Crescent Theatre', Walton touted the white-owned establishment's desegregated seating policy, which yielded what he described as a totally integrated and harmonious black and white audience. Maintaining this decorum were several 'colored ushers in uniform', who kept the patrons quiet during the shows. Walton expressed the hope that this newly integrated theatre would lead to more 'first-class colored moving picture houses' in the city so as to 'educate, develop and assist in bringing about in the future conditions as they should exist'.[44]

Data on the specific seating policies and practices of early Harlem theatres is hard to find, and often contradictory. But New York State anti-discrimination legislation sheds light on public policy, if not local practice. In January 1913, a bill was proposed by New York State Assemblyman A. L. Levy to eliminate 'discrimination on account of race, creed, or color, in the public places of New York State'. Proprietors or employees of amusement and other public sites would be liable for fines of up to $1,000, jail terms of up to thirty months and restitution of up to $500. Two years before this bill was introduced, *The New York Age* had reported the case of an African-American woman in Paterson, New Jersey, who had been awarded $500 compensation for being charged twenty-five cents instead of fifteen cents at a motion picture theatre. However, despite sporadic challenges to dominant white attitudes and segregation practices, *de facto* racist policies probably persisted in most theatres owned and managed by whites.[45]

Walton initially advocated a cautious activism aimed at challenging theatre segregation. As Harlem's black neighbourhood grew in size, however, and as theatre managers became bolder in drawing the colour line, he began to advocate boycotts and lawsuits. A 1909 article in the *New York Clipper* on the Coloured Vaudeville Benevolent Association emphasised a desire for the elevation of black performance standards by non-confrontation means.[46] When the Lafayette Theatre opened in December 1912 on Seventh Avenue between 131st and 132nd Streets, Walton attacked attempts by its white managers to establish a segregated seating policy.[47] As a result of this negative publicity, business dropped off at the Lafayette and other local businesses owned by its managers, resulting in a desegregation policy trumpeted in advertisements in *The New York Age*. A few months later, Walton described seeing 'colored and white theatregoers sitting side by side on the first floor of the theatre peaceably and quiet', and sarcastically recalled: 'I was a bit nervous, as I was fearful that a sensation would be caused by some white person swooning and becoming unconscious because of the presence of colored people.'[48] Although Walton does not explicitly refer to the 'There's a Reason' cartoon, he does mock the racist attitudes it depicted.

Black ownership of Harlem theatres, as distinguished from black management, apparently did not occur until 1921. Although in 1911 Walton told his readers that 'everyone familiar with the situation in New York City will readily admit that there is a crying demand for a large colored theatre in the colored residential district of Harlem',[49] Henry T. Sampson reports that it was not until 1921 that 'the first theatre in New York City, owned and managed by blacks, was constructed. The Renaissance, at Seventh Avenue and 133rd Street was built by the Sares Realty Company, headed by William Roach'.[50] Before this time, Walton's enthusiasm for desegregation breakthroughs such as the Crescent and Lafayette theatres was tempered by the fact that these theatres, catering to black audiences, were still largely owned by white people.[51] Thus it is no surprise that, as early as 1911, he publicised plans for a new black-owned theatre to be built on 138th Street. Although the project never materialised, Walton publicised it for months, including soliciting names for the new theatre from his readers. When the Crescent Theatre was sold the same year, he criticised African-American entrepreneurs for failing to buy the theatre which was increasingly catering to black audiences: 'It is up to the members of the race who have the money to invest to come out of their state of lethargy and take advantage of the many opportunities offered to make money as well as raise the standard of the race several points in the business world.' He concluded that 'Negroes are not well disposed to the idea of cooperative ownership', an attitude resulting in part from 'recent failures of our large fraternal orders [which] have done much to lessen the confidence of those who have money to invest, but who are afraid to venture even to the amount of $1.'[52]

In 1914, Lester Walton was able to practice what he had preached about local control of Harlem's cultural institutions. When the Lafayette Theatre was sold by its white owners, Walton leased the theatre and became its manager. In the following years, he developed a stock company and produced musical-comedies, dramas and operas for African-American audiences.[53] The success of the Lafayette encouraged the development of the nearby Lincoln Theatre, although at both theatres costs were high and audience tastes unstable for some time. In addition, as one theatre historian notes, there were 'few good serious plays of Negro life', and the quality of the acting varied widely. As a consequence, the Lafayette and other early black theatres would be 'prosperous one year and broke the next'.[54] Gradually, however, these theatres developed stronger acts and more loyal audiences, and became essential to African-American culture during the Harlem Renaissance. By the 1920s, white bohemians would 'Take the A-train' uptown to these theatres, as described in a popular song, for a look at the new and, to them, exotic African-American culture which had by then firmly taken root.

The late 1910s and 1920s saw a gradual increase in the role of African-American entrepreneurs in theatre management and eventual ownership. However, while these changes in theatre operation indicate increased black self-determination and economic power, filmic representations of African-Americans remained predominantly racist. Writing about the images of African-American troops in

France in a Hearst-Pathé newsreel in 1918, Walton launched one of his most bitter attacks on the white movie industry: 'As long as our motion picture people and many of the daily newspapers insist on carrying on a propaganda of misrepresentation and educate the general public to judge twelve million native Americans by the worst and lowest types of the race (an unfair test to which no other race is subjected) just so long will there be a race problem.'[55]

Walton's frustration with the white film industry some twelve years after he began writing about moving pictures is symptomatic of the limited progress in the filmic representation of African-Americans during the period, despite the increasing empowerment of black spectators and entrepreneurs in movie houses and elsewhere. Likewise, Walton's enthusiasm for new, independent African-American film production companies in the 1910s was tempered by the economic realities of the day. Most of these black-owned companies folded within a few years because they were under-capitalised and operating within a distribution system increasingly dominated by the emerging Hollywood studios.[56] But if the opportunities created by cinema's arrival in Harlem failed to inhibit negative representations of African-Americans, motion pictures remained important rallying points for the complex struggles over racial identity, self-expression, and social and economic justice out of which the Harlem Renaissance of the 20s emerged.

Conclusion

In a relatively short time, Harlem changed from a place where African-Americans had little or no access to theatres to a place where they patronised, operated and eventually owned them. The proliferation of nickelodeons and the conversion of legitimate theatres to moving picture houses in Harlem after 1905 did more than provide a new form of entertainment for the local community. Film functioned as a double-edged sword for both white and black residents in Harlem, threatening the economic survival of existing entertainments, while also creating new opportunities for white and, later, African-American entrepreneurs. Pre-war cinema in Harlem both responded to and moulded a neighbourhood that would shift from a genteel white suburb into a thriving centre for African-American business and cultural life. Cinema's coincidence with the wave of black migration that transformed early twentieth century neighbourhoods in many cities across the United States thus provides a fascinating perspective on both the history of American race relations and the social context of early cinema.

Notes

The authors would like to thank the following for their valuable advice on this chapter: Eileen Bowser, Antonia Lant, and Robert Sklar. We would also like to thank everyone who read earlier drafts, including Giorgio Bertellini, William Boddy, Noel King, Margot Latham, David Patterson, and all of the participants in Antonia Lant's seminar on early cinema and Robert Sklar's seminar on historiography.

1 Governor Peter Stuyvesant founded the village of *Nieuw Haarlem* in March 1658, which centred closely around the intersection of 125th Street and First Avenue. For fur-

ther information, see Fremont Rider, compiler and editor, *Rider's New York City* (New York: Henry Holt and Company, 1916).

2 In part, Mary Carbine's essay '"The Finest Outside the Loop": Motion Picture Exhibition in Chicago's Black Metropolis, 1905–1928' (*Camera Obscura* vol. 23, May 1990, pp. 9–41) presents a model for our work, with its emphasis on the intersections of film and race in one neighbourhood. Carbine proposes that the moving picture house provided a space for consciousness and the assertion of social difference as well as the consumption of mass entertainments. Describing the black migration north during the first decades of this century as arising out of 'a racially centered world view' (p. 12), she shows how African-Americans had a 'distinct ethnic and cultural heritage that [strongly] influenced exhibition and moviegoing practices' (p. 10) in a Chicago neighbourhood in which black people generally 'looked forward to freedom from whites in everyday life' (p. 13). She refers to several tensions between blacks and whites with regard to film exhibition, as well as tensions within the black community itself (things which were also true of Harlem). However, whereas Carbine discusses an already established local film culture, our work examines how moving pictures gradually gained a stronghold in Harlem by successfully competing with local entertainments and attracting newly arriving audiences, who would in turn affect the local functioning of film.

3 *Harlem Local Reporter* (hereafter *HLR*) 24 October 1896, p. 2.

4 The Columbus Theatre later became Proctor's 125th Street Theatre in August 1900. The Harlem Music Hall became Hurtig & Seamon's Music Hall in December 1898.

5 'Dime Museums', *HLR*, 7 June 1890, p. 1. As Jervis Anderson notes, genteel Harlem 'wanted nothing to do with loose morals', but even in these early days it was unable to keep out some gambling dens, saloons and burlesque houses. Cited in *This Was Harlem: A Cultural Portrait, 1900–1950* (New York: Farrar Straus and Giroux, 1982), p. 47.

6 David Nasaw, 'The "Indecent" Others', in *Going Out: The Rise and Fall of Public Amusements* (New York: Basic Books, 1993), p. 60.

7 Charles Musser, *The Emergence of Cinema: The American Screen to 1907* (New York: Scribner's, 1990), pp. 274–5.

8 *New York Clipper* (hereafter *NYC*) 25 August 1900, p. 572.

9 Charles Musser writes that generally, 'Perhaps the only form of exhibition that did not prosper during [1903–4] … was, ironically, the storefront theatre, which [suffered] as existing vaudeville theatres added motion pictures to their bill'. *The Emergence of Cinema*, p. 366.

10 Keith–Proctor took over the Harlem Opera House in September 1906 and quickly reopened it as Keith and Proctor's Harlem Opera House, with movies on its bill. *NYC*, 6 October 1906, p. 881 and 27 October 1906, p. 961.

11 The magistrate reportedly said, 'If any man should show that picture to my child I would kill him. The town is full of this sort of places and they are doing incalculable harm. The police should close every one of them.' *Moving Picture World* (hereafter *MPW*) 14 December 1907, p. 663. The nickelodeon was located at 110 West 116th Street The owner was held on $1,000 bail.

12 The following week the theatre's staff was arrested again. *MPW*, 21 December 1907, p. 683 and 28 December 1907, p. 703.

13 The film was produced by IMP. *MPW*, 13 November 1909, p. 678.

14 The article continues, 'That is, they have a seating capacity of two hundred and fifty, and give four shows an hour. Others are so small that only fifty at a time can be jammed into the narrow area. They run from early morning until midnight, and their megaphones are barking before the milkman has made his rounds'. *MPW*, 5 October 1907, p. 487.

15 'The Nickel Craze in New York', *Views and Films Index*, no. 76 (5 October 1907), p. 1.

16 The article lists eleven area nickelodeons and their offerings: The Eldorado, The Nicolet, The Vanity Fair, The Harlem Comedy, The Auditorium, The Avena, The Parisienne, Howe's Nicolet (Bronx), The Belle Parie and two Nicolands at 145th and 3rd Avenue – all reportedly doing good business with movies and illustrated songs or vaudeville. *NYC*, 9 May 1908, p. 324.

17 For further information on the African-American migration into Harlem, see James

Weldon Johnson, *Black Manhattan* (New York: Da Capo Books, 1930) and Kenneth T. Jackson, *The Encyclopedia of New York* (New Haven: Yale University Press, 1995). See also Jeffrey S. Gurock, *When Harlem Was Jewish, 1870–1930* (New York: Columbia University Press, 1979) and Walter Benn Michaels, *Our America: Nativism, Modernism, and Pluralism* (Durham, NC: Duke University Press, 1995).

18 Anderson, *This Was Harlem*, p. 63.

19 *New York Age* (hereafter *NYA*), 15 December 1910, p. 6.

20 Rev. Powell's views on moving pictures and the church form part of a larger discourse on film as a form of social uplift that appeared in the *MPW* at this time. For example, in an article titled 'Clergymen Patronize Moving Picture Exhibitions', the views of the Rev. H. E. Latham are printed for *MPW* readers: 'The moving picture theatre is here as an institution; as a progressive and improving form of entertainment, for it furnishes amusement cheaply; it instructs; it helps people to enlarge their view of life and things, and gives a higher and better form of pleasure to most of its patrons who would naturally be content with a lower'. *MPW*, vol. 6, no. 9 (15 March 1910), p. 329. While some white clergy were prepared to speak out in favour of motion pictures, the general approach of white churches was guarded at best. Film trade publications such as *MPW* did, however, refer to certain church-related activities in promoting film-going as a culturally and morally wholesome activity. See 'Moving Pictures in Church', *MPW*, vol. 7, no. 4 (23 July 1910), p. 202.

21 *The New York Age* stemmed from a downtown New York tabloid called *The Rumor* which began in 1890. Published by George Parger, *The Rumor* called itself 'A Representative Colored American Newspaper'. From 1903 onwards, Booker T. Washington subsidised the paper until he purchased it outright in 1907. According to Roland E. Wolseley, the relatively conservative middle-class paper was severely criticised by W. E. B. Du Bois and other black leaders who believed that it 'condemned the black man to segregation and subservience to whites'. *The Black Press, USA* (Ames: Iowa State University Press, 1971), p. 32.

22 W. E. B. Du Bois, *The Souls of Black Folk* (New York: Bantam Books, 1989, first published in 1903).

23 Walton played in a local band called The Frogs, which was formed in 1908. Henry T. Sampson produces a photo of Walton and The Frogs in *Blacks in Blackface: A Source Book on Early Black Musical Shows* (Metuchen, NJ: Scarecrow, 1980), p. 26.

24 Walton, 'Theatrical Comment', *NYA*, 23 February 1911, p. 6. Walton cited the Court Theatre in Brooklyn as an example of a theatre that had recently booked fewer black acts as a result of its conversion to film.

25 Walton, 'Degeneracy of the Moving Picture Theatre', *NYA*, 5 August 1909, p. 6.

26 *Ibid.* The film may have been William Paley's *Avenging a Crime; Or, Burned at the Stake* (1904), which Musser describes as one of Paley's most sensational films, involving a black man (played by a white actor in black face) who loses at gambling, kills a white woman and is caught and burned at the stake. Musser, *The Emergence of Cinema*, p. 402.

27 Walton, 'Motion Picture Concern Makes Film Ridiculing Race', *NYA*, 16 October 1913, p. 6. The company was the Al Bartlett Film Company.

28 James W. Johnson, 'Uncle Tom's Cabin and the Clansman', *NYA*, 4 March 1915, p. 6 and Walton, 'Colored Citizen's Weakness Shown in Photo Play Incident', *NYA*, 25 March 1912, p. 6.

29 Walton, '*The Bar Sinister*', *NYA*, 14 June 1917, p. 6.

30 Walton, 'The Difficulties of a Pioneer Film Company', *NYA*, 9 August 1917, p. 6.

31 Walton, 'Moving Pictures of Tuskegee', *NYA*, 10 January 1910, p. 6. The film was produced by a group of black Bostonian businessmen who came up with the idea of forming a film company 'to produce some pictures that would show colored people what colored people are doing'.

32 Exhibitions such as this may suggest the importance of African-American churches in the reception of early film. While activists like Walton had to struggle for rights in white-owned theatres, black churches had more freedom to show films, especially uplifting ones like *A Trip to Tuskegee*.

33 Walton, 'Moving Pictures of Clef Club Tour', *NYA*, 12 November 1914, p. 6. Walton

wrote that the management of the Crescent Theatre 'claims the distinction of being the first theatre in New York to exhibit pictures of the Johnson–Jeffries fight'. See 'Fight Pictures at Crescent Theatre', *NYA*, 14 July 1910, p. 6. The fight footage was banned in Washington, DC, Baltimore, and elsewhere due to fears of possible riots. On this film, see Eileen Bowser, *The Transformation of Cinema, 1907–1915* (New York: Scribner's, 1990), pp. 192, 201–2, 289n.

34 Miriam Hansen, *Babel and Babylon: Spectatorship in American Silent Film* (Cambridge, MA: Harvard University Press, 1991), p. 311. Even before the fight took place, the *MPW* discussed the question of who would get rights to the fight in view of the enormous international interest it had attracted. If Johnson, the African-American won, the *MPW* reported, then 'the pictures would be of comparative little value, especially amongst the white section of the community. Amongst the colored section, however, their value would be greater'. *MPW* vol. 6 no. 23 (18 June 1910), p. 1039.

35 Mary Carbine makes a similar point about segregationist attitudes cutting across racial lines in her discussion of film exhibition in Chicago. See Carbine, 'The Finest Outside the Loop', pp. 23–4.

36 Gilbert Osofsky, *Harlem: The Making of a Ghetto (Negro New York, 1890–1930)* (Chicago: Ivan R. Dee, 1996, first published in 1963), p. 68.

37 Ibid., p. 43.

38 W. E. B. Du Bois described this Northern reactionary rhetoric as a form of 'self-defense and self-preservation'. Cited in Osofsky, *Harlem*, p. 43.

39 Ibid.

40 Frank Driggs, liner notes for *The Sound of Harlem*, n.p. (Columbia Records, 1964). In 1926 the Alhambra's management changed hands and black audiences were welcomed by advertisements that read 'sit anywhere you please'. Cited in Osofsky, p. 43.

41 Osofsky, *Harlem*, p. 108 and 244n.

42 *NYA*, 21 January 1909, p. 6.

43 *NYA*, 9 December 1909, p. 6. The Crescent Theatre was located at 36–38 West 135th Street, near Fifth Avenue.

44 'Mission of Crescent Theatre', *NYA*, 6 January 1910, p. 6.

45 'Plan to Prevent Discrimination in Public Places in New York State', *NYA*, 30 January 1913, p. 1; 'Fined $500 for Drawing Line', *NYA*, 30 November 1911, p. 6.

46 Walton, *NYC*, 19 June 1909, p. 488.

47 Osofsky, *Harlem*, pp. 110–11.

48 Walton, 'An Evening at the Lafayette', *NYA*, 20 February 1913, p. 6.

49 Walton, 'A New Theater for Harlem', *NYA*, 30 November 1911, p. 6.

50 Sampson, *Blacks in Blackface*, p. 123.

51 Walton, 'Crescent Theatre Sold', *NYA*, 24 August 1911, p. 6.

52 *Ibid.*

53 Osofsky, *Harlem*, pp. 110–11.

54 Edith J. R. Isaacs, *The Negro in the American Theatre* (New York: Theatre Arts, 1947), pp. 44–5.

55 Walton, 'The Colored Soldier on the Screen', *NYA*, 24 August 1918, p. 6.

56 In addition to the Frederick Douglass Film Company, the most significant companies and individuals included the Foster Photoplay Company (formed in Chicago in 1910 by Bill Foster); Lincoln Motion Picture Company (founded in 1917 in Los Angeles by a group of black businessmen); and Oscar Micheaux, the first African-American to produce a feature-length film. See Daniel Leab, ' "All Colored" – But Not Much Different: Films Made for Negro Ghetto Audiences, 1913–1928', *Phylon* 36 (September 1975), pp. 321–9 and Mark Reid, *Redefining Black Film* (Berkeley: University of California Press, 1993), pp. 7–18, for an overview of early black motion picture companies. For more on Micheaux, see Henry T. Sampson, *Blacks in Black and White: A Source Book on Black Films* (2nd ed.) (Metuchen, NJ: Scarecrow Press, 1995); Manthia Diawara, (ed.), *Black American Cinema* (New York: Routledge, 1993); Pearl Bowser and Louise Spence, 'Identity and Betrayal: *The Symbol of the Unconquered* and Oscar Micheaux's "Biographical Legend" ', in Daniel Bernardi, (ed.), *The Birth of Whiteness: Race and the Emergence of U.S. Cinema* (New Brunswick: Rutgers University Press, 1996), pp. 56–80.

4 'The Formative and Impressionable Stage': Discursive Constructions of the Nickelodeon's Child Audience

Roberta E. Pearson and William Uricchio

Cultural élites paid relatively little attention to the cinema during its first decade in the United States, considering it as a scientific novelty, a didactic instrument or at worst a harmless amusement. But when the nickelodeons began, in the oft-repeated phrase, to spring up like mushrooms on every street corner, contention quickly arose over the new medium's social position. The broadening of the cinema's clientele to include the urban masses cast the audience in a synechdocal relationship to those marginalised elements, principally workers and immigrants, who were perceived as threatening American national identity, causing concern among state officials, urban reform groups, professional associations and the clergy.[1] This chapter addresses this cultural contestation by discussing a specific set of viewers, arguing that children bore a similar relationship to the larger cinema audience and thus, implicitly, to the urban population. The linkage of children with the larger urban population was not without its contradictions, particularly, as we shall see, since children constituted the object of competing period discourses. But in this essay we focus on the ways in which children, constituting a minority, albeit a substantial minority of the nickelodeons' clientele, served as a central point of reference as New York City's cultural élites strove to suppress or regulate the new medium.[2]

A variety of the period's discourses increasingly marked children off from the rest of the population, defining childhood as a demographic category and providing the larger framework for the debates around children and the cinema. During the last decades of the nineteenth century and the first decades of the twentieth century, the discursive construction of childhood, while still fluid, was in a period of institutional reification. Society's concern with the category of the child, institutionalised in the 1860s and 1870s in the form of various reform organisations such as the Society for the Prevention of Cruelty to Children, became increasingly evident in state mandates concerning labour, schooling, legal status and leisure time, all of which draw distinctions between children and adults. As we know from such films as *Children Who Labor* (Edison, 1912) and *The Cry of the Children* (Thanhouser, 1911), the campaign for child labour laws continued well into the twentieth-century's second decade, although by this time children constituted a fairly small percentage of the working population. The influx of immigrants in the decades around the turn of the century focused increased attention on raising the school leaving age and mandating school attendance, since schools were perceived as the primary instrument of Americanisation. The law began to distinguish between adult and young offenders during this period, as the juvenile courts system was established to deal with children under the age of sixteen.[3] Laws also governed children's leisure activities: section 1482 of the Greater New York Charter of 1901 prohibited unaccompanied children under the age of fourteen from attending the theatre at night.

Children clearly constituted a salient demographic category in the period of cinema's establishment as a mass medium and most discourses about audiences asserted that minors formed a significant proportion of the nickelodeon's clientele. In 1910, John Collier, secretary of the People's Institute, the New York City civic reform organisation that most concerned itself with the cinema, suggested that nationwide, from 500,000 to 600,000 children attended picture shows daily. He contended that, each month, pictures approved by the National Board of Censorship were seen by a number of children exceeding the total child population in the country between the ages of four and sixteen. Collier also reported a statistic derived from the People's Institute investigation of cheap amusements in Manhattan: at a number of public schools in the 'congested neighbourhoods', 60 per cent of pupils reported going to the nickelodeon once a week.[4] In 1911, the Russell Sage Foundation employed Michael Davis, formerly of the People's Institute, to conduct a survey of Manhattan entertainment venues. He reported that 900,000 people a week attended moving picture shows, of whom 225,000 were children, spending a weekly average total amount of $11,250. Davis asked 1,140 children between the ages of eleven and fourteen to report their cinema attendance: 62 per cent said they went once a week or more frequently, while 'a truly astonishing proportion, 16 per cent of the total, avowed that they go daily'.[5] In 1914, the National Board of Censorship estimated that 180,000 children attended Manhattan nickelodeons daily.[6]

The variations among these figures point to the difficulty of obtaining valid quantitative data, but the reformers' discourse provides illuminating qualitative data. In fact, the reformers themselves were ultimately more concerned about the qualitative than the quantitative impact of the cinema. John Collier characterised the nickelodeon as 'a family theatre par excellence. Next to this, it is a children's theatre'.[7] But how did this theatre and its films affect the children? Then, as now, children were seen as particularly susceptible to media effects by virtue of their 'formative' and 'impressionable' minds, two words which occur again and again in the discourse of the period. The Women's Municipal League claimed that the 'bulk of [the nickelodeon proprietor's] patronage consist of children and immigrants – the formative and impressionable elements in our population'.[8] In 1910, *The American Review of Reviews* compared the influence of books and motion pictures: 'The exclusion of improper books from public libraries and circulating libraries is pretty closely attended to. Yet no group of libraries in the world have [sic] ever possessed the influence over susceptible children, and over all minds in the formative and impressionable stage, that the motion picture exerts today. It is probably the greatest single force in shaping the American character'.[9]

As these sources reveal, reformers believed that other groups, such as immigrants, shared childlike characteristics. These discursive parallels with other marginalised populations constructed the child as other, as separate from and inferior to the dominant white male. Said Michael Davis in *The Exploitation of Pleasure*, 'We ought to have motion-pictures specially produced as instruments of education – physical, intellectual, spiritual – for the adult as well as the child, and for America's child, the immigrant of many races'.[10] Maud McDougall explained the necessity for using the new medium to address children and immigrants. Asserting that children constituted 20 to 25 per cent of the audience and immigrants another 'very large percentage', McDougall continued, 'Immigrants and children! The entire raw material of future citizenship. No wonder that the "high-brows" – parents and teachers, legislators and entertainers – are concerned over the influence of these cheap shows'.[11] Dr Howard King, one of the 'high-brows' McDougall probably had in mind, wrote in *The Journal of the American Medical Association*: 'Moving picture shows in tenement districts and labour settlements should exhibit pictures that tend to elevate the mind and improve the moral condition of their audiences. Pictures portraying scandal, illicit amours and criminal cupidity very often have a debasing effect on a mind that is already morally warped though environment and surroundings, thereby bringing to the surface a latent criminality.'[12] King's statement sums up élite concerns: the cinema, in terms of both venues and films, had a powerful effect on the 'impressionable' and 'formative' minds of others whose age, or condition (living in tenements, being a worker, not being an American) or gender debarred them from the capacity for rational thought assumed to be inherent in the adult, native-born, white male. Said New York City's Fire Commissioner Joseph Johnson, after his department carried out an investigation of the city's nickelodeons: 'It is a panicky crowd which patronizes the moving-pictures houses of our city – mothers and children in the predominance – many of them of foreign birth'.[13]

In common with most dominant constructions of 'the other', the élite rhetoric of the period characterised children, women and immigrants as simultaneously vulnerable and dangerous.[14] Their less developed faculties of discrimination, their tendency to panic, their physical frailty, both marked them off from and granted them the protection of the dominant. Their perceived inferiority resulted in the custom of rescuing the 'women and children first', part of the Victorian cult of domesticity which sentimentalised these groups' supposed innocence. But this perceived inferiority had less positive implications. The public sphere had to be protected from destabilisation by these irrational others: children have never been allowed to vote, serve on juries or hold public office, activities also forbidden to women until the success of the suffrage campaign and to this day to non-citizens may not vote until they prove their suitability through passing a citizenship exam. But while the public sphere of the adult, native-born males remained inaccessible, these others were increasingly participating in the newly established alternative public sphere of the urban cheap amusements such as amusement parks, ice-cream parlours, dance halls and the nickelodeon. As the most high profile of these venues, the nickelodeon had the potential to exacerbate both the others' dangerous natures and their vulnerability. Depending on its deployment, it could serve as a force for good or for evil; it could uplift or degrade.

The issue of children and the moving pictures encompassed the demographic and legal construction of childhood, the binary discourses characterising children as simultaneously vulnerable and dangerous, and concerns about the cinema's perceived effects and cultural status. As part of the battle to control a new mass medium, the focus on children had widespread civic implications, involving not simply questions about the mental and physical health of the country's future citizens, but also an institutional redefinition of the public sphere at a contentious moment in American history. Children's saliency to the reformers' discourse also had profound implications for the film industry. Not only did children constitute at least a quarter of the nickelodeons' clientele, but their incorporation into the audience formed a crucial part of the strategy of building the mass audience that would make the cinema an acceptable medium. Because children stood in a crucial relationship to the rest of the audience, particularly those other others, women and immigrants, the discursive contestation around children's cinemagoing had wider reverberations.

Then as now, the concerns of the élite about the moral and physical dangers the nickelodeon held for its supposedly most vulnerable audience included the problem of film content. Given its desire to create a mass audience, the film industry produced films it thought suitable for all, rather than targeting particular audience segments as it does today. Many critics, however, shared a never precisely articulated 'magic bullet' theory of media effects and believed that many films were not at all suitable for children. The 'magic bullet' theory, first formulated in the early stages of mass-communications research in the 1940s and still widely retained, holds that audiences have no defence against media messages, and respond indiscriminately to what they see or hear. The 'formative' and 'impressionable' minds of children would, of course, be particularly susceptible to the 'magic bullet'. According to Lucy Robertson Jones, Chairman of the Yorktown Municipal Women's League: 'about a quarter of the films from which the ordinary programmes are made up are such as to degrade the taste or corrupt the morals of young people. These films introduce them to a world of chicanery and intrigue, of horseplay and gambling house brawls, of infidelity and "forced embraces" (to use the language of the scenarios), of bomb throwing, suicide and incendiarism'.[15]

Jones' fears paralleled earlier moral panics about other popular media forms, such as the dime novel, but some asserted that film's imagistic base rendered it even more of a threat to the nation's young. In 1911, Richard Barry claimed that 'where once the dime and nickel novels suggested ways of crime to unbalanced youth the moving picture has come to make a more ready and more potent appeal. The printed word is never so ardent with an impressionable mind as the acted word'. According to Barry, film viewing had disastrous consequences for some young people. He reported that a sixteen-year-old girl committed suicide after seeing a film in which a girl who turned on the gas was rescued by her lover, that two boys, after seeing *Jesse James at Bay*, went into the hills with .22 calibre rifles, shot a dog, wounded a little girl, and fired on pursuing policemen and three other men, and that a fourteen-year-old boy arraigned for stealing jewellery confessed he had conceived the idea of being a burglar from a motion picture.[16] Reports of such direct media effects on children's behaviour seem to have been as numerous in film's second decade as they are in its tenth, but then as now some saner voices were heard.[17] Speaking of his research for the People's Institute report on cheap amusements, John Collier said:

In the truant class I found that every mortal boy jubilantly acknowledged the soft impeachment of motion pictures. My impulse was to blame the truancy on motion pictures but older heads on the committee reminded me that truants had existed long before motion pictures caught their roving eye. So did juvenile delinquency, I may add, and when I read in the newspapers that a boy has robbed, hurled stones, or run away from home 'because he saw it in a motion picture', I am inclined to wait for the evidence.[18]

Despite the absence of any satisfyingly conclusive empirical evidence, many reformers argued that the cinema constituted just as powerful a force for good as it did for bad. While some critics claimed that the potent cinematic image could turn children into criminals, others argued that it could just as well turn them into scholars. In 1909, William Allen Johnston pointed out that, 'Children attend them after school hours; and the exhibits are often highly educational, it is asserted. Not only that, but the lessons of the screen are more forcibly impressed upon the youthful mind than the dry exercises of the schoolbook'.[19] Anecdotal evidence seemed to confirm these impressions. In the course of their investigations for the People's Institute's report on cheap amusements, Michael Davis and Josephine Redding attended a nickelodeon where 'Paul Revere rode madly for nearly half-an-hour; between the scenes Longfellow's poem was shadowed onto the curtain, and the children shouted its lines in unison'.[20]

Élites may have disagreed as to the effects of film content, but they were unanimous about the deleterious effects of film venues, which were seen as posing physical and moral threats to children's well-being. Here the corporeality of the audience was at issue, and while many complained about hygiene, the possibility of eye damage, and the danger of fire and panic, the supporters of moving pictures launched no counter-attack. The People's Institute report on cheap amusements asserted that: 'Often the sanitary conditions of the showrooms are bad; bad air, floors uncleaned, no provision of spittoons, and the people crowded closely together all make contagion likely'.[21] Women's and children's apparent physical frailty put them in particular jeopardy. The critic Walter Pritchard Eaton, in an article aptly titled 'The Menace of the Movies', wrote:

> In this dust-laden atmosphere ... the audience, mainly women and children, are seated for an hour or more, breathing in contamination from the breath of others and from the lack of cleanliness in the place.... We would not think for a moment of permitting schoolrooms to get into the condition in which most of the moving picture halls are, yet it must not be forgotten that a great many children spend several hours each week in these places and that no precautions at all are taken to keep them from being sources of danger for one another.[22]

Moving pictures were also perceived as posing greater hazards to children's eyes. The People's Institute report declared that 'children are fond of crowding forward right next to the curtain where the eye strain is severe'.[23] Fire Commissioner Johnston's view that women and children constituted a particularly panicky part of the audience was widely held. When calling for better lit venues, *The Film Index* maintained that 'women and children become nervous in a darkened auditorium and are unnecessarily startled by unusual noises, such as the sputtering of the lamp of the projecting machine, and ... mischievous boys take advantage of the darkness to create disturbances that annoy the audience'.[24]

This last comment indicates the dual characterisation of children as the other: vulnerable women and children panic easily but dangerous boys create disturbances that might precipitate panic. This duality is most marked in the discourse about the so-called 'moral dangers' of the nickelodeons, a euphemism for the sexual threat believed to be ever present in the new public sphere of the cheap amusements. Even John Collier, that most progressive of progressive reformers, could not resist writing in melodramatic terms about this issue: 'The main evil lies in the complete darkness in which many picture shows are run. It is an evil pure and simple; unnecessary; detrimental to the artistic effect of the pictures themselves, and destructive of the social interchange which ought to go on in a family and neighbourhood gathering place like a motion picture show.'[25] Reports of the evils visited on children through attending the nickelodeons abounded. In June 1908, Vincent Pisarro of the Society for the Prevention of Cruelty to Children (SPCC) said:

> [The moving picture show] is a grave menace to their well being. ... Such is the craze for their entertainments that children are easily tempted to wrongdoing to see them. ... The secret distribution of free tickets to children by the smooth-tongued young rakes who run these shows is working untold harm. For a coveted season ticket many a boy has turned pickpocket, turning his plunder over to the crook who runs the show and many a girl has sold her first innocence for the same price. Add to these allurements the darkness of the auditorium during the exhibition, with its opportunities for 'puppy-love' affairs, and you have an ideal breeding ground for degradation which even the worst of the so-called 'dancing academies' can not rival.[26]

Five years later, despite the vast transformations in the industry that were making the cinema an acceptable mass entertainment, the SPCC still claimed that the nickelodeons were a menace to the innocent. In May 1913, a spokesman for the SPCC was quoted in the *New York Times* as asserting that 'Degenerates have found these moving picture resorts the easiest means of making the acquaintance of children, and numerous crimes against both boys and girls have resulted'. The SPCC had prosecuted 114 such cases in the previous year.[27]

Although period mores forbade explicit articulation of the problem, it is clear that children were seen as potentially willing participants in sexual experimentation as well as being the innocent dupes of depraved male sexuality. In this era, the line between virtue and depravity was thin and porous, as attested to by the prevalent trope of the 'fallen woman', excluded from hearth and home because of sexual misdemeanours. Illicit sexual contact, for boys and girls as well as adult females, resulted in 'ruin', forever preventing a child's integration into the adult public sphere and therefore posing a problem for the state. But were the numerous reports of such 'ruin' simply a case of moral panic, or did the nickelodeons really tempt children to sin? Again, little evidence survives, but two days after New York City's Mayor George B. McClellan revoked nickelodeon licenses in 1908, a Mrs Smyther wrote to him urging him to continue his campaign:

> Thank God you have at last awakened to the horrors of those moving picture dens. Being a cheap entertainment many little girls can get the price and go there and spend

hours. My heart has been broken by my daughter spending her Sunday at that dreadful 14th Street theatre. Through the influence of some of the men she met there she has run away from home with another girl. While we have her back she came to us ruined and will never be the same child again. In the name of humanity stand firm against those places. Do not let it blow over as it usually does for a few dollars breaking our homes and hearts. I could give you the names of many if I dared but what's the use. We have no money to fight with but must suffer and weep. Asking God to help you am Mrs. Smyther. [28]

Mrs Smyther writes in the melodramatic style of the period's discourses around 'illicit' sexuality, casting her daughter, her husband and herself as the innocent victims of the piece. But was the young Miss Smyther simply an innocent victim or might she have been an active agent in her own 'ruin'? Did she see the nickelodeon as a rare opportunity to escape the parental home, as Kathy Peiss has suggested was the case for many of the city's females?[29] If the 'dreadful 14th St. theatre' had not 'ruined' her, would the same fate have befallen her at the neighbourhood dancing academy or ice-cream parlour? Despite the prevalent discourse of innocence, reformers seem to have believed that many youngsters, like Miss Smyther, were potential perverts, needing very little to detour them from the straight and narrow road of propriety. The moral panic around the nickelodeon and the other so-called 'cheap amusements' resulted precisely from the period's dual construction of children as both innocent victims and potentially dangerous participants in illicit activities, be they sexual or criminal.

Reformers formulated various strategies for the protection of children in the nickelodeon audience. The most repressive proposed their total or partial exclusion from the nickelodeon, striking at the economic base of the film industry, which depended on children for a significant portion of its revenues. Many in this faction were clergymen, such as Canon William Chase, one of the film medium's most vociferous opponents, who launched his attack against the nickelodeons as early as October 1907. According to Chase, 'the open saloon is not so dangerous to our young people as is the apparently clean and innocent Sunday show, for its evils are understood. The Sunday show drives out of the mind all holy thoughts which have sanctified the day'.[30] In January 1908, the *New York Times* reported that, at a meeting of the American Sabbath Union at Marble Collegiate Church,

> Canon Chase ... will call the attention of those present to the moving picture show and penny arcade situation. Most of the clergy assert that these places do more harm in one Sunday than the vaudeville operators do in a year, because there are at least 500 of them in the city, open from early morning until late at night, and because they are so cheap as to attract thousand [sic] of young persons. Their very obscurity, the clergymen say, increase their harmful influence, because they do not attract the element of the public that would be apt to take action to suppress them.[31]

Chase's campaign against the nickelodeons was part of the larger effort to impose the so-called 'Blue Sunday' on the metropolis, by prohibiting almost all forms of entertainment on the 'Lord's Day'. Clearly, the clergy were feeling the competition. The *Tammany Times*, print organ of New York City's powerful Democratic political machine, reported that many of the complaints Mayor McClellan had received about moving pictures came from clergymen, who believed 'that the shows keep children from Sunday schools'.[32]

Legislators seemed reluctant to impose an outright ban on children's nickelodeon attendance, but, working with legal precedents marking young people as a separate demographic category, they defined sixteen as the 'age of consent' for nickelodeon attendance. The 1911 Code of Ordinances of the City of New York prohibited the admission of unaccompanied minors under the age of sixteen to any place where moving pictures were shown under a common show licence. This ordinance was aimed directly at the nickelodeons, whose proprietors paid $25 for a common show licence, rather than at vaudeville theatres, whose proprietors paid up to $500 for a theatrical licence. The film industry had good reason to contest this law, but so did many of the reformers. Not only did they see the cinema's potential for good, but they argued that exclusion was impossible to enforce and led merely to disrespect for the law on the part of devoted young cinephiles who would find some means of gaining access to the moving picture shows despite the prohibition. The National Board of Censorship argued in 1913 that 'Unaccompanied children go in large numbers to the picture theatres. Some States have forbidden this by law, but the prohibition has not been successful.... Laws which prohibit the admission of unaccompanied children under any and all conditions are unenforceable and demoralising. They contribute to the prevalent disrespect for the law'.[33] Worse still, such laws resulted in the exposure of children to those very moral dangers that so agitated reformers. In 1913, W. B. Rogers, deputy chief of New York City's Bureau of Licenses and partially responsible for nickelodeon regulation, urged the New York State Senate to rescind a state-wide prohibition against unaccompanied minors attending moving picture shows. The present law, Rogers declared, was 'one of the best allies of the white slave traffic'. When conducting an investigation of moving pictures for New York City's Mayor Gaynor, Rogers saw 'men and women of the underworld ... waiting in front of moving-picture places, and they were only too glad to heed the request of minors for an escort, taking advantage of acquaintances thus formed with young girls to lead them to lives of vice'.[34]

Exclusionary policies that attempted to define children as a separate audience were not only unenforceable but actually exacerbated existing problems. Reformers seem to have realised that exclusion was unworkable and sought not to define children out of the audience but, rather, to define them as junior consumers of targeted products by developing special venues and special films for children. The Recreation Committee of the Yorkville branch of the Women's Municipal League persuaded three local nickelodeons to give special Friday afternoon and evening performances of films approved by the Committee, and asked churches, schools and settlements to recommend the shows. The Committee noted that this experiment had taught them several lessons about the nickelodeons' operating procedures. The proprietors, they said, knew 'nothing about the pictures they exhibit except their title and class ("drama", comedy or educational)'. The proprietors accepted whatever the film exchanges provided, demanding only that the programme be 'properly balanced', i.e., contain an equal number of comedy and 'drama' reels, but they seldom showed even one educational film. The Committee's requests for special films upset 'the regular circuit arranged by each exchange for its films'. The exchanges, which derived no profit from the arrangements, could 'not always be relied on to take the trouble'. The success of the young people's shows depended on persuading the exchanges to 'book for the Friday performances only films endorsed by our Committee. The Committee does not know how to accomplish this'.[35] The Committee's comments confirm the view of early film historians that both film exchanges and nickelodeon proprietors selected films for a mass audience and had difficulty varying their procedures to cater for a target audience. Several other reform organisations, such as New York City's Educational Alliance and the People's Institute, also experimented with special children's shows, but such programmes do not seem to have become regular practice, most probably because of the industry's inability to address specialised needs.[36]

Censorship was the reformers' most lasting legacy to the film industry, but this strategy, too, ran into the mass-audience problem. The National Board of Censorship of Motion Pictures was established in 1909 through co-operation between the People's Institute and the Motion Picture Patents Company, the trust that represented the interests of the country's leading film manufacturers. The Board's close links to the industry rendered it sympathetic to the mass-audience concept. The Board proclaimed in 1913 that: 'The programs in commercial picture theaters are not selected for children, but for a general audience of men, women and children. So long as trade conditions make this necessary, the film programs cannot be strictly adapted to the child mind'. The censors could not ensure that the nickelodeons showed only films appropriate for children, but the Board proposed another solution: 'As soon as the schools begin to use motion pictures extensively, the theatres will be compelled to adapt to the new conditions and make a special bid for child patronage, otherwise they will lose the patronage of the children, and in large measure of the parents of children as well'.[37] This suggestion may well have reflected the interests of the film industry. In 1910, the Motion Picture Patents Company established an exchange branch, the General Film Company, which by 1911 owned practically all of the country's exchanges.[38] The General Film Company in turn established an educational unit that produced lists of films suitable for use in the schools. This not only increased the industry's profits and enhanced its respectability, it defined children as a target audience, but only during school hours, leaving them free to attend the ordinary nickelodeons during their leisure time.[39]

As late as 1916, when the establishment of the mass audience was well under way and élite attacks on the medium had somewhat abated, the censors, who had by this time renamed themselves the National Board of Review of Motion Pictures, again insisted that their judgment of films could not be predicated solely on their suitability for children: 'There is a vast range of subjects entirely suitable for the mature, which are unsatisfactory for children. It has been demonstrated again and again that it is equally fallacious to reduce all pictures to the plane of the intelligence of the child. The National Board refuses to attempt to do this. It judges primarily from the standpoint of the adult'. On this occasion it suggested another solution: the selection of pictures 'suited to young people under sixteen and their increasing use in entertainments or theatres expressly for children on selected days'. Perhaps implicitly acknowledging that this strategy had already been tried and failed, the Board said that ultimately only parents could ensure that children were not exposed to improper films: 'This phase of the problem will be solved when parents assume their responsibility and allow boys and girls to attend only those motion pictures which are suitable to their intelligence'. The Board noted that it was now furnishing a list of appropriate films on a monthly basis.[40]

We have argued in this chapter that the industry's critics saw children as being in a synechdocal relationship to the larger audience, which in turn bore a similar relationship to the multicultural urban populations that élites perceived as posing great threats to social stability. For this reason, reformers' discourse centred on the moral and physical threats that the nickelodeons posed to young audiences, while many of their suggestions for improvement centred on somehow constituting children as a separate audience. The industry's discourse recognised children as a demographic category, but its industrial practices made it difficult to treat them as a separate audience with regard to film content. Given this problem, children would derive the most effective protection from the regulation of existing exhibition venues rather than of film content. In 1913, the National Board of Censorship reported that 'A law now proposed in New York State … allows the admission of unaccompanied children to picture theaters where the program is strictly confined to films with accompanying music and recitation, but without vaudeville; where the unaccompanied children are segregated away from adults; where a matron … is constantly present; and where the interior is adequately lighted throughout the course'.[41] We have been unable to ascertain whether these suggestions became law, but it is certainly true that, in the same year, New York City's Board of Aldermen finally passed a much-contested ordinance regulating moving picture venues. Although it did not specifically mention children, this ordinance addressed many of the reformers' concerns regarding the moral and physical hazards of the nickelodeon. The ordinance required that the 'space occupied by each person shall be separated from the adjoining space by an arm or other suitable device' and that lighting be at all times of such intensity that 'a person with normal eyesight' could 'read the Snellen standard test type at a distance of 20 feet'. No longer would children sit crowded on benches in dark nickelodeons, easy prey for unscrupulous adults. And no longer would they be subjected to physical dangers. Motion pictures now had to be adequately fireproofed, have aisles wide enough and exits numerous enough to deal with a panicky crowd, have adequate ventilation and be 'kept clean and free from dust'.[42]

Censorship ameliorated but did not entirely allay the concerns of cinema's critics. While the film industry acceded to both the construction of children as a demographic category and to the construction of children as 'other', its industrial organisation, indeed its very survival, was predicated on the concept of the mass audience. Not until the collapse of the Hollywood studio system and the fragmentation of the mass audience in the 60s did the industry agree to the strategy suggested by many of the nickelodeon period's reformers and establish a ratings system that acknowledged children as other with regard to film content. During the nickelodeon period, the regulation of exhibition venues provided the most effective means of both protecting and disciplining that simultaneously vulnerable and dangerous other, children. Hence the discursive construction of children as other eventually served the needs of both reformers and film industry. We would argue that it also serves the needs of early film historians. Focusing on the synechdocal relationship of children to the larger audience and its other others, immigrants and women, and the synechdocal relationship that this audience bore in turn to the urban populace further illuminates the social and cultural contestation over the moving picture during its first decade as a true mass medium.

Notes

1 For more on period perceptions of audiences, see William Uricchio and Roberta E. Pearson, *Reframing Culture: The Case of the Vitagraph Quality Films* (Princeton: Princeton University Press, 1993) and 'Constructing the Mass Audience: Competing Discourses of Morality and Rationalization in the Nickelodeon Period', *Iris* 17 (Autumn 1994), pp. 43–54.

2 Despite their discursive centrality, film historians have paid relatively little attention to children, with the exception of the work done by Richard DeCordova and Lea Jacobs on children's matinées in the United States in the 20s and Terry Staples on children's matinées in the United Kingdom in the 30s.

3 E. Fellows Jenkins, 'Department of Philanthropy, Charities and Social Problems', *Annals of the American Academy of Political and Social Sciences*, vol. 26 (November 1905), pp. 774–5.

4 John Collier, 'The Problem of Motion Pictures', reprinted from the *Proceedings of the Child Welfare Conference*, Clark University, June 1910, New York Public Library for the Performing Arts, p. 3.

5 Michael M. Davis, *The Exploitation of Pleasure* (New York: Sage, 1911), pp. 28–9, 34.

6 F. Robertson Jones, Chairman, 'Yorkville Branch', *Women's Municipal League of New York Yearbook, 1914* (no publisher), p. 42.

7 John Collier, secretary of the People's Institute, to members of the Committee of Cheap Amusements, 25 December 1908, Community Service Society Files, Box 180, Theatre Investigations Folder, Rare Books and Manuscripts Library, Columbia University Library.

8 Michael M. Davis, Jr. and Josephine Redding, 'Cheap Amusement Investigation A Vitally Important Matter', *The Women's Municipal League Bulletin*, March 1908, p. 10.

9 'The Moving Picture and the National Character', *The American Review of Reviews*, September 1910, p. 320

10 Davis, *The Exploitation of Pleasure*, p. 56.

11 Maud McDougall, 'The Mission of the Movies', *The Designer*, January 1913.

12 Howard, D. King, MD, 'The Moving Picture Show: A New Factor in Health Conditions', *The Journal of the American Medical Association*, 14 August 1909, p. 520.

13 Joseph Johnson, 'Fire-Proofing A City', *American Review of Reviews*, December 1913, pp. 699–707.

14 The other is often constructed in terms of a binary opposition since the moment of first encounter, for example, Native Americans have been represented as either 'savage savages', fit only for extermination, or as 'noble savages', inherently inferior yet capable of being assimilated by the dominant. Much the same holds true of contemporary Hollywood's representation of African-Americans: blacks are either savage, drug-dealing murderers (for example, Wesley Snipes in *New Jack City*) or noble, long-suffering do-gooders (Morgan Freeman in almost any role). There is a vast literature on the topic which space constraints prohibit us from citing here.

15 F. Robertson Jones, 'Yorkville Branch', p. 44.

16 Richard Barry, 'Moving Picture Bubble', *Pearson's Magazine*, January 1911, p. 133.

17 For example, Maud McDougall made much the same claims as Barry.

18 Collier, 'The Problem of Motion Pictures', pp. 3–4.

19 William Allen Johnston, 'The Moving Picture Show, the New Form of Drama for the Million', *Munsey's Magazine*, August 1909, p. 636.

20 Davis and Redding, p. 11.

21 'Cheap Amusement Shows in Manhattan: Preliminary Report of Investigation', p. 4, Subject Papers, Papers relating to the formation and subsequent history of the National Board of Review of Motion Pictures, Box 170, Rare Books and Manuscripts Department, New York Public Library.

22 Walter Pritchard Eaton, 'The Menace of the Movies', *American Magazine*, September 1913, p. 592.

23 'Cheap Amusement Shows in Manhattan', p. 4

24 *The Film Index*, 12 June 1909.

25 Collier, 'The Problem of Motion Pictures', pp. 4–5.

26 *The New York World*, 27 December 1908.

27 *New York Times*, 30 May 1913.

28 Letter from Mrs Smyther to Mayor George McClellan, 26 December 1908, George B. McClellan Collection, Manuscript Division, Library of Congress.

29 See Kathy Peiss, *Cheap Amusements: Working Women and Leisure in Turn-of-the-Century New York* (Philadelphia: Temple University Press, 1986).

30 *New York Times*, 14 October 1907.

31 'Moving Picture Men Score One in Court', *New York Times*, 3 January 1908.

32 The *Tammany Times*, 19 December 1908.

33 National Board of Censorship of Motion Pictures, *Suggestions for a Model Ordinance for Regulation of Motion Picture Theatres* (no date, probably 1913), p. 4.

34 *New York Times*, 20 February 1913.

35 F. Robertson Jones, 'Yorkville Branch', pp. 42–4.

36 See, for example, George Blaisdell, 'At the Sign of the Flaming Arcs', *Moving Picture World*, 4 January 1913, p. 34, on the People's Institute's special shows for schoolchildren.

37 National Board of Censorship of Motion Pictures, *Suggestions for a Model Ordinance*, p. 4.

38 Eileen Bowser, *The Transformation of Cinema, 1907–1915* (Berkeley: University of California Press, 1994), pp. 81–2.

39 For more on the industry's relations with the schools during this period, see Uricchio and Pearson, *Reframing Culture: The Case of the Vitagraph Quality Films* (Princeton, NJ: Princeton University Press), p. 49.

40 *The Standards and Policy of The National Board of Review of Motion Pictures* (reissued 1 October 1916) (New York: National Board of Review of Motion Pictures, 1916), p. 21.

41 National Board of Censorship of Motion Pictures, *Suggestions for a Model Ordinance*, p. 4.

42 *The City Record*, 3 July 1913, pp. 6503–4.

PART TWO
The Politics of Audiences

5   Why the Audience Mattered in Chicago in 1907

Lee Grieveson

In the midst of its 'crusade' against 'nickel theaters' in early 1907, the *Chicago Tribune* carried a front-page report on a fire that had broken out in one of the city's theatres of this kind.[1] The theatre, like 'practically all the others', was without 'adequate protection'. 'Disorder followed', and, in the 'panic' that ensued, one audience member was trampled on.[2] Behind the concern about physical safety, and the call for governmental regulation of building codes, lay concerns about moral danger. In other theatres, the paper noted, 'the fire panic was lacking but the continuous performance panic of cheap songs, tawdry singers, and suggestive pictures reigned'. Typically in early writing on such nickel theatres, an 'intrepid man or woman' would visit a theatre in the poorer region of the city to report back on the sights (and, frequently, on the smells) of these recently developed spaces. This work became a subcategory of what Walter Rauschenbusch termed a 'new literature of exploration', which was visible not only in aesthetic discourse but also in reform efforts to shine light on the moral darkness of the city through vice commissions, police investigations, tenement house commissions and moral crusades against prostitution.[3] In a manner typical of the genre, the *Tribune* began its exploration by claiming: 'Here is what was seen', and describing, first, the series of 'suggestive' pictures shown on the screen. In *Bad Son*, as the *Tribune* journalist describes it, the eponymous son goes to a gambling den, loses money and then enlists in the French navy. He then joins in a mutiny in which an officer is killed, enters a Turkish harem and at last returns home. In *Burglars at the Ball*, burglars steal silver and jewellery from a house where a masked ball is in progress, but are finally caught and clubbed by the police. The *Tribune* noted, however, that boys in the audience felt that 'the burglars could have made their "getaway" if they had been a little smoother'. Another film showed a 'mob' of French waiters on strike, waving such banners as 'Down with the Bosses' and 'The Striker Forever', and fighting with the police.[4]

As the aside about boys watching *Burglars at the Ball* suggests, an account of the audience watching these films was even more important to this narrative of exploration than a description of the films themselves. 'The crowd', the *Tribune* assured its largely white, middle-class readers, 'was watched closely'. They were mainly 'the children of the poor. They were of the families of foreign laborers and formed the early stage of that dangerous second generation which is finding such a place in the criminals of the city'.[5] The disorderly, 'panicky' and potentially criminal 'crowd' in those fetid, dark, smelly nickel theatres emerged at this moment as a critical site for investigation, not only for papers like the *Tribune* but also for a series of reform organisations attempting to gather knowledge about the audience. This knowledge focused almost exclusively on children of an urban immigrant population, and was clearly predicated on the development of the nickel theatres which had opened moving pictures to a working-class and immigrant audience who had not previously frequented theatrical-style entertainments. This chapter will examine the production of knowledge about this audience in Chicago at this precise moment, and will pose the questions: how was this audience made visible?[6] Why did it need to be watched so closely? And how did these discourses about child audiences function?[7]

To pre-figure my argument, I wish briefly to outline the two strands of my account. First, I want to suggest that the regulatory intervention into the new nickel theatres was part of a wider regulatory regime which focused on concerns about immigration, governance and citizenship, enforced in differing ways, by such regulatory agents as settlement workers, citizen groups, probation officers and juvenile courts. These concerns about governance and citizenship were particularly acute in relation to children, who were positioned as citizens-in-formation, as *tabula rasa* for the imprinting of values, behaviours and ideals of what the *Chicago Tribune* called 'good citizenship', and thus frequently cast in a synechdochal relationship to an audience and population that threatened disorder in terms mainly of class and ethnicity.[8] As critical legal theorist Alan Hunt suggests, regulatory interventions are frequently responses to the 'discovery' of some social problem, and this concern about the child audience was part of a complex articulation of discourses on race, ethnicity, urban unrest and youth that gelled into the figure of the 'delinquent' in the late nineteenth and early twentieth century.[9] The audience of the new nickel theatres emerged as a problem of knowledge as part of debates about youthful delinquency that were themselves informed by wider concerns to do with the emergence and proliferation of an ungovernable urban lower-class and immigrant population. The production of knowledge about these potentially wayward audiences can be linked, then, to the more general procedures and apparatuses of government through which, in Michel Foucault's conception, the attributes of modern citizenries have been formed.[10]

The further point I want to develop from this perception of the relationship between debates about audiences and debates about population and governance concerns the shaping of the discourse of cinema. Debates about the social functioning of moving pictures – what moving pictures are for, how they should function in society – had at this time a material effect on the formation of cinema as a social construct. As Alan Hunt observes, the collection of knowledge 'plays a central role in the formulation of regulatory policies and strategies'.[11] The concerns about audiences made cinema liable to intervention; discourses make possible institutions which, in turn, sustain those discourses. In this sense, the emergence of a police censorship board in Chicago in late 1907 figures as the endpoint of my account here. The police censorship board prohibited 'immoral or obscene' films and required the police department to issue a permit before any picture was shown. As a prototype for the establishment of state censorship boards in the 1910s, it was a critical aspect of the structure of governance set in place for the emerging cinema.

Schools for Crime

The first nickel theatre opened in Chicago in mid-1905. There were a handful in operation by January 1906, and theatres multiplied quickly thereafter, primarily along the main thoroughfares of immigrant neighbourhoods. In February 1907 it was estimated that there were 158 nickel theatres in the city, visited by 100,000 people a day.[12] By the end of 1906, there were attempts to gather knowledge about this new development in the city. Sherman C. Kingsley, a prominent charity administrator, undertook an investigation of the nickel theatres and penny arcades in the poorer sections of Chicago. His report, published in *Charities and the Commons* in January 1907, pronounced them 'objectionable'.[13] Alongside other Charity Organisation Society workers, Kingsley called for the building of more playgrounds in the city's slum districts to counteract the problematic influence of nickel theatres. Under the proper guidance, Kingsley argued, the child's 'instinct for play' could become a force for 'character building', inculcating the correct 'social virtues' and allowing 'moral growth' to occur.[14] Kingsley's concern to develop supervised playgrounds for the inner-city youth was part of a broader strategy of Progressive reform linked to new ideas about adolescence and play that were closely connected to anxieties about the urban, immigrant working class.[15] Play-reformers believed that the correct management of the juvenile lifecycle and the proper provision of play facilities would socialise children into the roles, behaviours and values expected of workers and citizens. From Kingsley's objections, it appears that moving pictures were perceived as a factor which might well interfere with this process.

Another report on Chicago's nickel theatres, carried out by the Chicago City Club, was also undertaken in late 1906 and published in April 1907. The City Club was a civic reform organisation aiming to bring together those upper- and middle-class white men 'who sincerely desire to meet the full measure of their responsibility as citizens ... who are united in the sincerity of their desire to promote public welfare'.[16] The report suggested that the theatres were 'distinctly harmful to the children of the city', because of the immoral environment and the immoral content of many moving pictures, and also because moving pictures had a hypnotic effect on children and could thus induce criminal acts.

The City Club asked the Chicago Juvenile Courts and probation officers about the effect of moving pictures on the criminality of children. They reported that 'daring hold-ups, shop lifting and murders depicted by moving picture machines were getting the children of the city into trouble'.[17] The report on nickel theatres thus participated in a discourse on delinquency that had a fairly recent provenance and was predicated on concerns about the wayward children of the urban lower classes.[18] The creation of special judicial and correctional institutions for the labelling, processing and management of 'troublesome' youth brought attention to – and in doing so, invented – new categories of youthful misbehaviour around the turn of the century.[19]

The first juvenile court in the United States was founded in Chicago in 1899, in part as an expression of anxieties about the development of a criminal underclass. The superintendent of the Illinois Reform School reasoned that, since it was the aim of the criminal class 'to undermine the confidence of the community and to weaken the strength of the Commonwealth', crime could be reduced by 'stopping production' of criminals and regulating the upbringing of children who had criminal propensities.[20] Such propensities were frequently found, commentators suggested, among lower-class immigrant groups. '[I]t is not at all unlikely', one penologist wrote, 'that juvenile delinquency of the most serious kind in the United States is in some measure to be set down to the boundless hospitality of her shores'.[21] Reformers hoped to convert the mainly recent immigrant juvenile delinquents into law-abiding citizens through the development of a reformatory system.

The City Club's reliance on the juvenile courts and probation officers for information and Kingsley's concern to enact play reform indicate that their reports were closely connected to the developing discourse on delinquency. Nickel theatres emerged as problems of knowledge in relation to debates about youthful delinquency that were quite closely linked to concerns about an ungovernable urban immigrant population. This concern became more explicit when the Juvenile Court Committee themselves undertook investigations of Chicago's nickel theatres in early 1907 and again in 1909. The Juvenile Protective Association also conducted highly critical investigations in 1909 and 1911.[22]

The early reports on nickel theatres and juvenile delinquency posited a model of spectatorship akin to hypnosis. This model was deeply affected by debates over crowd psychology, sociology and the emerging field of social psychology. The pioneering work of Gustave LeBon and Gabriel Tarde in the late nineteenth century attempted to develop a theory of the 'popular mind' in order to control it. In the preface to his *Psychology of the Crowd*, for example, LeBon stated that 'knowledge of the psychology of crowds is today the last resource of the statesman who wishes not to govern them – that is becoming a very difficult matter – but at any rate not to be too much governed by them'.[23] For LeBon and Tarde, individuals were suggestible – capable of being influenced by others – via a process of transference that was heightened in relation to images. Their work greatly influenced Edward A. Ross, whose books *Social Control* (1901) and *Social Psychology* (1908) defined the parameters of the debate in the US.[24] For Ross, suggestibility was 'not a weakness produced by civilization', but was intimately related to factors of age, race, ethnicity and gender, and 'at its maximum in young children'. Ross also maintained that 'hysteria, the mental side of which is exaggerated suggestibility, is much more common in women than in men'.[25] Given the long-standing association between independence and worthy citizenship, suggestible subjects were frequently seen as being beyond the borders of the citizen ideal. Groups identified as being most vulnerable to suggestibility were also likely to go on to imitate what they saw. 'Suggestion and imitation', Ross wrote, 'are merely two aspects of the same thing, the one being the cause, the other effect'.[26] It is this combination of effects that made moving pictures both harmful to these groups and, more importantly, a potential problem for society. LeBon went so far as to suggest that moving pictures should be placed in governmental hands.

The City Club report was published on 13 April 1907, just three days after the *Tribune* had begun its crusade against the nickel theatres. This is unlikely to have been a coincidence. The *Tribune* almost certainly had access to the report prior to publication, and some of its staff may well have been involved in the City Club. The paper's readership was largely white, native born and middle class, and its stance, which developed through the spring of 1907 in a series of editorials, news reports and letters to the editor, mirrored the positions outlined in the City Club report. The nickel theatres, the *Tribune* argued,

> minister to the lowest passions of childhood. They make schools of crime where murders, robberies and holdups are illustrated. The outlaw life they portray in their cheap plays lends to the encouragement of wickedness. They manufacture criminals to the city streets.[27]

These schools of crime, the *Tribune's* argument ran, 'manufactured' not 'good citizens' but criminals. The nickel theatre's potential usurpation of the role of the school as the primary instrument of Americanisation was viewed with considerable unease.[28] The *Tribune's* first contribution to the growing debate about nickel theatres concluded by asserting that the theatres should not be 'tolerated for a day in a community where truth and honor and good citizenship are urged as worthy of the aspirations of childhood'.[29]

Three days later, in an article titled 'Nickel Theaters, Crime Breeders', the paper set in play the stance that would effectively structure its understanding of the effects of moving pictures on young audiences. Moving pictures, the paper argued, affected the audience differently according to gender: young girls could be seduced into sexual immorality, young boys influenced to commit criminal acts.

Two examples from the paper illustrate this. The paper reported that one fourteen-year-old boy 'walked out from these pictures of murder and robbery, which he gazed at for hours, with his eyes popping and his mouth open in wonderment, went home, secured his father's revolver and walked on the street ready to kill'. Accosted by the man he attempted to rob, the boy was taken to juvenile court where 'His mother wept for him and promised to teach him better'. His sentence was suspended 'on the promise that he would never again venture into a 5 cent theater'.[30] In a report the day after the 'Nickel Theaters, Crime Breeders' piece, the paper asserted that 'There were a number of little girls who should have been playing with dolls who were ruined through going to the nickel theatre'. This was illustrated with an example of a girl who had run away from home with a man named Sorenson, the manager of a 'tawdry' nickel theatre on Halstead Street:

> The young girl was 15 years old and from all the evidence in the case was of pure and unsophisticated mind until she began looking at the scenes of love and passion supplied by Sorenson's tawdry place. Day by day she frequented the place. . . . The man saw her pretty cheeks and fresh young face and laid his nets. Finally there came a day when she did not go home and when the police found her she was living in a room in a West Madison street hotel with Sorenson.

The conclusion of the story would perhaps be salutary to other girls and parents: 'She wept when she saw her mother', the paper noted, 'but it was too late. She was sent to the Erring Women's Refuge'.[31]

Although, according to the *Tribune*, moving pictures affected male and female members of the audience differently, it suggested that there was a consistency of effect in matters of class and ethnicity. The *Tribune* staff were concerned that moving pictures and nickel theatres would, in their words, sow 'the seeds of class hatred', a concern that was no doubt exacerbated by the urban unrest that had plagued the city for some years.[32] George Kibbe Turner, writing about Chicago in April 1907, termed this a 'wave of crime'.[33] There had been a series of disturbances in the city, which could perhaps be traced back at least to 1903, when a streetcar strike had led to violence and when there had been a series of highly publicised confrontations between police and a gang of working-class bandits. The city witnessed a series of major strikes between 1904 and 1906.[34] The *Tribune* suggested that audiences at the city's nickel theatres were mostly children 'of the families of foreign labourers ... [who] formed the early stage of that dangerous second generation which is finding such a place in the criminals of the city'. These moviegoers were part of a population that seemed to many middle-class Americans at this time visibly out of control. Moving pictures and nickel theatres were identified as problems of governance, in close connection with the wider fears about 'mobs', 'crowds' and rioting addressed by Tarde, Le Bon and Ross. They became what Steve Redhead terms a 'site of intervention' in the disciplining and policing of working-class culture'.[35] Reform groups articulated a set of 'regulatory strategies' for cinema, transforming the knowledge gained about audiences into the form of procedures, ordinances and statutes.[36] The following two parts of this essay address the debates over this.

Uplift Theatres, Big Lizards from Java and Films with Hustle

On 2 May 1907, less than three weeks after the publication of the Chicago City Club's report on Chicago's nickel theatres, a special meeting of the club was convened to debate its findings and to work out a policy for regulating the nickel theatres. At the meeting, Judge Julian Mack, a juvenile-court judge, argued for the complete exclusion of children under thirteen from these theatres, a stance already adopted by the *Tribune*, based on comments by juvenile-court Judge McKenzie Cleland and on the research of the Juvenile Protective League. Arguing against this, Jane Addams, founder of the Hull House settlement, suggested that moving pictures and nickel theatres could be productive of social virtue and moral growth if more closely supervised by the police and by citizen groups.[37] Addams placed the cinema in a category reserved by others for playgrounds, as a potentially positive force in the reshaping of subjectivity and of the urban environment. The debate in the City Club effectively established two distinct and opposing positions on the nickel theatre business: on the one hand, a coercive approach aimed, if not at the total eradication of nickel theatres, at least at prohibiting children from visiting them; on the other hand, an attempt to shape the institution in such a way as to help mould a population of cultivated, moral and socially responsible city dwellers.

The debate about the City Club report had visible and productive effects in relation to the nickel theatre business: Addams set up a nickel theatre within the confines of Hull House, attempting to reorient the business away from commercialised pleasure towards some form of municipal or reform-generated control. The *Chicago Tribune*, reporting positively on this, noted that moving pictures would now be 'operated in connection with settlement work'.[38] Such work was

84

closely associated with the assimilation of immigrants into American society and culture. The settlement house movement itself emphasised the role of environmental factors in shaping the lives of the immigrant masses, and attempted to create a physical environment that would help mould responsible citizens. Education was seen as central to the assimilation of immigrants and to the creation of a new American 'type'. In her autobiography, *Twenty Years at Hull House,* Addams wrote generally of the aims of Hull House in this respect. 'It seemed to me', she observed, 'that Hull House ought to be able to devise some educational enterprise which should build a bridge between European and American experience in such ways as to give them both more meaning and a sense of relation'.[39] For a short period of time, moving pictures were seen as one element of this strategy of acculturation and education, linked mainly to the education of boys and the shaping of their 'moral codes' in line with those of the 'more fortunate boys' who read the 'chivalric tales' of Homer and Stevenson.[40]

The *Moving Picture World* termed this 'the uplift theater' when it opened on 16 June 1907. It was located on Halstead Street, like Sorenson's tawdry nickel theatre, the two perhaps existing for a few months side by side as diametrically opposed understandings of the social functioning of cinema. The uplift nickel theatre showed mainly 'actualities' and travel pictures, interspersed with lectures. The educational value of moving pictures had been discussed from the moment they were first exhibited, but what emerged here was a strong sense of how this educational role could be moved to centre stage in the cinematic institution as a whole, with the nickel theatre in effect becoming like a school. Many defenders of moving pictures argued that it could become an important educational tool. Thomas Edison, for example, claimed that 'I look for the time, and it's not far distant, when every college and school in the world will boast of its projecting machine and library of educational films'. Travelling exhibitor Lyman Howe asserted that 'The day is not far distant when every schoolroom will have its moving picture machine . . . I have the same forecast from more than 500 teachers who now realize the educational possibilities of the animated camera'.[41] Far from being schools of crime, the argument ran, moving pictures and nickel theatres were in reality valuable adjuncts to the school.

The uplift theatre closed after just three months. Gertrude Britton, the manager of the theatre, blamed the closure on the inability to obtain suitable films: 'Funny pictures of the kind desired by Hull House theater were difficult to find. Those of the "slap stick" and vulgar variety were numerous but not wanted'.[42] This is one example of how industrial strategies influenced a stance on the social functioning of cinema, effectively marginalising a conception of it as linked to education and acculturation. Addams, too, acknowledged this, arguing in 1909 that the aims of Hull House in regard to nickel theatres were better served by assisting the Juvenile Protection Association in their campaign to gain knowledge about nickel theatres and thus to improve them.[43] It is worth noting also that Addams's work had a general and long-term influence on the beginning of large-scale mass communications research.[44] The Payne Fund Studies on moving pictures and youth, which developed out of the research agenda of the department of sociology at the University of Chicago in the late 20s, deliberately harked back to Addams's 1909 book *The Spirit of Youth and the City Streets* in their projected volume titled *Boys,*

Movies and City Streets.[45] A published volume of that series, entitled *Movies, Delinquency and Crime,* paid close attention to the question of the immigrant spectator in an analysis of the connection between cinema and delinquency.

There may have been a more prosaic reason for the demise of the uplift theatre. It was seemingly unable to attract a large enough audience. The *Moving Picture World* had a report in June on the theatre which, significantly, quoted children disaffected with the show:

> 'Bet your life its pretty, all right, and its lasts good and long and dat *Cinderella* show was swell, but its slow to make a go of it on dis street', he said. 'Things has got ter have some hustle. I dont say its right, but people like to see fights 'n' fellows getting hurt, 'n' love makin', 'n' robbers, and all that stuff. This show here ain't even funny, unless those big lizards from Java was funny.'[46]

Audiences, even supposedly malleable children, voted with their feet. The uplift theatre itself was seemingly not immune to the industry's commercial aesthetic and, in any case, it was located next door to Sorenson's tawdry nickel theatre.

Policing the Cinema

On 23 April 1907, in the midst of this intensified surveillance of moving pictures and nickel theatres, Police Commissioner Theodore Bingham announced an investigation of New York City's penny arcades and nickel theatres.[47] By July, Bingham had recommended that the Mayor revoke the licences held by scores of penny arcades, nickel theatres and cheap vaudeville houses because they admitted children unaccompanied by parents, showed obscene pictures or violated building and fire regulations.[48] Linked to a discourse of efficiency, scientific investigation and expertise, police interest in the cinema was also explicitly concerned with questions of morality. Policing in the US was in any case often linked to moral issues. Raymond Fosdick, an authority on European and American policing, suggested in 1920 that 'Nowhere in the world is there so great an anxiety to place the moral regulation of social affairs in the hands of the police [as in the United States]'.[49] The concern to regulate morality was part of the profound influence of what Robert Fogelson calls 'the catchall tradition of American policing', linked to a broader regulation of the urban environment through such activities as suppressing vice, curbing juvenile delinquency and looking for missing persons.[50] The transformation of the police during the early twentieth century into a semi-military force was linked to larger changes in the structure of urban governance. Most police work, Sidney Harring has suggested, 'consisted of patrolling the city for deviations from middle-class standards of public order'.[51] Nickel theatres and moving pictures would emerge as significant police issues in relation to morality and urban governance.

In Chicago in November 1907, a momentous city ordinance was passed which made it unlawful to show moving pictures without first securing a permit from the chief of police.[52] All moving pictures were to be submitted to a ten-man police censorship board and would be banned from Chicago if the police found them to be 'immoral or obscene'.[53] This ordinance set in place the legal parameters for municipal and state censorship and, thus, had an enormous impact on the system of state censorship that emerged in the US through the 1910s. It introduced a shift away from the literal policing of the space of nickel theatres, visible in Bingham's investigation in New York City and also in many cases where the police actually stopped the exhibition of certain moving pictures, towards the policing of the films that could be exhibited.[54] This was an important innovation in the development of a governance of cinema.

The constitutionality of the board was challenged by an exhibitor, Jake Block, who had been denied a permit for two films, *The James Boys in Missouri* and *Night Riders,* in late 1908. Block argued that the law deprived him of rights under the Constitution and that the films he had shown in his theatre were 'moral and in no way obscene'.[55] His case was denied and the constitutionality of the police censorship board was upheld in 1909 by the Illinois Supreme Court. It was the purpose of the law, Chief Justice James H. Cartwright argued, 'to secure decency and morality in the moving picture business, and that purpose falls within the police power'.

In upholding the constitutionality of the board, Justice Cartwright explicitly invoked the need to protect youthful audiences. 'On account of the low price of admissions', he noted, nickel theatres

> are frequented and patronized by a large number of children, as well as by those of limited means who do not attend the productions of plays and dramas given in the regular theaters. The audiences include those classes whose age, education and situation in life especially entitle them to protection against the evil influence of obscene and immoral representations.

He concluded that exhibition of the pictures 'would necessarily be attended with evil effects upon youthful spectators'.[56] The concern about the effect of moving pictures and nickel theatres on children, and indeed on those of 'limited means', that emerged so forcefully in early 1907, contributed both to the creation of a police censorship board and to the defence of its constitutionality in the state Supreme Court.

In 1909, reformers in Chicago lobbied for and won the right to institute an eleven-person censorship board to sit alongside the police censorship board. This dual board gave way in 1914 to a single board made up entirely of reformers. The new board introduced the 'pink permit' system whereby children could be entirely barred from movies that received an 'adults only' rating, one of the first age-rating systems in the country.[57] This brings the narrative I have outlined here full circle: the reform-generated concern about nickel theatres contributed directly to the creation of a police censorship board, which in turn gave way to private forms of governance carried on through reform boards. The withdrawal of direct state action was further facilitated by an internal 'reformation' of cinema signalled by the formation of the National Board of Censorship in 1909. Shifts in signifying practices, particularly the emergence of formations of narrative capable of (in part at least) directing the moral and emotional response of movie-goers, can be linked to the intensified reform concern shown from early 1907. These shifts have been connected by Miriam Hansen to an 'invention of spectatorship' as a standardisation of the diverse and sometimes unpredictable acts of reception that threatened various forms of disorder.[58] This invention, underpinned by the regulatory intervention I have described in this chapter, was critical to the emergence of what we call Hollywood.

Notes

Thanks to Peter Kramer, Murray Smith, Vanessa Martin, Howard Booth and Thomas Austin for help with the writing of this chapter. Thanks are due in particular to Peter for his characteristically insightful reading of an earlier draft.

1 The *Chicago Tribune*, 3 May 1907, p. 2.
2 The *Chicago Tribune*, 15 April 1907, p. 1.
3 Walter Rauschenbusch, *Christianity and the Social Crisis*, 1907, quoted in Paul Boyer, *Urban Masses and Moral Order in America, 1820–1920* (Cambridge, MA: Harvard University Press, 1978), p. 127. For more on this linkage of social and aesthetic discourse on the 'underworld' of the city, see my 'Mapping the City: Early Moving Pictures of the "Underworld" of New York City', *OverHere: A European Journal of American Culture*, vol. 17, no. 1 (Summer 1997).
4 The *Chicago Tribune*, 15 April 1907, p. 1.
5 *Ibid.*
6 It is important to note that Chicago served as a port of entry for immigrants and had a broader mixture of classes than other American cities. Some of the concern about lower-class and immigrant audiences was specific to Chicago and New York City. It cannot be taken as representative of wider patterns. It is, however, true that the system of regulation of moving pictures and nickel theatres set in place in both Chicago and New York City came to have wider applicability and greater ramifications for the film industry in the US.
7 Let me make clear at the outset that I will not be discussing audiences themselves, or how they responded to either films or these projects to gather knowledge about them and to speculate on the effects of moving pictures on them. That is a separate project. My concern here is to trace out the emergence and proliferation of discourses about audiences, a concern that is consistent with Michel Foucault's general work on the relations between knowledge and power within specific discursive formations. Power and knowledge are, for Foucault, frequently intertwined: 'power produces knowledge ... power and knowledge directly imply one another ... there is no power relation without the correlative constitution of a field of knowledge, nor any knowledge that does not presuppose and constitute at the same time power relations'. Michel Foucault, *The History of Sexuality, Volume 1: An Introduction*, trans. Robert Hurley, 1978 (London: Penguin Books, 1990), pp. 92–7. Within cinema studies, I am also drawing on the work of William Uricchio and Roberta E. Pearson. See their 'Constructing the Audience: Competing Discourses of Morality and Rationalization During the Nickelodeon Period', *Iris*, no. 17 (Autumn 1994), and also their chapter (Chapter 4) in this volume.
8 The *Chicago Tribune*, 10 April 1907, p. 10. Roberta E. Pearson and William Uricchio also suggest that the child audience bore a synechdochal relationship to the larger cinema audience and urban population in Chapter 4 in this book.
9 Alan Hunt, *Explorations in Law and Society: Toward a Constitutive Theory of Law* (London: Routledge, 1993). See, in particular, 'Law as a Constitutive Mode of Regulation', pp. 301–33. On the emergence of the category of the delinquent, and its links to wider debates about immigration and urban unrest in this period, see Anthony M. Platt, *The Child Savers: The Invention of Delinquency* (Chicago: The University of Chicago Press, 1969); Steven L. Schlossman, *Love and the American Delinquent: The Theory and Practice of 'Progressive' Juvenile Justice, 1825–1920* (Chicago: The University of Chicago Press, 1977); and Mary E. Odem, *Delinquent Daughters: Protecting and Policing Adolescent Female Sexuality in the United States, 1885–1920* (Chapel Hill, NC: The University of North Carolina Press, 1995).

10 Graham Burchell, Colin Gordon and Peter Miller (eds), *The Foucault Effect: Studies in Governmentality* (London: Harvester Wheatsheaf, 1991).

11 Hunt, *Explorations in Law and Society*, p. 317.

12 For details, see Kathleen D. McCarthy, 'Nickel Vice and Virtue: Movie Censorship in Chicago, 1907–1915', *Journal of Popular Film*, 5, no. 1 (1976), p. 39; the *Moving Picture World*, 29 June 1907, p. 263; and Charles Musser, *The Emergence of Cinema: The American Screen to 1907* (Berkeley, LA: University of California Press, 1990), pp. 422–4, 428.

13 Sherman C. Kingsley, 'The Penny Arcade and the Cheap Theater', *Charities and the Commons*, XVIII (January 1907), quoted in Kenneth L. Kusmer, 'The Functions of Organized Charity in the Progressive Era: Chicago as a Case Study', *The Journal of American History*, vol. LX, no. 3 (December 1973), p. 663.

14 Kingsley, in Kusmer, 'The Functions of Organized Charity', p. 663.

15 Roy Rosenzweig, *Eight Hours For What We Will: Workers and Leisure in an Industrial City, 1870–1920* (Cambridge: Cambridge University Press, 1983), pp. 143–4. See also the discussion in Boyer, *Urban Masses and Moral Order*, pp. 240–5. The first annual convention of the Playground Association of America took place in Chicago in 1907.

16 City Club of Chicago Statement of Purpose, quoted in Maureen A. Flanagan, 'Gender and Urban Political Reform: The City Club and the Woman's City Club of Chicago in the Progressive Era', *American Historical Review*, 95, no. 4 (October 1990), p. 1032. Flanagan also provides details of the membership of the City Club.

17 The *Moving Picture World*, 29 June 1907, p. 263.

18 Anthony M. Platt, *The Child Savers*; Ian Hacking, 'The Making and Molding of Child Abuse', *Critical Inquiry*, 17 (Winter 1991), pp. 265–6.

19 See Platt, *The Child Savers*, and, on juvenile courts more generally, see Schlossman, *Love and the American Delinquent*, pp. 55–78.

20 J. D. Scouller, quoted in Platt, *The Child Savers*, p. 32.

21 William Douglas Morrison, quoted in Platt, *The Child Savers*, p. 37.

22 For brief details on these reports see McCarthy, 'Nickel Vice and Virtue', p. 53; Alan Havig, 'The Commercial Amusement Audience in Early 20th-Century American Cities', *Journal of American Culture* (Spring 1982), pp. 2–4; and David Nasaw, 'Children and Commercial Culture: Moving Pictures in the Early Twentieth Century', in Elliot West and Paula Petrik, *Small Worlds: Children and Adolescents in America, 1850–1950* (Kansas: University Press of Kansas, 1992), pp. 19–22.

23 Gustave LeBon, *The Crowd*, 1895 (New York: Viking, 1960), p. xxi. For a discussion of this work, see Robert Nye, *The Origins of Crowd Psychology: Gustave LeBon and the Crisis of Mass Democracy in the Third Republic* (London: Sage Publications, 1975).

24 Edward Ross, *Social Psychology: An Outline and Source Book* (New York: Macmillan, 1908); Edward Ross, *Social Control: A Survey of the Foundation of Order*, 1901 (Cleveland: Case Western Reserve University Press, 1969). For an insightful discussion of this work, see Dorothy Ross, *The Origins of American Social Science* (Cambridge: Cambridge University Press, 1991).

25 Ross, *Social Psychology*, pp. 13–16. On how a notion of 'civilisation' was entwined with a discourse of race, see Gail Bederman, *Manliness and Civilization: A Cultural History of Gender and Race in the United States, 1880–1917* (Chicago: The University of Chicago Press, 1995).

26 Ross, *Social Psychology*, p. 13.

27 The *Chicago Tribune*, 10 April 1907, p. 10.

28 For more on discourses about moving pictures and schools see William Uricchio and Roberta E. Pearson, *Reframing Culture: The Case of the Vitagraph Quality Films* (Princeton, NJ.: Princeton University Press, 1993). The *Chicago Tribune* commented favourably in summer 1907 on vacation schools using 'dramatic recitals' to 'offset the allurements of the 5 cent theaters'. The *Chicago Tribune*, 13 June 1907, p. 3.

29 The *Chicago Tribune*, 10 April 1907, p. 10.

30 The *Chicago Tribune*, 13 April 1907, p. 3. The boy, the *Tribune* sorrowfully noted, was 'not a product of poverty row, but came of a good family, and had gone wrong through

looking too long on the scenes of evil depicted in the Halstead Street theaters'. Halstead Street was a street densely populated by different immigrant groups. Jane Addams chose a house on Halstead Street as the site for the settlement house Hull House because it was one 'of those large foreign colonies which so easily isolate themselves in American cities'. Jane Addams, *Twenty Years at Hull House* (New York: Signet, 1960), p. 76. Nickel theatres in the hands of 'foreigners', as numerous commentators attested, could even manufacture criminals from 'good' families.

31 The *Chicago Tribune*, 14 April 1907, Section I, p. 5.

32 The *Chicago Tribune*, 15 April 1907, p. 4.

33 George Kibbe Turner, 'The City of Chicago: A Study of the Great Immoralities', *McClure's* (April 1907), in Arthur and Lila Weinberg (eds), *The Muckrakers* (New York: Capricorn Books, 1964), p. 389.

34 See Sidney L. Harring, *Policing a Class Society: The Experience of American Cities, 1865–1915* (New Brunswick, NJ.: Rutgers University Press, 1983), pp. 228–33. See also Turner, 'The City of Chicago', pp. 404–5.

35 Steve Redhead, *Unpopular Cultures: The Birth of Law and Popular Culture* (Manchester: Manchester University Press, 1995), p. 43.

36 Alan Hunt writes: 'Not only is knowledge "produced" but it must also be transformed into a form that is capable of being expressed as a regulatory policy or strategy, which in turn is capable of being incorporated into legislative form'. Hunt, *Explorations in Law and Society*, p. 319.

37 See the account in the *Moving Picture World*, 11 May 1907, p. 147.

38 The *Chicago Tribune*, 16 June 1907, p. 3.

39 Jane Addams, *Twenty Years at Hull House*, p. 172.

40 Jane Addams, *The Spirit of Youth and the City Streets* (New York: Macmillan, 1909), pp. 80–1.

41 Thomas Edison, quoted in *The Nickelodeon*, 1 August 1910, p. 64; Lyman Howe, quoted in Charles Musser and Carol Nelson, *High-Class Moving Pictures: Lyman H. Howe and the Forgotten Era of Traveling Exhibition, 1880–1920* (Princeton: Princeton University Press, 1991), p. 174.

42 Gertrude Britton, quoted in the *Moving Picture World*, 29 June 1907, p. 262.

43 Addams, *Twenty Years at Hull House*, p. 267. Alan Havig suggests that Louise De Koven Bowen, who was head of the Juvenile Protective Association, had done much of the research for Addams's *The Spirit of Youth*. Havig, 'The Commercial Amusement Audience', p. 2.

44 Dorothy Ross has suggested that the empirical stance of the department of sociology at the University of Chicago in the late 20s was indebted to the work of Hull House prior to that. 'The inspiration ... came largely from Hull House and the urban charity movement. Hull House widened the sympathies of its academic visitors and the writings of Jane Addams were regularly consulted.... More specifically, *Hull House Maps and Papers* (1895) began the urban studies and use of maps for which Chicago sociology later became famous.' Ross, *The Origins of American Social Science*, pp. 226–7.

45 Lea Jacobs suggests this in her 'Reformers and Spectators: The Film Education Movement in the Thirties', *Camera Obscura*, no. 22 (January 1990), p. 34. On the Payne Fund Studies on the effect of moving pictures on young audiences see also Garth S. Jowett, Ian C. Jarvie and Kathryn H. Fuller (eds), *Children and the Movies: Media Influence and the Payne Fund Controversy* (Cambridge: Cambridge University Press, 1996).

46 The *Moving Picture World*, 29 June 1907, p. 262.

47 This investigation followed on from a conference between the Department of Health and Fire. The aim, the *Moving Picture World* prophesied, was 'to subject these places to a more rigorous supervision'. The *Moving Picture World*, 4 May 1907, p. 137.

48 The *Moving Picture World*, 20 July 1907, p. 312.

49 Raymond Fosdick, *American Police Systems*, 1920, quoted in Robert M. Fogelson, *Big-City Police* (Cambridge, MA: Harvard University Press, 1977), p. 108.

50 Fogelson, *Big-City Police*, p. 88.

51 Harring, *Policing a Class Society*, p. 29.

52 For details on this ordinance, see 'Police Supervision in Chicago', *The Nickelodeon*, January 1909, p. 11. It was passed on the 4 November and came into effect on the 15 November 1907.

53 The category of the immoral was, as Edward De Grazia and Roger Newman show, 'a legal net big and durable enough to condemn almost any picture'. The suppression of 'immoral' movies would continue for more than fifty years. Edward De Grazia and Roger K. Newman, *Banned Films: Movies, Censors and The First Amendment* (New York: R. R. Bowker Company, 1982), p. 10.

54 For example, exhibition of the controversial *The Unwritten Law: A Thrilling Drama Based on the Thaw–White Case* (Lubin, 1907), was stopped by police in early 1907 in Worcester, Houston and Superior, Wisconsin. See details in Rosenzweig, *Eight Hours for What We Will*, p. 205; The *Moving Picture World*, 20 April 1907, p. 93; and the *Moving Picture World*, 27 April 1907, p. 119.

55 Quoted in De Grazia and Newman, *Banned Films*, p. 177. For further discussion of the implications of this case see my 'The Birth of Fiction, 1907–1915', in Leonardo Quaresino, ed., *The Birth of Film Genres* (forthcoming).

56 Justice James H. Cartwright, quoted in De Grazia and Newman, *Banned Films*, p. 178.

57 De Grazia and Newman, *Banned Films*, p. 9; McCarthy, 'Nickel Vice and Virtue', p. 45.

58 Miriam Hansen, *Babel and Babylon: Spectatorship in American Silent Film* (Cambridge, MA: Harvard University Press, 1991), pp. 15–16.

6   The Revolt of the Audience: Reconsidering Audiences and Reception during the Silent Era
Steven J. Ross

Why should academics care about movie audiences or the ways in which they respond to films? It is clear why producers, distributors and exhibitors care: favourable audience reactions can mean millions of dollars to a company. But why should scholars worry about the nature of reception? The answer is not money, but power: the power of film to shape the ways in which millions of Americans think about class and class conflict. What if working-class audiences got so fed up with the denigrating images of labour activism which they saw on the screen that they went out and made their own movies? And what if their highly class-conscious movies proved so powerful that strikes and political actions seen on the screen inspired similar actions off the screen?

This is not idle speculation. It actually happened during the early decades of the twentieth century as working-class audiences revolted against the anti-labour, anti-left images they saw at the movies. Their revolt assumed several forms: some movie patrons registered their anger by walking out of or boycotting theatres that showed politically offensive films; others struggled to control exhibition by renting or opening their own movie theatres; still others attempted to take audience reception to its ultimate level by producing their own movies. Coming from a variety of backgrounds, a small group of worker film-makers – a term I use to describe individual workers, labour unions, worker-owned companies, or members of radical, worker-oriented organisations like the Socialist party who made movies – revolted against anti-labour movies by producing films that depicted a unified working class using strikes, unions and socialism to transform a nation. Bureau of Investigation chief J. Edgar Hoover considered these class-conscious productions so dangerous that he sent secret agents to spy on worker film-makers. Censors and government agencies also feared the potential impact of this audience revolt and moved to limit the growth of an independent working-class film movement.

Emerging during an era of rampant class conflict, silent films played an important role in shaping, not merely reflecting, the course of these struggles. In the workplace, such labour organisations as the American Federation of Labour, the Industrial Workers of the World and the Western Federation of Miners battled with employers for the loyalties of millions of unorganised wage earners. In the political arena, Socialist party candidates challenged Democrats and Republicans for control of a wide range of local and national offices. In 1912, for example, Socialist presidential candidate Eugene V. Debs received nearly one million votes.

Workers, radicals and their opponents understood that movie-goers were also voters and what people saw on the screen could sway their behaviour at the ballot box. Indeed, films advocating the abolition of child labour, aid for widowed mothers and greater factory safety heightened public consciousness and helped to ease the passage of laws aimed at remedying these problems.[1]

The experiences of working-class audiences, and the groups that opposed them, demand that academics reconsider the ways in which they have looked at audiences and reception. Film scholars usually discuss reception in terms of theatregoers' reactions to a particular film. Recent works in the field reveal how ethnic, class, racial and gender identities shaped audience responses to specific movies. While taking us far beyond the old hypodermic-needle approach to reception, these works still suffer from one critical problem: they see audiences in the relatively narrow role of always responding to films made by others, and responding in rather limited ways.[2]

In order to assess the changing political content and impact of film, we need to expand our ideas about 'audiences' and the arenas in which reception occurs. The power of movies often extended far beyond the four walls of the theatre and affected more than just immediate ticket-holders. When it came to shaping the ideological character of movies about class conflict, groups outside the theatre often exerted far more influence on producers than paying audiences sitting in movie houses. The former, whom I call reactive pressure groups, included a wide array of capitalists, censors, clergy, politicians, police, reformers, civic leaders, government officials, union and radical leaders, and the rank-and-file members of their organisations. These diverse bodies reacted to what they saw as ideologically dangerous cinematic images by pressuring producers and studios to alter the political content of their films. In some cases, as with worker film-makers, reactive groups emerged from the ranks of paying audiences; in other instances, they were people or organisations who feared the enormous power and propaganda potential of film.

We also need to broaden our view of 'reception' to include actions taken by groups outside the movie theatre. Censoring films, pressuring film-makers to make certain kinds of ideological statements, producing films to combat offensive images seen on the screen, or putting into action lessons learned from watching films are all examples of such a broadly conceived notion of reception.

The main focus of this chapter is on exploring the relative power (and powerlessness) of paying audiences and reactive pressure groups to set the political agenda of American film. One of the oldest myths in the film industry is that audiences get the films they want: producers' desires for profit leads them to make films they believe audiences will pay to see. In truth, producer decisions about what films to make were not part of a democratic interaction with audiences. Some people exercised far more power than others. When it came to films dealing with class conflict, reactive pressure groups had a greater impact than paying audiences in influencing producer decisions about what movies to make. Indeed, the power of reactive pressure groups grew more pronounced after 1918–19 (the end of the First World War), while the power of paying audiences was largely limited to choosing from among the kinds of films producers wanted to make.

This is not to say that paying audiences passively accepted whatever they were given by movie industry leaders. Beginning in 1907, worker film-makers made newsreels, short movies and feature films designed to amuse, educate and politicise the great mass of American movie-goers. Although relatively few in number, worker films precipitated bitter battles over the political content and direction of American cinema. Between 1907 and 1930, when the class character of movies – and the nation – was still being formed, working-class audiences and film-makers fought with movie industry personnel and a wide variety of reactive pressure groups – federal agencies, capitalist organisations and local and state censors – to define the kinds of images and political subjects film-goers would be allowed to see. The outcome of these struggles was critical to our own times, for the victors were able to set the ideological visions of class relations that would dominate American cinema for the next seventy years.

My exploration of audiences and reception is divided into two sections. The first focuses on working-class audiences as receivers and producers of mass culture during the pre-war era. The second examines the power of reactive pressure groups to reshape cinematic politics and thwart the growth of the worker film movement during the late 1910s and the 1920s.

The Revolt of the Working Class

There has been considerable debate among cinema scholars, especially in recent years, over the class composition of early audiences. I would suggest that a close reading of labour, radical and industry periodicals reveals that from the rise of the first nickelodeons in 1905 until the rapid spread of luxurious movie palaces in the early 1920s, working-class Americans comprised the bulk of paying audiences. Pre-war periodicals repeatedly spoke of movies as 'entertainment for the masses' and movie houses as 'theaters of the poor workers and their wives and children'. 'Motion pictures', observed Los Angeles socialist Chester Wright, 'find their support in the nickels and dimes of the working class'.[3] Early surveys described the overwhelmingly working-class character of movie audiences: at least 72 per cent of New York audiences in 1910 and 63 per cent of Waltham (Massachusetts) audiences in 1914 came from blue-collar backgrounds. Even as late as 1924, representatives of the Motion Picture Theatre Owners' Association insisted that 80 per cent of their audience were 'poor or only moderately well off'.[4]

Middle-class Americans certainly attended movies during these early years, but their numbers have been greatly exaggerated because many contemporary observers, as well as recent scholars, wrongly classified all white-collar workers as middle class. This is not a premise that all white-collar workers shared. We need to be careful not to impose current assumptions about class identity on to the past. The class status of white-collar workers was hotly contested throughout the first three decades of the new century. Many of these workers were the sons and daughters of blue-collar parents, and they lived in working-class neighbourhoods and married working-class men and women.[5]

While early audiences were predominantly working class, not all workers or neighbourhood theatres were the same. Recent works by Roy Rosenzweig, Kathy Peiss, Lizabeth Cohen, Greg Waller and Kathryn Fuller show how exhibitors often

94

catered to the ethnic, religious, gender, age and racial character of their patrons.[6] Missing from this scholarship, however, is a discussion of the ways in which theatre owners catered to the political desires of their more class-conscious clientele. Exhibitors in Los Angeles, New York and Cleveland, for example, built a large and steady following among unionists and socialists. Long Beach, California exhibitor, R. H. Poole, advertised himself and his theatre as 'a staunch friend and in sympathy with the cause of Labor'. Cleveland theatre owner William Bullock repeatedly boasted about his union background and loyalty to labour's cause, and local unionists, noted one labour paper, 'seem to appreciate it the way they crowd into the American'. The class loyalties of audiences also helped politicise activities within the theatre. Unions at times sent speakers into neighbourhood houses to talk about ongoing strikes and solicit donations from sympathetic patrons.[7] Likewise, exhibitors in large cities like New York and Chicago and in small towns like Yolo, California, and Aurora, Illinois, catered to socialist patrons by showing such radical films as *From Dusk to Dawn* (1913) and *The Jungle* (1914), and allowing Socialist candidates to address audiences prior to election day.[8]

Given the predominantly working-class character of early audiences, it is not surprising that many early films focused on their lives. Movies were far more politically engaged and ideologically varied in the pre-war era than at any subsequent time in the industry's history. Indeed, movies reflected the political diversity and concerns of an era in which Americans voted in large numbers for candidates from the Populist, Socialist, Progressive and Prohibition parties. Movies about class struggles and the problems of working-class life had grown so numerous by 1910 that reviewers began talking about the rise of a new 'Labour–Capital' genre.[9] Labour–capital films were highly polemical productions that examined collective actions and struggles among strikers, unionists, radicals, employers, police and government troops.

In trying to make sense of and solve the class conflicts that beset the nation, labour–capital film-makers advanced one of five basic ideological perspectives: radical, liberal, conservative, populist and anti-authoritarian. Radical films presented scathing critiques of capitalism and proposed socialism or some radical variant as the best solution to the ills of society. Liberal films condemned the exploitation of innocent workers and called for reform measures that would foster greater cooperation between labour and capital. Conservative films depicted worker activism in the worst possible light and rarely explained the causes of strikes or employee discontent. Populist films preached a gut-level hatred of monopolists and showed how they undermined the well-being of ordinary citizens. Anti-authoritarian films mocked the authority of those who gave workers the hardest time: employers, foremen, police and judges. Between 1905 and April 1917, when America entered the First World War, producers turned out at least 274 labour–capital films. Of the 244 films whose politics I could determine, 112 (46 per cent) were liberal, 82 (34 per cent) were conservative, 22 (9 per cent) were anti-authoritarian, 17 (7 per cent) were populist and 11 (4 per cent) were radical.[10]

Audience reception of these films was deeply influenced by their political and ideological loyalties. Class-conscious movie-goers of all ages reacted passionately and sometimes physically to films that praised or disparaged the efforts of labour and radical movements. A six-year-old boy attending a New York showing of *Tim Mahoney, The Scab*, in May 1911, grew so disgusted by its anti-union message that he 'forgot himself and cried out: "Gee, I'd hate to have a scab for a father"'. That same month, union audiences in Brooklyn 'registered an emphatic protest' by walking out of a theatre showing *The Strike at the Mines* (1911), an 'exhibition of fake pictures showing alleged outrages by miners during a strike'.[11] Not surprisingly, pro-socialist films prompted positive reactions among left-oriented audiences. During the 'final stirring scenes' of *The Jungle* (1914), Los Angeles movie-goers 'seemed to rise en masse and the big Auditorium resounded with their cheers'. In the Bronx, a 'thousand men, women, and children crowded the new Rose Theater' in 1912 to see a programme that featured 'moving pictures and slides of the Lawrence [Massachusetts] strike, the last May Day parade, and pictures portraying the class struggle and working class life'.[12] Paying audiences elsewhere responded to images that spoke to their political beliefs by cheering or booing, by engaging in fist fights with patrons of differing political persuasions, by coming back for repeat performances, or by storming out of theatres.

Reception also assumed more highly organised responses. Concerned that the spread of anti-labour images would impede their ongoing campaign to recruit among working-class movie-goers, American Federation of Labour (AFL) and Socialist party leaders called on wage earners in 1910 to boycott theatres that screened films which attempted 'to prejudice the public mind against organizations of labor'. AFL convention delegates urged local unions 'to use all legitimate means ... to discourage the exhibition of such moving pictures that falsely pretend to represent instances in connection with our movement'.[13] Labour and radical leaders, like their counterparts in business and government, believed that what was seen on the screen could affect actions off the screen. 'Motion pictures are something more than an instrumentality for recreation', the AFL's Executive Committee explained in 1916. 'They are an agency for education, for dissemination of current information ... [and] have a determining influence in directing and educating public thought and opinion.'[14] Unionists and socialists feared that conservative filmmakers, if left unopposed, would seize control of the screen and dominate cinematic discourses about the goals and struggles of unions and radicals.

The initial calls for labour and radical organisations to boycott theatres showing anti-labour films met with modest success. Workers could, and did, walk out of especially offensive movies. But the film distribution system, which frequently appeared dominated by the Movie Trust and its allies between 1908 and 1912, made it difficult for audiences to exert much control over what was shown in local houses. A sympathetic Long Island exhibitor explained to his union patrons in 1911 that theatre owners had 'little to say about what attractions shall appear on their curtain'. They simply had to take, usually sight unseen, whatever was sent to them by the central film exchanges. Similar complaints were echoed all across the country. The 'moving picture trust now control fully 30% of the business', lamented one Los Angeles theatre man, 'within the next year it will control most of it'.[15]

Small groups of determined wage earners revolted against Movie Trust control by opening their own movie theatres. In December 1909, Chicago radicals opened a movie house aimed at spreading 'Socialist propaganda ... [to] the thousands of people who attend five and ten cent theaters'.[16] Nineteen months later, radical movie-goers in Los Angeles opened the Socialist Movie theatre and promised to exhibit films that would 'offset the anti-labor films so generously displayed by the trust houses'. As one of the owners explained: 'Our theater is the result of the rebellion of the audiences against what was given them'. Films depicting the 'worker, hat in hand, in front of the forging boss, has at last worked on our nerves; we want a theater that will portray working class life without insulting us'.[17]

Adopting the slogan, 'Labor and Socialist Pictures Every Day', the theatre owners showed a mixture of commercially produced pro-labour features and locally produced news films of strikes, Labour Day parades, socialist political campaigns and women's suffrage rallies. These latter news films, gushed one reporter, were 'an eye-opener and show vividly what possibilities lie within the working class'. The Socialist Theatre also served as an important political space. Local unions, socialists and suffragists frequently spoke to audiences about the most important issues of the day. Speeches by Wage Earner's Suffrage League leaders like Laura Cannon, who stressed the interconnectedness of gender and class, were 'a decided hit with the patrons of the house, judging from the very good receipts at the box office'.[18]

Working-class audiences also engaged in more modest efforts to use movie theatres to promote their particular political agenda. Trade unionists in Kansas, Oklahoma, Pennsylvania and New York countered anti-labour propaganda by renting local theatres and entertaining the public with free screenings of pro-labour films – usually accompanied by several speeches. Likewise, Socialist locals arranged special showings of *The Jungle* and other radical films as a means of reaching people who 'would not have been attracted by any other means within our knowledge'. Workers also exerted control over the screen by promising exhibitors to purchase a certain number of tickets if a particular film was shown; other times, they simply rented films and a projector and screened movies at local parks, auditoriums or labour temples.[19]

The impact of worker forays into exhibition was limited by one key fact: audience power was still confined to choosing from among the kinds of films producers wanted to make – and not many wanted to make militantly pro-union or socialist films. The revolt of the audiences took a major step forward when workers and radicals grew so fed up with the anti-labour images they saw on the screen that they went out and produced their own films. The modest costs of making movies ($400 to $1,000 a reel in many instances) allowed workers, as well as a wide range of other groups, to participate in this fledgling industry. The people who led the worker efforts were not film-makers who were radicals, but radicals and unionists who quickly grasped the extraordinary propaganda value of film. Beginning with a few modest actualities in 1907, worker film-makers produced features and newsreels that challenged the dominant political and economic order by offering viewers alternative ways of understanding and resolving the harsh battles between employers and employees. And they did so in a brilliant manner designed to entertain as well as educate. Presenting their political messages within the popular form of love stories and melodramas, worker features played to mass audiences, not just unionists and radicals, in first-run and neighbourhood theatres throughout the country.

The worker film movement went through two main stages: a fragmented pre-war period in which a small number of individuals and organisations made a few inexpensive theatrical films and news films, and, a more well organised, better funded post-war effort in which incorporated companies and large worker organisations turned out features, non-theatrical films and newsreels on a more regular basis. Although worker film-makers came from a variety of backgrounds (moderate and militant trade unionists, socialists and communists) and espoused a variety of solutions to the problems of the day, they shared one central belief: that movies could help forge a common working-class consciousness by showing often divided wage earners that their common interests were far greater than their differences. Such films as *A Martyr to His Cause* (1911), *From Dusk to Dawn* (1913) and *What Is to Be Done?* (1914) exposed millions of people in all industries and in all parts of the country to the same set of images and messages at roughly the same time. They showed the sweatshop labourer in New York, the coal miner in Pennsylvania, the mill hand in Georgia and the cannery worker in California that exploitation and injustice could be stopped if working people joined together and exercised their collective power – through workplace militancy, trade unionism, socialism and/or political action. Worker films provided wage earners with a means of envisioning a different kind of nation, one in which an empowered working class could guarantee every citizen a right to a decent standard of living, a safe workplace and a government free from corruption.[20]

Worker film-makers hoped that their movies would move the masses. They were not disappointed. Motion pictures and news footage 'depicting the class struggle and conditions of the working class' were greeted with 'many rounds of enthusiastic applause' by audiences throughout the country.[21] *From Dusk to Dawn* played to packed houses for months and proved especially popular, as one New England exhibitor observed, 'with unionists, union sympathisers, and Socialists'. Movie fan and Socialist presidential candidate Eugene V. Debs described how audiences in Terre Haute (Indiana) were 'gripped and held at truest interest' by a 'series of stirring scenes and harrowing exhibitions which can never be forgotten'. The 'great demand growing in the [Mid] West for labour union and Socialist pictures', reported the *Cleveland Citizen*, proved that audiences *wanted* to see radical films about class conflict.[22]

Audience reception also assumed far more powerful forms as images of resistance to capitalist domination on the screen inspired similar actions outside the movie theatre. Illinois tailor P. H. Reesburg told how seeing *The Jungle* 'made Socialists of many ... and sausage haters of others'. Movie projectionist Walter Millsap was so deeply affected by *From Dusk to Dawn* that he left Yolo, California, to join producer Frank Wolfe at the newly-founded socialist colony of Llano del Rio. Watching *The Blacklist* (1916), a militantly pro-union movie 'in which the events of a strike were depicted, one being the burning of the superintendent's house by strikers', prompted Connecticut mill workers to launch a strike at their factory. Leaders of the Boot and Shoe Workers' Union insisted that labour films helped spur their members to fight for higher wages.[23]

Worker films elicited equally passionate responses from individuals and groups outside the working class. While many reformers believed that immigrants and workers 'lacked the intellectual, educational, and cultural resources to resist' the detrimental effects of movies, others feared that workers would understand all too well the radical messages flashed on the screen. The growth of a powerful medium that appealed directly to working-class audiences – many of whom were also voters – frightened a wide range of politicians, capitalists, civic leaders and government officials. 'From the Syndicalist's point of view', Walter Eaton wrote in 1915, 'the movies should be regarded as a blessing, as an aid in the growth of class-consciousness, for they are rapidly segregating the theatrical amusement of the proletariat from the theatrical amusement of the master class, and drawing the line of social cleavage more and more sharply'.[24]

Censors, perhaps the most powerful of all reactive pressure groups, were deeply troubled by the ability of worker films to heighten class consciousness and inspire class action. Studies of censorship have generally stressed how authorities used their powers against films they believed displayed too much sex, crime or violence. But movies dealing with radicalism and class conflict proved even more worrisome and were suppressed in their entirety rather than simply cut in a few selected places. This was especially so in cities where censorship was controlled by the police. Royce Baker, Detroit's censor, made his position explicitly clear in 1913 when he warned producers: 'Never show strikers rioting, destroying property, or committing depredation or violence'.[25]

Representing but a handful of films in comparison to the thousands pouring out of the rapidly expanding movie industry, worker films encountered stiff opposition from censors throughout the country. Los Angeles censors came within one vote of banning *From Dusk to Dawn* (1913) on the grounds that it 'was produced for the purpose of furthering the "socialistic" cause and for the glorification of the teachings of a political party'. Censors in Minot banned the film without offering any explanation. Springfield's Chief of Police banned film posters that 'showed policemen with drawn clubs in the act of arresting striking workmen'. Chicago censors tried to ban the film because they 'did not like the scenes showing the police beating up the strikers'.[26]

The power of reactive pressure groups proved so great that they made it difficult for paying audiences to see the kinds of films they wanted. The National Board of Review of Motion Pictures chairman, W. D. McGuire, told of several instances in which films were 'condemned by state censorship boards because they presented arguments favorable to labor'. Socialist film critic Louis Gardy warned in 1914, that censorship was a dangerous 'weapon of reaction' used to 'uphold all the viciousness of the present system and stifle any movement which may bring a better day'.[27]

Worker film-makers responded to these attacks by embarking on an ambitious campaign to produce more class-conscious movies. Heartened by the box-office success of *From Dusk to Dawn*, Frank Wolfe announced plans in 1914 to build a movie studio at the socialist colony of Llano del Rio and turn out a dozen 'Socialist pictures a year'. Two years later, Upton Sinclair, buoyed by the continuing popularity of *The Jungle*, announced similar plans to start a socialist film company which would produce movies for the masses and make a fairly good profit in the process.[28] These efforts to reach the screen on a more regular basis were suspended in April 1917 when the United States entered the First World War.

For the next several years, international conflicts supplanted domestic class conflicts as the focal point of American life and film – or so it seemed.

Audiences, Reactive Pressure Groups, and the Shaping of Post-war Ideology

Working-class audiences often appeared to enjoy watching worker films that showed wage earners defeating employers, electing Socialists to important offices and becoming the heroes and heroines of their own entertainment. But despite a successful beginning, worker films – as well as commercially made liberal and radical films about the class struggle – gradually disappeared from the screen. Between 1921 (when national fears of Bolsheviks and labour radicalism began to subside) and 1929, producers turned out at least eighty-two labour–capital films – an average of nine a year as compared to the 262 labour–capital films (twenty-eight a year) released between 1908 and April 1917.[29] On the other hand, an analysis of the American Film Institute Catalogue indicates that between 1921 and 1929 'society' films about the glamorous life of the wealthy outnumbered labour–capital films 308 to 67.[30] How do we account for this change? Did the worker film movement fail because post-war audiences grew tired of labour–capital films? Did wage earners now prefer fantasies about class harmony to fantasies about class conflict? If audiences had *really* wanted to see films about class struggles would not producers have responded to their desires?

My answer to these questions is: not necessarily – an answer that seemingly flies in the face of conventional wisdom. For many years, film scholars argued that post-war audiences wanted to forget the hardships of war and focus on prosperity and the fast life. 'The working man as a subject for films disappeared after the war', insisted Lewis Jacobs. 'The way of the rich was becoming the way of the land', explained Benjamin Hampton, 'and people were suddenly interested in etiquette, in social forms, in behaviour, in the standards and clothes and beauty lotions and habits that would help them to be like the people they admired'.[31]

While these assertions are partially true, they overlook the critical fact that paying audiences never had a real opportunity to voice their preferences. When deciding whether or not to make films about class conflict, movie industry leaders were far more influenced by reactive pressure groups than by paying audiences. The power of the latter was largely confined to choosing among the kinds of films producers wanted to make.

The First World War and post-war years marked a critical turning point in the class focus and ideology of American film. The worker film movement failed not because paying audiences lost interest in class-conscious films, but because the opposition of reactive pressure groups proved too powerful. Federal authorities, local and state censors and capitalists placed enormous pressure on movie industry leaders to alter the kinds of films and ideological statements they could make. Consequently, while audiences *may* have wanted studios to produce more labour–capital films, producers were reluctant to make them.

Understanding the power of paying audiences and reactive pressure groups to shape the political direction of post-war film requires that we answer two interconnected questions: why did the movie industry cut back on labour–capital films and why did the worker film movement fail?

The Committee on Public Information (CPI), the government's propaganda agency, was the first wartime reactive pressure group to alter the ideological focus of American film. Worried that negative foreign responses to American social problem films would weaken support for the Allied war effort, CPI chairman George Creel ordered his censors to deny lucrative export licences to films that portrayed 'strikes and lynchings, riots, murder cases, graft prosecution, and all the public washing of the Nation's dirty linen'.[32] Such liberal labour–capital films as *Intolerance* (1916) and *The Eternal Grind* were banned on the grounds that they dealt 'with a phase of American industrial life' that was a 'blot on American institutions' and 'bad testimonials to the value of democracy'.[33]

Creel also moved to alter domestic productions by asking film-makers to make happy movies 'that presented the wholesome life of America, giving fair ideas of our people and our institutions'. These patriotic 'requests' were accompanied by subtle threats to draft movie industry employees (then exempt from military service) and to institute greater federal control over the industry. While industry leaders may have resented government pressures, they acceded to Creel's demands. In July 1918, Famous Players–Lasky president Adolph Zukor pledged that henceforth his company would produce only movies 'of a cheerful nature' that would present 'the ideals and aims of American democracy to the rest of the world'.[34]

The end of foreign war in November 1918, was greeted by the outbreak of class war at home. Hoping to raise living standards eroded by wartime inflation, 4 million workers took part in 3,500 strikes in 1919. In Seattle, a general strike of 60,000 workers paralysed the city for several days. In Boston, the police walked off their jobs demanding higher pay and union recognition. By the end of 1919, 4.1 million wage earners belonged to unions, a 49 per cent increase since 1916. Government and capitalist fears of labour radicalism were further compounded by the spread of Bolshevism throughout Europe and by the ability of two American Communist parties to enlist 160,000 members. Attorney General A. Mitchell Palmer responded to these perceived threats by inaugurating a vicious campaign of illegal arrests and deportations – known as the Red Scare – aimed at suppressing domestic radicalism.[35]

Fears of unbridled class conflict led other federal agencies to pressure producers into making certain kinds of political films. In the months following the Armistice, officials from the Department of Labour, concerned that movies with radical or 'labor themes' could 'do our country incalculable harm', asked all producers planning to make such films to send them copies of their scripts before beginning production. Government endorsements were promised for those who cooperated, whereas censorship was implied for those who did not.[36] In December 1919, movie industry leaders, facing equally subtle threats of censorship if they failed to comply, pledged to join the government's Americanisation campaign and 'use the power of the motion picture screen to spread anti-Red teachings' and 'combat social unrest'.[37]

And comply they did. Between 1918 and the end of 1922, when labour militancy and pressure from reactive pressure groups was most intense, American film companies (excluding worker film-makers) turned out 142 labour–capital films. Of the 126 whose politics could be determined, 68 per cent took a strongly conservative view towards labour–capital conflict, 23 per cent were liberal, 5 per cent were populist, 4 per cent anti-authoritarian, and none were radical. This reflects a dramatic shift from the earlier ideological sympathies of film-makers. Between 1905 and April 1917, 46 per cent of labour–capital films were liberal, 34 per cent were conservative, 9 per cent were anti-authoritarian, 7 per cent were populist, and 4 per cent were radical.[38]

The declining number and shifting political sympathies of labour–capital films were not simply the result of capitulating to federal pressure. Two other factors promoted a change in the kinds of movies producers were willing to make: costly threats from censors and the desire of powerful studios and theatre chains to alter the class composition of movie audiences. Throughout the post-war era, censors remained deeply troubled by the power of film to affect public consciousness. The 'motion picture', New York censors insisted in 1922, 'does more to influence the lives of the people in our country than newspapers, books, or magazines'.[39] As strikes, violence and anti-union open-shop drives swept the nation, censors repeatedly used their powers to suppress films and newsreels which they perceived as advocating or inciting class conflict. Censorship was most pronounced in areas where strikes and organising activities were most intense. Pennsylvania, West Virginia, New York, Ohio, Kansas, Maryland, Washington and South Carolina empowered censors to prohibit all 'inflammatory scenes and titles calculated to stir up ... antagonistic relations between labor and capital' or 'revolutionize our form of government through insidious propaganda'. It was not just radical worker productions that authorities feared. Liberal films like *The Whistle* (Famous Players–Lasky 1921) and newsreel footage of strikes taken by Hearst, Gaumont and Fox were also cut or banned by the censors.[40]

While producers never really knew what paying audiences wanted to see, they did know what censors did not want them to see: liberal or radical labour–capital films. Censorship boards, which operated in 100 cities and nearly a dozen states by 1926, had the ability to cost producers a great deal of money either by banning films or demanding so many cuts that it would be impossible to get them to exhibitors in a timely fashion. The power of censors was greatly heightened in the 1920s by the rise of a new type of movie industry, metaphorically known as Hollywood, that was a stark contrast to the competitive, decentralised movie business of previous decades. The rapid growth of a highly capitalised studio system in the post-war era shifted control of production, distribution and exhibition operations into the hands of a few powerful, vertically integrated companies. Such oligarchical studios as Paramount, Fox, Warner Bros and MGM understood the need to please reactive pressure groups, for they could cost them far more money than paying patrons. Studio ownership of many first-run theatres and block-booking policies meant that any film held up by censors would result in lost revenues for all parts of their business. Under enormous pressure from Wall Street 'advisors' to turn a profit, studios responded to threats from censors and government agencies either by halting production of labour–capital films or making them so conservative that no censor would object. Between 1924, when industry self-censorship grew more intense, and 1929, only thirty-seven labour–capital films were produced by commercial film-makers; of the 35 films whose politics could be determined, 74 per cent were conservative and 16 per cent liberal.[41]

It would be wrong to attribute these changes solely to the power of external pressure groups. Studio decisions to shift from producing labour–capital films that stressed conflict between the classes to cross-class fantasies ('society films' as some critics called them) which focused on love and harmony between the classes, were also affected by industry-wide efforts to increase revenues by building a new cross-class audience. Theatre-owning studios and innovative exhibitors like Abraham Balaban and Sam Katz believed they could retain their loyal working-class patrons and attract prosperous members of the 'old' and 'new' middle classes, as well as the rapidly expanding ranks of white-collar workers (whose class status was not entirely clear), by creating a new entertainment experience which transcended traditional class boundaries. They did this by erecting luxurious movie palaces in suburbs and 'safe' parts of the city, and by offering audiences lavishly produced cross-class fantasies – for example, *Saturday Night* (1922) and *Orchids and Ermine* (1927) – which promoted glamorous but ultimately conservative visions of consumption and class interaction. In these films, if not in life, working class, middle class and upper class were joined by their love of consumption and, sometimes, of each other. Yet beneath the veneer of cross-class fantasy lay a vision of class relations more in tune with the dominant pro-capitalist ideology espoused by censors and Republican politicians than with the ideas expressed in liberal or radical labour–capital films.[42]

One might well argue that producers gave paying audiences what they wanted to see. The New York business offices of Famous Players–Lasky certainly thought so. What 'the public demands today', they told Cecil B. DeMille, 'is modern stuff with plenty of clothes, rich sets, and action'. But others thought they were wrong. 'Seventy-five per cent of the motion pictures shown today are a brazen insult to human intelligence', heart-throb Rudolph Valentino told a reporter in January 1923.[43] Many movie-goers agreed with Valentino. When asked what kinds of films they wanted to see, audiences at New York's Rialto, Rivoli and Criterion Theatres replied in a 4:1 ratio that they preferred 'simple true-to-life stories rather than spectacular and fantastic ones and pictures that instruct and provoke thought rather than pictures whose sole purpose is amusement'. A majority of readers responding to a *Saturday Evening Post* survey in 1928 said that they preferred 'A Simple Story Well Told' to 'Pictures That Have Lavish Settings, Costumes, Fashions'.[44]

Certainly, no one *forced* audiences to watch these films. Patrons wanting to see more class-conscious films could sometimes do so at their neighbourhood theatres. But these theatres held less and less appeal for the millions of movie-goers who quickly grew accustomed to the luxuries offered by the movie palaces that showed cross-class fantasies. And few palaces, given their efforts to attract cross-class audiences, were willing to screen contentious labour–capital films. 'Pictures that are favorable to the working class', the editors of the *Butte Bulletin* explained in 1922, 'have difficulty in getting a place to have them shown, as the picture palaces are owned and controlled by the capitalist class'.[45]

Determined to give viewers a political choice, militant working-class audiences once again revolted against conservative film-makers by organising their own production companies and opening theatres in which to show pro-labour pictures. The most prominent of these companies were launched between July 1918 and 1922 by socialists, militant trade unionists and communists in Hollywood, Seattle, New York and Chicago. 'Other groups have sprung up in the past months in the Middle West', a labour periodical reported in May 1920, 'and New York has three or four groups which propose to enter upon the competitive field to supply pictorial propaganda'.[46]

Like their pre-war predecessors, the leaders of this movement were not film-makers *per se*, but working people who wanted 'to counteract the anti-labor temper of many of the present productions' by offering the public positive portrayals of socialism and unionism. After several years of turning out a modest number of newsreels and news films, worker film companies succeeded in raising enough capital to produce two feature films. *The New Disciple*, released in 1921 by the Seattle-based Federation Film Corporation, used a conventional love story between a factory worker and a factory owner's daughter to tell an unconventional story of how workers and farmers defeated capitalists, company goons and Red Squads by joining together to organise worker cooperatives. *The Contrast* (1921), produced by New York's Labour Film Services, was an equally class-conscious melodrama that showed impoverished West Virginia coal miners overcoming company lockouts and the murder of union leaders to defeat avaricious coal owners and win their strike. These films were followed by a handful of features, such as *Labor's Reward* (1925) produced by the American Federation of Labour, *The Passaic Textile Strike* (1926) produced by the International Workers' Aid (IWA), several feature-length documentaries produced by the IWA, and a number of newsreels.[47]

Unfortunately, the increased monopolisation of distribution and exhibition facilities by studios and theatre chains made it hard for an independent producer to place films in first-run theatres. Worker film companies and working-class audiences responded to this situation by creating an alternative distribution system that relied on labour, radical and ethnic organisations around the country to arrange local screenings. The revolt of the audiences grew more widespread in the early 1920s as unionists and radicals in Seattle, Bremerton (Washington), Kansas City, Newmannstown (Pennsylvania), New Adams (Illinois) and a number of mining communities around the nation opened their own movie houses. In addition to showing a regular array of Mary Pickford, Douglas Fairbanks, Charlie Chaplin and Harold Lloyd movies, these theatres made special efforts to screen labour–capital films 'in which labor's side of the plot was presented in a true light'.[48]

When given the opportunity to see worker productions, paying audiences responded in impressive numbers. *The New Disciple* (1921), the only worker film to play in many first-run houses, attracted one million viewers in its first year and set attendance records in Montreal, Buffalo and Detroit. *Labor's Reward* was seen by 479,500 people in the course of its initial forty-week run. IWA leaders, who screened Russian-made films along with their own productions, reported averaging about 100,000 patrons for each of their seven programmes. Audience demand for labour films in Los Angeles was so great and products so limited that the Barn Theatre arranged a special return screening of *From Dusk to Dawn* (1913) in September 1922.[49]

Given the fact that worker films were aimed at politicising as well as entertaining audiences, the success of these films – and the worker film movement in general – needs to be measured not simply by attendance figures or the numbers of films produced. The power of worker films is best revealed by examining the responses of paying audiences and the fervid efforts of reactive pressure groups – capitalists, federal agencies and censors – to keep these movies off the screen. As in the pre-war era, labour and radical activism on the screen inspired labour and radical activism off the screen. Trade unionists in Streator, Illinois, who were fighting an open-shop battle similar to the one portrayed in *The New Disciple*, 'found hope in the story of a like situation'. Washington state labour leader William Short told how repeated screenings of *Labor's Reward* prompted an upsurge in requests for organisational help, while jubilant AFL officials reported that the film increased 'demand for union made goods'. Union and radical leaders throughout the country offered equally impressive stories about the power of worker films to affect audiences. As one Midwestern unionist explained: 'Men who won't read papers, men who you can't talk to for any length of time will go to see that picture, and when they get through they are better trade unionists, they understand the situation better, they take a more active interest, and they do better work amongst their fellows thereafter'.[50]

If worker films proved so popular with audiences why did they disappear from the silent screen? The answer, in brief, is that worker film-makers encountered powerful opposition from a wide range of reactive pressure groups who feared the impact of their films and fought to get them off the screen. Throughout the late teens and 1920s, government authorities repeatedly used their powers to suppress radicalism – and that meant radical films as well as radical movements. Told by one of his secret agents that worker films were being made 'for the purpose of inciting class feelings', Bureau of Investigation head J. Edgar Hoover assigned agents to monitor the activities of key figures in the worker film movement and to send him reviews of their films. Hoover also called on the Military Intelligence Division of the War Department, the US Post Office, the New York City Police Department, Connecticut's Department of Americanisation and numerous private citizens to aid him in his investigations.[51]

Capitalists were equally determined to stop worker productions. Mine owners and manufacturers pressured local and state boards to censor films and newsreels depicting labour and radical activities. W. D. McGuire, head of the National Board of Review of Motion Pictures, told how the creation of a censorship board in strike-plagued West Virginia was traced 'directly to the capitalistic interests and originated from the fact that several pictures were shown indicating the success of trade unionism as opposed to capitalism'. In Seattle, where working-class militancy was especially pronounced, labour spies kept employers appraised of worker reactions to labour–capital films and the activities of the Federation Film Corporation.[52] The Erie (Pennsylvania) Chamber of Commerce, 'fearful that workers here should take inspiration' from *The Passaic Textile Strike*, persuaded local exhibitors to cancel a scheduled screening.[53]

The most damaging attack on the worker film movement came from local and state censors. The appearance of worker-made films in the 1920s led censorship boards to exercise the kind of class power that federal officials only threatened.

Kansas censors banned *The Contrast*, reported one labour paper, 'because the board felt that the exhibition would inspire class antagonisms that would be damaging to the public interest'.[54] Heeding Justice Department warnings about groups who 'produce films which teach lessons which are destructive of the fundamentals of our government', the New York Motion Picture Commission, and its counterparts across the nation, pledged to stop the exhibition of films which 'seek to undermine and revolutionize our form of government through insidious propaganda'. The board severely cut or banned such movies as *The Contrast, The Jungle* (reissued by the LFS in 1922), *The Passaic Textile Strike* and the IWA's *Breaking Chains* (1927) and *The Miners' Strike* (1928), which offered positive images of domestic strikes or the revolutionary activities of foreign workers.[55] Chicago authorities banned the IWA's *Prisoners for Progress* on the grounds that it might 'tend to incite riots and disorder', while Durham (North Carolina) officials refused to allow *Labor's Reward* to be screened in the municipal auditorium.[56]

Given such intense opposition by censors, combined with the skyrocketing costs of production, it is hardly surprising that few worker film-makers were able to produce a first, let alone a second feature. By the mid-1920s it was clear to studios and worker film-makers alike that censors were unlikely to allow any liberal or radical labour–capital film to pass without severe changes. Threats of censorship made it difficult for worker film companies to finance their productions. Bearing in mind that companies like the Labour Film Services and Federation Film Corporation were financed through stock sales, investors were reluctant to back a movie that might never reach the screen. 'All capitalists whom I have tried to interest in financing the [labour] play', lamented aspiring worker film-maker Carl Clancy, 'refuse to invest in it because they say it so strongly boosts the closed shop, and the cause of organised labor'. The prospect of spending several years raising money and the logistical nightmares involved in battling censors and getting their films into theatres discouraged prospective labour film-makers from pursuing their goals. Likewise, few studio executives were willing to risk their careers by making such controversial films.[57]

Audiences may have wanted more of these films, but industry producers were reluctant to make them and exhibitors were reluctant to show them. The certain opposition of reactive pressure groups proved more powerful than the unpredictable tastes of paying audiences. In the end, the power of paying audiences was confined to choosing whether or not to see the kinds of films producers wanted to make. Since a handful of powerful studios controlled over 90 per cent of the films produced and distributed in the late 1920s, as well as many of the nation's luxury houses, their films were the ones to which audiences grew accustomed. Worker film-makers never got a fair chance to test their films in the marketplace. 'The producer's success is not dependent upon the merit of his production', studio critic William Seabury wrote in 1926, 'but upon his control of theaters'. Studio control of theatres, added a *New York Times*' reporter, deprived the public 'of the power to influence exhibitors in the choice of films'. Unable to finance productions or arrange distribution and exhibition deals, the nation's first worker film movement came to an end. From the 1930s onwards, Hollywood studios and conservative reactive pressure groups continued to set the dominant cinematic visions of class relations in America.[58]

Power and Powerlessness

Movies have never been simply about entertainment. From the start, films served as powerful weapons of political propaganda that helped to mould the consciousness of a nation. To understand why certain political films get made and others do not, why certain ideological perspectives are sanctioned and others avoided, we need to move away from romanticised notions of audience power. The power of paying audiences, as I have argued, was generally limited to choosing from among the kinds of films producers wanted to make. Yet, audiences could and did exercise a modest degree of power in recasting the political content of films and the settings in which they were shown. Throughout the silent era, working-class audiences revolted against the dominant forces of exhibition and production by opening class-conscious movie theatres and making class-conscious films. Their revolt, however, was ultimately quashed by the combined power of movie industry leaders who sought to eliminate all independent competitors, and conservative reactive pressure groups who fought to keep what they deemed as politically dangerous films off the screen.

This is not to suggest that there was a clear conspiracy among one or two powerful bodies. Censors, federal agencies, Wall Street investors and employers' associations all played crucial roles in setting the political agenda of American film not so much by telling studios what films to make, but by collectively proscribing the limits of what they *could not* make.

Only by broadening our notions of spectatorship and reception to include groups and arenas far beyond the movie theatre can we begin to understand the complex factors that have shaped – and continue to shape – the ideological direction of American cinema.

Notes

1 For a discussion of class conflict between 1900 and 1930 and the role movies played in shaping attitudes towards class, see Steven J. Ross, *Working-Class Hollywood: Silent Film and the Shaping of Class in America* (Princeton: Princeton University Press, 1998).
2 For recent works that explore the ways in which ethnicity, race, class and gender effected audiences, see Roy Rosenzweig, *Eight Hours For What We Will: Workers and Leisure in an Industrial City, 1870–1920* (New York: Cambridge University Press, 1983); Kathy Peiss, *Cheap Amusements: Working Women and Leisure in Turn-of-the-Century New York* (Philadelphia: Temple University Press, 1986); Greg Waller, *Main Street Amusements: Movies and Commercial Entertainment in a Southern City, 1896–1930* (Washington, DC and London: Smithsonian Institution Press, 1995); Kathryn H. Fuller, *At the Picture Show: Small-Town Audiences and the Creation of the Modern Movie Fan Culture* (Washington, DC and London: Smithsonian Institution Press, 1996). For excellent overviews of reception and spectatorship, see Janet Staiger, *Interpreting Films: Studies in the Historical Reception of American Cinema* (Princeton: Princeton University Press, 1992); Linda Williams (ed.), *Viewing Positions: Ways of Seeing Film* (New Brunswick: Rutgers University Press, 1995).
3 *Film Index*, 5 September 1908; *New York Call*, 14 January 1912; *California Social Democrat*, 19 September 1911.
4 J. R. Dennison quoted in Chicago *Daily Worker*, 10 September 1925; New York survey figures are taken from Michael M. Davis, *The Exploitation of Pleasure: A Study of*

Commercial Recreation in New York City (New York: Sage, 1911), pp. 21–31; Waltham figures are taken from Alan Havig, 'The Commercial Amusement Audience in Early 20th-Century American Cities', *Journal of American Culture*, 5 (Spring 1982), 8.

5 I date the emergence of movie-going as a regular part of middle-class life later than most film scholars. For a more extensive discussion of middle-class audiences and the problematic class identity of white-collar workers, see Ross, *Working-Class Hollywood*, pp. 14–15, 19–20, 175–94, 286 n. 23.

6 See sources cited in note 2.

7 *Los Angeles Citizen*, 13 April 1917; *Cleveland Citizen*, 23 February 1907.

8 Ross, *Working-class Hollywood*, pp. 27, 288 nn. 46–7.

9 For references to what reviewers referred to as 'Labor', 'Labor–Capital', 'labor movement stories' or 'proletarian playlets', see advertisements and reviews in *Motography*, 12 July 1913; *Film Index*, 12 September 1908; *New York Call*, 12 January 1912. For more elaborate discussions of silent films about working-class life, see Kay Sloan, *The Loud Silents: Origins of the Social Problem Film* (Urbana and Chicago: University of Illinois Press, 1988); Peter Stead, *Film and the Working Class: The Feature Film in British and American Society* (London: Routledge, 1989); Kevin Brownlow, *Behind the Mask of Innocence* (New York: Alfred A. Knopf, 1990); Steven J. Ross, 'Cinema and Class Conflict: Labor, Capital, the State and American Silent Film', in Robert Sklar and Charles Musser (eds), *Resisting Images: Essays on Cinema and History* (Philadelphia: Temple University Press, 1990), pp. 68–107; Steven J. Ross, 'Struggles for the Screen: Workers, Radicals, and the Political Uses of Silent Film', *American Historical Review*, 96 (April 1991), pp. 333–67; Ross, *Working-Class Hollywood*.

10 For a more extensive discussion of these films and the methodology used to compile these figures, see Ross, *Working-class Hollywood*, pp. 56–85, 297–8 n. 3.

11 *New York Call*, 31 May 1911; 15 May 1911.

12 *Los Angeles Record*, 30 June 1914; *New York Call*, 28 August 1912.

13 *Film Index*, 10 September 1910; *Report of the Proceedings of the 30th Annual Convention of the American Federation of Labor for 1910* (Washington, DC, 1910) (hereafter, *AFL Proceedings*), p. 338. For denunciations of conservative films and calls for theatre boycotts by unionists and socialists, see *Chicago Daily Socialist*, 30 August 1910; *New York Call*, 24 August 1910; *Moving Picture News*, 8 October 1910; *Los Angeles Citizen*, 2 September 1910; *Cleveland Citizen*, 10 December 1910.

14 *AFL Proceedings 1916*, p. 116.

15 *New York Call*, 10 July 1911; [Girard, Kansas], *Appeal to Reason*, 7 October 1911. For overviews of the early distribution system, see William Marston Seabury, *The Public and the Motion Picture Industry* (New York: The Macmillan Company, 1926), pp. 8–21; Howard T. Lewis, *The Motion Picture Industry* (New York: D. Vann Nostrand Co., 1933), pp. 3–27.

16 *Chicago Daily Socialist*, 13 December 1909.

17 *California Social Democrat*, 9 September 1911; [Girard, Kanas], *Appeal to Reason*, 7 October 1911.

18 *Los Angeles Citizen*, 8 September 1911; *California Social Democrat*, 16 September 1911; *Los Angeles Citizen*, 22 September 1911.

19 Alvin Huff to Upton Sinclair, 1 November 1915, Thomas Brandon Collection, file J216, Film Studies Centre, Museum of Modern Art, New York (MOMA). For examples of labour and radical-sponsored screenings, see *Film Index*, 27 May 1911; *New York Call*, 28 August 1912, 20 July 1913; Sloan, *Loud Silents*, pp. 61–2.

20 For a more detailed look at the worker film movement and its films, see Ross, *Working-Class Hollywood*.

21 *Chicago American Socialist*, 8 August 1914; *Los Angeles Citizen*, 24 October 1913; see also *Cleveland Citizen*, 31 May 1913.

22 *Los Angeles Citizen*, 19 September 1913; Chicago *Party Builder*, 14 March 1914; *Cleveland Citizen*, 31 May 1913.

23 P. H. Reesburg to Upton Sinclair, 18 January 1915, quoted in Thomas Brandon, 'Populist Film', Chapter 1, p. 30, file C34, MOMA; R. J. Caldwell to National Board of

Censorship, 7 December 1916, Box 105 (Supreme Test), National Board of Review of Motion Pictures Collection, Special Collections Department, New York Public Library (hereafter, NBRMP); *New York Call*, 27 May 1912. For Millsap's experiences, see Walter Millsap, 'Llano del Rio Colony', pp. 20–1, transcript, UCLA Oral History Project, 1969, Special Collections, UCLA The confused Caldwell wrote to the NBRMP complaining about *The Supreme Test*; but the scenes he described came from *The Blacklist*.

24 David Nasaw, *Going Out: The Rise and Fall of Public Amusements* (New York: Basic Books, 1993), p. 174; Walter Prichard Eaton, 'Class-Consciousness and the "Movies"', *Atlantic Monthly*, 115 (January 1915), p. 53.

25 Baker's edict is cited in Brownlow, *Behind the Mask*, p. 160. Censorship of early motion pictures is discussed in Brownlow, *Behind the Mask*; 'An Unamerican Innovation', the *Independent*, 86 (22 May 1916), p. 265; 'The Motion Picture in Its Economic and Social Aspects', special issue of *The Annals*, 78 (November 1926), pp. 46–186; Robert Fischer, 'Film Censorship and Progressive Reform: The National Board of Censorship of Motion Pictures, 1909–1922', *Journal of Popular Film*, 4 (1975), pp. 143–50; Kathleen D. McCarthy, 'Nickel Vice and Virtue: Movie Censorship in Chicago, 1907–1915', *Journal of Popular Film*, 5 (1976), pp. 37–55; Morris L. Ernst and Pare Lorentz, *Censored: The Private Life of the Movie* (New York: Jonathan Cape and Harrison Smith, 1930); Lamar T. Beman (ed.), *Censorship of the Theater and Moving Pictures* (New York: H. W. Wilson Co., 1931); Edward de Grazia and Roger K. Newman, *Banned Films: Movies, Censors, and the First Amendment* (New York and London: R. R. Bowker Co., 1982); Francis G. Couvares (ed.), *Movie Censorship and American Culture* (Washington, DC and London: Smithsonian Institution Press, 1996).

26 Los Angeles *Western Comrade*, December 1913; *New York Call*, 28 September 1913; Chicago *Party Builder*, 7 March 1914; for Minot, see *ibid.*, 12 July 1914; 4 February 1916.

27 William D. McGuire to Thomas Ince, 3 January 1917, Box 4, NBRMP; *New York Call*, 2 July 1914. Repeated calls by labour and radical organisations for an end to censorship fell on deaf ears. See *ibid.*, 12 July 1914; 4 February 1916.

28 Chicago *Party Builder*, 21 March 1914; for Sinclair's plans, see Upton Sinclair to W. H. Weyland, 2 February 1916, file J216, Brandon Coll., MOMA.

29 See note 10 for methodology used in compiling these figures.

30 I compiled these figures by counting the number of 'society drama', 'society melo-dramas', 'society comedies' and 'society comedy-dramas' listed in the AFI Catalogue. Kenneth W. Munden (ed.), *The American Film Institute Catalogue of Motion Pictures Produced in the United States. Feature Films 1921–1930*, 2 vols (New York and London: R. R. Bowker, 1971).

31 Lewis Jacobs, *The Rise of the American Film* (New York: Teachers College Press, 1968), p. 395; Benjamin Hampton, *A History of the Movies* (New York: Covici-Friede Publishers, 1931), p. 221. Lary May also attributes the shift in the class focus of films to changing audience tastes: Lary May, *Screening Out the Past: The Birth of Mass Culture and the Motion Picture Industry* (New York: Oxford University Press, 1980).

32 [George Creel], *Complete Report of the Chairman of the Committee on Public Information 1917, 1918, 1919* (Washington, DC, 1920), p. 7.

33 Quotations taken from 'Films Rejected for Export', Records of the Committee on Public Information, Record Group 63, 30-B3, National Archives, Washington, DC; see also files for *The Eternal Grind* and *Intolerance*.

34 [Creel], *CPI Report*, p. 103; *New York Call*, 9 July 1918; on Creel's subtle threats of cen-sorship, see *New York Evening Call*, 31 December 1917. For a more extended discussion of the CPI, see Ross, *Working-Class Hollywood*, pp. 123–6; Stephen Vaughn, *Holding Fast the Inner Lines: Democracy, Nationalism, and the Committee on Public Information* (Chapel Hill: University of North Carolina Press, 1980).

35 For labour and radical activities during these years, see Foster Rhea Dulles and Melvyn Dubofsky, *Labor in America* (Arlington Heights: Harlan Davidson, 1993); James R. Green, *The World of the Worker: Labor in Twentieth-Century America* (New York: Hill and Wang, 1980). The Red Scare and government repression are discussed in Robert K.

Murray, *Red Scare: A Study in National Hysteria* (Minneapolis: University of Minneapolis Press, 1955).

36 David Niles, Chief, Motion Picture Section, Department of Labour, quoted in *Variety*, 29 November 1918.

37 *Los Angeles Times*, 3 January 1920; *New York Times*, 12 January 1920.

38 There were at least 274 labour–capital films produced between 1905 and April 1917; percentages reflect the 244 films whose politics I could determine.

39 State of New York, *Annual Report of the Motion Picture Commission* (Albany: J. B. Lyon Co., 1922), p. 6.

40 Ernst and Lorentz, *Censored*, p. 42; [NY] *Moving Picture Commission 1922*, p. 10; see also Beman, *Censorship*, p. 213.

41 For recent works that explore the rise of Hollywood and its oligarchic studio system, see Douglas Gomery, *The Hollywood Studio System* (New York: St. Martin's Press, 1986); Thomas Schatz, *The Genius of the System: Hollywood Filmmaking in the Studio Era* (New York: Pantheon, 1988); Richard Koszarski, *An Evening's Entertainment: The Age of the Silent Feature Picture, 1915–1928* (New York: Charles Scribner's Sons, 1990); for an older but very useful study, see Hampton, *History of the Movies*.

42 For the rise of movie palaces, cross-class fantasy films and industry efforts to build new cross-class audiences, see Douglas Gomery, *Shared Pleasures: A History of Movie Presentation in the United States* (Madison: University of Wisconsin Press, 1992); Ben M. Hall, *The Best Remaining Seats: The Golden Age of the Movie Palace* (New York: De Capo, 1988); May, *Screening Out the Past*, pp. 147–66; Ross, *Working-Class Hollywood*, pp. 173–211.

43 Cecil B. DeMille, edited by Donald Haynes, *Autobiography of Cecil B. DeMille* (Englewood Cliffs, NJ: Prentice-Hall, 1959), p. 212; *New York Call*, 26 January 1923.

44 *New York Call*, 25 June 1923; results of the *Saturday Evening Post* survey are reprinted in Howard T. Lewis, *Cases On the Motion Picture Industry* (New York: McGraw-Hill, 1930), pp. 134–6.

45 *Butte Bulletin* quoted in *New York Call*, 27 October 1922.

46 *New York Call*, 28 May 1920.

47 *Chicago New Majority*, 20 June 1920. For a more detailed history of worker films and worker film companies during the post-war era, see Ross, *Working-Class Hollywood*, pp. 143–72.

48 *Seattle Union Record*, 22 January 1921. The creation of these alternative networks and the rise of worker-owned theatres are discussed in *Seattle Union Record*, 4, 28 February 1921; *United Mine Workers' Journal*, 31 (15 March 1920), p. 14; 31 (1 April 1920), p. 17; *Chicago New Majority*, 10 December 1921; *Los Angeles Citizen*, 7 April, 21 July 1922; Ross, *Working-Class Hollywood*, pp. 166–8, 208–11, 219–20.

49 For distribution and attendance, see *Seattle Union Record*, 16 December 1922; Ross, *Working-Class Hollywood*, pp. 167–8.

50 *Chicago New Majority*, 1 March 1924; AFL officials quoted in Jonathan Dembo, *Unions and Politics in Washington State 1885–1930* (New York: Garland Publishing Company, 1983), p. 426; *AFL Proceedings 1926*, pp. 163–4. For reception of worker films by mainstream newspapers and trade and labour periodicals, see Ross, *Working-Class Hollywood*, p. 169.

51 Robert A. Bowen to J. E. Hoover, 7 January 1921, Investigative Case Films, reel 926, 212657, Records of the Bureau of Investigation, National Archives, Washington, DC. The Bureau Records are the best single source of information about the Labour Film Services. Agents apparently rifled the LFS offices and sent copies of correspondence to Hoover. For a more complete set of citations, see Ross, *Working-Class Hollywood*, pp. 326–7 n. 66.

52 W. D. McGuire to R. Murray, 21 April 192, Subjects Correspondence (Stelze), Box 43, NBRMP. For Seattle labour spy reports, see 'Report of Agent 106', 21 November 1919, folder 18, 14 January 1920, folder 20, 30 April 1920, folder 24, Box 1; 'Report of Agent 17', 25 March 1920, folder 4, 6 June 1920, folder 7, Box 2, Broussais C. Beck Papers,

Special Collection, University of Washington; 'Report of Agent # [no.] 172', 20 April 1920, folder 6, Box 1, Roy John Kinnear Papers, UW.

53 Chicago *Daily Worker*, 7 January 1927.

54 *AFL News Service* quoted in *Los Angeles Citizen*, 23 September 1921.

55 [NY] *Moving Picture Commission 1922*, pp. 9, 10. Among the foreign films distributed by the IWA and censored by state officials were *Russia Through the Shadows* (1921), *The Fifth Year* (1924), *Russia and Germany: A Tale of Two Republics* (1924), *Potemkin* (1926) and *The End of St. Petersburg* (1928).

56 Chicago *Daily Worker*, 18 March 1925; for Durham, see *AFL News Service*, 13 March 1926.

57 Carl Clancy to Frank Morrison, 29 July 1919, Records of the American Federation of Labour Convention for 1919, reel 29, American Federation of Labour Records: The Samuel Gompers Era (microfilm collection). The decline of the worker film movement is explored more fully in Ross, *Working-Class Hollywood*, pp. 212–39.

58 William Marston Seabury, *The Public and the Motion Picture Industry* (New York: Macmillan Company, 1926), p. 45; *New York Times*, 10 July 1927. In 1928, the Federal Trade Commission charged the ten distributors who handled 89 per cent of all films in the United States with violating anti-trust laws; a year later, it charged four studios with the same offence for producing 90 per cent of American feature films. *New York Times*, 28 April, 21 June 1928; Hampton, *History of Movies*, pp. 317, 364–8. For a brief look at labour–capital films from 1930 to the present, see Ross, *Working-Class Hollywood*, pp. 240–57.

7 Viewing the Viewers: Representations of the Audience in Early Cinema Advertising
Kathryn Helgesen Fuller

Bert Cook was an itinerant film exhibitor who toured small towns in upstate New York between 1897 and 1911, presenting a programme of films and illustrated songs in lodge halls, church basements, opera houses, country fairs and on amusement-park midways. His Cook and Harris High Class Moving Picture Company was a small troupe that played only the very smallest of venues. Ninety per cent of his shows played in towns of fewer than 4,000 people.[1]

Cook continued to work in the film industry for over fifty years. After finishing as an itinerant exhibitor in 1911, he then operated stationary nickelodeons until 1917, and from 1918 until the late 1940s, worked as a projectionist. His early success as an exhibitor depended in large part on his ability to attract audiences. He needed to pay attention not only to the quality of his films and to the performance that his company mounted, but also to the quality of his promotional materials.

Advertising was a key component of Cook's travelling movie show, as it was the prime means for him to explain the character and content of his programme and thus attract audiences. Playing one-night stands, he had insufficient time to place advance notice in local weekly newspapers. Cook's advance agent would show sample handbills and couriers (four-page handouts that doubled as show programmes) to sponsoring organisations and opera house managers to persuade them to sign contracts. Handbills would then be distributed around town by the sponsors selling tickets. Young boys would pass them out on the street, tack them up on doors and display them in store windows. Because advertising was Cook's chief tool of communication and sales to potential audiences and hall managers, it is interesting to analyse it in some detail in order to see what it might reveal about Cook's show and his relationship to his audiences.

Successful advertising was also important to Cook because competition was fierce. More than half a dozen other itinerant exhibitors travelled the same territory of upstate New York villages and played the same films. The fact that Cook survived in the exhibition business, when so many of his rivals failed, is a sign that he must have been doing something right. Yet his advertising differed from what we might consider to be typical motion picture promotion.

The focus of Bert Cook's advertising images was not his films, as we might anticipate from later movie posters. Instead, the bulk of his illustrations featured images of his audiences. His handbills offered viewers an idealised picture of his prospective audience engaged in the movie-going experience. The two main images on his couriers in 1906 were a photograph of himself and a drawing of an audience watch-

The Twentieth Century Production.

Cook & Harris
HIGH CLASS
Moving Picture Company.

There are Many Imitators, but only One Genuine

ELKS' OPERA HOUSE,
Richfield Springs,
Under the auspices of Richfield Encampment, No. 86, I. O. O. F.

FRIDAY
Afternoon and Evening,
April 28.

School Children's Matinee
AT 4:00 P. M.

Reserved Seats on sale at Hyde's Book Store, commencing Tuesday, April 25th, at 9:00 a. m.

A Cook and Harris poster from 1905.

ing a film. Bert beamed out from the advertisement, young and earnest in his cheap cutaway coat with an artificial daisy in his lapel, proudly presenting the show. The large, amateurishly sketched illustration depicted the interior of a small three-tiered opera house, filled with clean-cut, sober men and women. They were plainly rendered, and plainly dressed – no jewellery or cutaway coats, just workmen's jackets, high-necked dresses and simple faces as befitted a small-town audience. There were no children, old people or obvious ethnic or racial differences depicted among the opera house viewers. It was a very homogenous assembly.

All eyes looked intently at the stage, which was filled with a large screen set in a picture frame draped with curtains. On the screen was the image of an American naval warship, bristling with guns, with flags waving in the breeze, steaming straight out towards the viewers. The audience appeared neither fearful nor excited for, despite appearances, the ship was not literally leaving the screen to drown them in its wash. No projector, projectionist, beams of light, lecture on stage or musical accompaniment were visible. The film appeared to be presented with rear-screen projection, or as if by magic, without further explanation. On the back page of the courier, Cook admonished sceptics to 'Remember – this is not a stereopticon or magic lantern exhibition, but the very latest marvel in the world famous moving pictures'. Cook assumed that his audience was familiar with moving pictures and with the visual shorthand which meant that this picture represented a movie show, and thus viewers would know what to expect without further cues.[2]

Bert Cook took such pride in his advertising that it must have been an affront to him when, in December 1906, his new advance agent, Art Richardson, blamed his difficulty in securing bookings for Cook's show on a combination of his inadequate film attractions and poor advertising illustrations: 'You had better get the San Francisco Fire off your 3-sheets, its getting old and stale. And get a new cut on your Courier. And get a 9-sheet stand. Hadley [a competitor] has got an all new line of paper this season – swell'. Richardson continued: 'It makes me sick to see the little picture-shows getting all kinds of money just because they got swell paper. Get a nice flashy 3-sheet, a 6-sheet, a nice special 3-color half sheet with your picture on [it] and fix up your Courier. And then your business will increase 90 per cent. You wait and see'.[3]

Within a few weeks, Richardson had completely lost patience with Cook's reluctance to change, writing: 'This job is too hard. I have no paper to show the society and the minute they see the San Francisco fire they give me [a] wise look, put their tongue in their cheek and say no I guess not. . . . Now for god sake get this off your Courier and get some paper. That is one big hoodoo you have got on your show'.[4] When Richardson scolded Cook about the 'hoodoo', he meant not only the dated San Francisco Fire film but also the courier image of the audience. Richardson saw the illustration as outmoded, and one which identified Cook as a small-time operator.

I was sufficiently intrigued by Cook's choice of advertising images to search for their origin and to find out how widespread their use was. I was puzzled to discover just how long Cook clung to them when the others had moved on. How typical was he of early film exhibitors? My research led me to explore the representation of audiences in early film advertisements. What were the functions of these images for film exhibitors and spectators? I am limited in answering these questions because the papers of so few itinerant exhibitors have survived, other than those of the prominent Lyman Howe. Itinerants' operations and their interactions with film and poster suppliers are sketchily documented in Sears, Roebuck catalogues and in such showmen's trade papers as *Billboard* and the *New York Clipper*. Cook is intriguing to study for his career as a small-time exhibitor who survived year after year in a challenging business. His case is also special because of the wealth of information we have about his operations.

In this chapter I will argue that audience images were integral to the selling of the movie-going experience to the earliest film viewers, and were used by most of the early film exhibitors (urban and rural showmen, itinerants and those who performed on the regular bill of vaudeville theatres). Advertisements depicting an opera house auditorium full of fascinated spectators were at one and the same time ingenious marketing tools, an attempt at audience education, and clever depictions of what Tom Gunning has described as the 'cinema of attractions'. But while most exhibitors chose these images in the period up to 1900, they quickly dwindled thereafter, coinciding with the decline of film exhibition in vaudeville theatres and of the cinema of attractions. Cook is, to date, the only exhibitor I have been able to identify who continued to feature audience images (in his case, until 1907), but perhaps other small-time or rural showpeople did the same. While film form and the relationship of the audience to the screen image evolved greatly during cinema's first decade, Cook appeared to lay stress, through his advertising, on the continuities in the movie-going experience rather than on dramatic changes. His example suggests new avenues of inquiry concerning the relationships between audiences, exhibitors and the movie show.

Audience Images as Educational Tools

In 1896, the posters and advertisements of the earliest film exhibitors featured depictions of an enthralled audience watching the show. Such imagery had rarely been used in theatrical, circus and vaudeville advertising, where the focus was on the stage performance and poster viewers assumed that they shared the same spectatorial position as the audience. Audience images in entertainment advertising were found, however, in the promotion of mechanical novelties like the stereopticon slide and phonograph shows.

As early as the seventeenth century, T. A. Kircher, the inventor of the magic lantern, had taken great care to educate his audiences about the nature of his apparatus and show. Charles Musser notes that

> Kircher's text indicates that the revelation of the technical base of projection to the audience was a necessary condition of screen entertainment. The instrument of projection had to be made manifest within the mode of production itself, so that projected images did not appear as magic but as 'art'. Images were subsequently described as 'lifelike', not as life itself. This demystification, however, cannot be assumed. Into the 19th century, mediums used projected images, concealed their source, and claimed these images were apparitions.[5]

In the late nineteenth century, posters for Emile Reynaud's Theatre Optique, which featured a projecting praxinoscope using hand-drawn images on gelatine strips, was advertised both with a luminous screen image of Pierrot and with a theatre illustration of inventor, apparatus, projected image and admiring audience, viewed in full detail from a position backstage.[6] Even single-viewer moving image devices, such as the Mutoscope and Kinetoscope, were advertised not with a preview of the film image to be seen but with a picture of an attractive, smiling woman turning the crank and raptly gazing into the machine's aperture.[7]

Advertisements for mechanical novelty entertainments could have focused on the apparatus, the exhibitor, the projected image, or on some combination of the three. There was no imperative to depict the audience, so their repeated inclusion is both interesting and significant. Because these mechanically reproduced noises and shadows were described as 'lifelike', with their movement, their sound and their verisimilitude noted, exhibitors were drawn to associate and connect the entertainment images to live audience members. Exhibitors addressed potential customers directly in these images, in order to assure viewers that they would be part of a socially acceptable throng of people, and to explain what was going to happen during a film exhibition.

Two of the earliest and most famous film advertisements featured audiences rather than solely on-screen images. The Cinematographe Lumière poster from early 1896 depicted the first row of the intimate theatre set up in the basement-level Salon Indien at the Grand Café in Paris. In this image, seven well-dressed middle-class people (a couple, two children, an older man and woman and a gendarme) all laugh uproariously at the antics of the young boy in the film *L'Arroseur arrosé*. The children raise their arms in glee.[8] Another well-known early Lumière poster featured a crowd milling around outside the café, anxiously awaiting a turn to go inside to see the show. 'The image must certainly have piqued public curiosity', two poster historians note, 'by relying on presentation of the who rather than the what of the matter'.[9]

The poster for the New York City exhibition of Edison's Vitascope at Koster and Bial's music hall in April 1896 similarly featured an audience. The interior of the theatre was shown in half-light. The first ten rows of the auditorium were visible as the audience members turned their faces upward to view the film. The audience members were not depicted as elegantly dressed; the women wore small straw hats and street clothes. No projector was in sight, but a beam of light poured towards a screen set in a large gold picture frame. The screen displayed the Gaiety Girls, dancing in short dresses in a garden setting, in lifelike colours which no hand-tinted film could match. A testimonial on the poster to 'Edison's Greatest Marvel' read: 'Wonderful is the Vitascope, Pictures life size and full of color, makes a thrilling show'.[10] The prevalence and significance of this audience imagery was so widely assumed in 1896 that newspaper accounts of the inaugural film exhibition at Koster and Bial's were also illustrated with drawings of the audience in attendance that evening, and not of the film images.[11]

The image on the screen in some early advertisements seemed mystical, being so large and fantastically inserted into a realistic opera house setting. However, other posters showed the projectionist and the beam of light stretching from the projector towards the screen to explain the trick behind the magic and demonstrate how the movie show operated.[12] Whether or not apparatus was depicted to explain how the image was thrown on to the screen, these images all showed audiences held in rapt attention by the film, but they were pictured as neither frightened nor mystified. Popular historical accounts of the earliest film exhibitions have emphasised how spectators would flee in alarm from images of crashing waves which they believed were descending from the screen. Such films as *Black Diamond Express* are described even today by some scholars as featuring a train 'rushing toward the camera and visually assaulting the spectator'.[13] Despite the prevalence of these accounts of audience alarm, few contemporary advertising images portrayed this reaction. Perhaps exhibitors considered it bad advertising. Even if it was only a myth, this notion that spectators might have found films overly realistic, frightening, threatening or attractive was a popular joke among film industry people. Filmmakers satirised naïve audience members who confused film images with reality in films like *Uncle Josh at the Picture Show* (1902) and in cartoons and quips in the exhibitor trade journals. Nevertheless, exhibitors refrained from using anything in their advertising images that belittled their customers.[14]

How much did these poster images, like the 'cinema of attractions', exaggerate or minimise aspects of the movie-going experience, and what aspects reflected a realistic portrayal of what happened in the theatre? Charles Musser notes that 'early cinema's presentational approach was concerned with display, exhibitionism, and the offering of spectacular, realistic or novel effects'.[15] Film subjects were not presented totally realistically, but were isolated, sometimes magnified for display, for the benefit of the spectator. The benefit the advertising image had on future ticket sales was more important to exhibitors than representing the actual movie-going experience. Movie-show advertising images portrayed a panorama of the half-lit opera house, full of upstanding, well-behaved, well-dressed and attentive audience members, who were fully visible to the viewer and to each other. Typically, during an actual entertainment, the auditorium was plunged into complete darkness for the show. Thus, audience members could not see each other across the hall. While posters, such as Bert Cook's, promised viewers a steaming ship, a rolling train or other such images projected on a huge, stage-filling screen, an image which was meant to impress viewers with film's ability to depict size and power in motion, in reality Cook often projected films on a nine-foot-square portable screen. While early film exhibitions were depicted in posters as technologically advanced and perfect in projection, often critics of actual performances reported that film images were marred by poor focus, murkiness, jumpiness, rainy streaks, images that moved too slowly or too quickly, and the bothersome flicker that hurt spectators' eyes. A newspaper account of an early Vitascope exhibition in Wilkes Barre, Pennsylvania, related:

> There is an unsteadiness of movement which is far from natural, though it is understood that Mr. Edison will have this remedied in a comparatively short time. The apparatus in use is somewhat crude, due no doubt to the hurried manner in which it has been prepared. That material which surrounds the machinery should be of sufficient thickness to prevent the light escaping and to a certain extent illuminating the room, for to get good results from the Vitascope there must be absolute darkness in the house.[16]

Despite any disparities between poster versions of the early film-viewing experience and the real thing, the essential truth portrayed by the posters was the centrality of audiences to the movie show. Early movie posters ingeniously captured and reflected the cinema's engagement with and awareness of its viewers. As Tom Gunning notes, 'spectatorial identification with the viewpoint of the camera is a linchpin of early cinema'.[17] Gunning postulates that these audiences went to the show to see the mechanical apparatus and each other as well as to watch films, and that audiences had an undisguised awareness of their active position as viewers, not an anonymous absorption into the film narrative.[18] Thus, early advertisements, which showed the opera house audience as well as the projector and beam of light, made the mechanical aspects of motion picture exhibition visible to the spectators and to prospective customers and explained the lure of the 'cinema of attractions'.[19] Film viewers were a continuously visible and tangible presence in early film through their physical presence in the theatre, as the subject of address of the film, and as participants in the (albeit somewhat idealised) movie-going experience depicted in posters and advertisements.

The Brief Life of the Audience Image

Audience images held educational meanings for both film viewers and film exhibitors, but this phase of explication was short-lived. After the Spanish–American War film shows in 1898, the fascinated audience image appeared much less frequently in exhibitors' advertising, and was replaced by the exhibitors' focus on dramatic images of screen action and spectacle. Audiences became invisible in movie advertising just as direct acknowledgement of the camera and audiences began to disappear from film. It is, therefore, interesting that Bert Cook retained this style of advertising image into the following decade.

Audience images made a brief but spectacular series of appearances in the Sears, Roebuck catalogue, due to Alva Roebuck's interest in photography and popular entertainment. The Sears Fall 1897–8 catalogue featured a 'Department of Special Public Entertainment Outfits and Supplies', which was introduced with a large panoramic illustration of an opera house audience. More than 100 men and women in fashionable street clothes intently gazed at a lecturer. Both a Graphophone and an elaborate image of a pitched naval battle, projected on a huge screen, shared the stage with him. The stereopticon projector and projectionist were fully displayed, as was the beam of light leading to the slide image.[20] Viewers of this illustration saw the audience, the apparatus, the screened image, the presenter and operator simultaneously. Sears promoted the Optigraph moving picture machine with a sketch of an opera house interior. Some of the women were depicted in elegant evening dress. Viewers' attention was also drawn to the projector, rendered in very crisp outline, as it apparently operated itself.[21]

Several pages later, the Sears catalogue brought all its entertainment equipment together into combination deals. The company promoted outfits that featured stereopticons, phonographs and moving picture projectors. The firm offered purchasers free posters promoting one or a package of two or three entertainments. The stereopticon slide show was symbolised by a drawing of a prospector panning for gold in the Klondike. The image had no frame or stage, no audience, no hint of the mechanical apparatus at work. A second illustration featured the Graphophone talking machine (phonograph), set up in a parlour or on a small stage. Three human forms appeared to be emerging from or blown out of the machine's horn: a tuxedoed entertainer, a woman and an Irish comic. The text underneath read, 'It talks – it laughs – it plays – it sings'. As phonographs had been popular for the better part of a decade, if too expensive for home purchase, the advertisement assumed that readers were aware that the machinery produced and reproduced the singers and their voices for listeners' amusement.[22] However, the new moving picture equipment was illustrated with an audience image and not

A poster from the Sears, Roebuck and Co. catalogue, Fall 1897–8.

with a depiction of film content. The advertisements showed an opera house filled with numerous women and men in suits and evening dress, who watched a screen. The film projector was set up prominently at the front of the image. It shot out a beam of light that became the screened image of the film *The Kiss.* No lecturer or projectionist was shown – it looked like the machine itself was presenting the entire entertainment.[23]

Sears catalogues in 1901–2 and 1902–3 contained no movie audience images at all, although they still carried Edison and Optigraph film projectors. Novelty was no longer a selling point, and small itinerant exhibitors could no longer command opulent opera house audiences. The illustration of the Department of Public Entertainment Outfits and Supplies featured a man exhibiting a stereopticon

Sears, Roebuck and Co. catalogue, Fall 1897–8.

image of a train moving through a rural landscape. His audience consisted of about fifty men and women, holding programmes, sitting on wooden kitchen chairs in a club room or parlour. Film exhibition was becoming more corporate and professionalised and the travelling exhibitor, with his close connection to his audience, was becoming ever more marginalised and reduced to amateur status or, as in this image, practically domesticated. Perhaps it was the growing relation of this audience image to the decline in prestige and appeal of itinerant film exhibition that so irked Bert Cook's advance agent Art Richardson.

A different evolution in focus occurred in the advertising of a leading travelling film exhibitor, Lyman Howe. His entertainment troupes toured widely in the East and advertised extensively through posters, couriers and handbills in each town they visited. When Howe first incorporated motion pictures into his programme, he immediately adapted the enthralled opera house audience imagery into his advertising and stationery. This was a logical extension of the previous promotion of his own phonograph and stereopticon slide shows as well as a bow to the Lumière and Edison examples. As the films themselves became more important than the mechanics of projecting and viewing them, his advertising imagery similarly evolved.

A poster from 1893 for 'Howe's Wonderful Phonograph Concert' featured the brightly-lit interior of a well-appointed, two-tier opera house, filled with about 150 elegantly dressed men and women. Lyman Howe himself stood on stage near the foreground of the poster, next to the phonograph. He lectured and held a cylinder, in anticipation of changing the one on the machine. There was, however, no indication of any music emanating from the phonograph. Howe did not gaze at his patrons, but looked directly out at the poster viewers, presenting himself as authoritative, respectable and professional, with the audience's attention solely directed towards him and his machine.[24]

In 1896, Howe created new audience images to advertise his latest entertainment device, a moving picture projector he called the Animotiscope. His business stationery featured an illustration of the interior of a large, two-tiered opera house. A simply drawn and plainly dressed audience paid rapt attention to an anonymous lecturer on stage and to a beam of light which became the large projected image on the picture-framed screen. For his autumn 1897 courier, Howe chose a drawing of a three-tiered opera house in which the audience was enthralled by the dramatic, extremely large on-screen image of a train. No projector, light beam, projectionist or lecturer was seen here, nor was musical accompaniment indicated. The on-screen image seemed particularly powerful and almost magically large in size. 'Life Motion – Realism!' the poster touted, 'Astonishing! Thrilling! Refined!' In September 1898 (as Bert Cook was to later do), Howe added a photograph of himself to the upper-left corner of his programmes and changed the on-screen image to a warship, calling his show Lyman H. Howe's Wargraph exhibition.[25]

Having used these audience images since 1893, in 1898 Howe began to change them. In the autumn season, his theme was 'New Marvels in Motion Pictures'. He still utilised the enthralled audience imagery, but he began to focus ever more intently on the film. His stationery and poster focus zoomed in from the auditorium panorama to the opera house screen. There, variously, were shown naval battle scenes, African wildlife and exotic magicians' trick films. As before, audience members filled the first two rows of seats and the side box nearest the stage, gazing intently at the film. But the rest of the auditorium and audience were cropped out. The image would have made little sense if viewers had not already been familiar with the earlier advertisements, and if they did not understand what portions of the illustration were missing.[26] A few symbolic or residual audience members now represented the entire enthralled audience, and the poster viewers' perspective shifted from the detached, omniscient observer to one seated in the middle of the theatre. This effect further focused poster viewers' attention on the screen. Describing a film's action and plot became more important to attracting paying customers than relating the full story of what transpired in the opera house.

By autumn 1899, and throughout the next decade, Howe used only his own photograph in his stationery, posters and couriers, effectively turning himself into his own brand-name image, even though he no longer met the public by travelling with

A Howe Poster, c. 1898.

his troupes. In 1906, compared to Bert Cook's continued use of the opera house image on his couriers, Howe used a large portrait of himself with a small drawing of a cameraman shooting a scene. By 1912, his advertising featured scenes from his travel films, and they resembled the movie posters which film producers had begun distributing in the preceding two years.[27]

Cook's Use of the Audience Image

One notable exception to the disappearance of audience imagery in early film advertising was Bert Cook's practices between 1897 and 1907. Charles Musser has noted that 'despite many stable elements, the cinema underwent a staggering array of fundamental changes between 1895 and 1907'.[28] Similar changes affected both early film advertising and audiences' movie-going experiences. Historians tend to study evolution and discontinuity – change over time – but it is also valuable to examine continuities. Bert Cook's advertising demonstrated remarkable continuity during this period of tumultuous change in the movie industry from the 'cinema of attractions' to the rise of narrative film, and from itinerant exhibition to the spread of nickelodeon theatres. Certainly, audiences in the small towns Cook visited semi-annually would have felt comfortably familiar with his trademark handbills and his show. Familiarity can breed contempt, however, as advance agent Art Richardson's tirades about Cook's tired advertising in late 1906 demonstrate. The aspects of continuity and stability that a film exhibitor–businessman might work hard to achieve could also be construed by critics as a showman's backwardness, laziness and outmoded ideas. If the 'cinema of attractions' was truly attractive to audiences, why should exhibitors have been so eager to abandon it? Perhaps Cook enjoyed providing familiar visual thrills the way some amusement seekers ride a favourite roller coaster ten times in a row without diminishing their pleasure.

Bert Cook was a pioneer of early motion picture exhibition who began his entertainment career in the mid-1890s, as a young tintype photographer's assistant, giving phonograph concerts and singing illustrated songs (popular tunes accompanied by stereopticon slides portraying the songs' narrative). In 1897, he joined his friends John Sherwood and William Pearce in forming the Sherwood Concert Company to exhibit projected motion pictures. The group's stationery featured the popular opera house audience image. In 1899, Cook, now business manager of the Pearce Moving Picture Company, adopted as his courier illustration an almost amateurishly rendered image of an opera house audience. The stiffly drawn but enthralled viewers watched a huge, stirring, patriotic film scene depicting Admiral George Dewey's warship, the *Olympia*, steaming into Manila Bay. Cook had obtained it from the stock woodcuts of the Onondaga Engraving Company of Syracuse. The on-screen image of the warship also featured a large bust of Admiral Dewey floating above, facing away from the ship. The two images were disconnected by relative size, but linked like a pictogram: Dewey + ship = patriotism. The on-screen image was not simply a naturalistic portrayal of a ship, nor a lifelike portrayal of the admiral, but a surreal, symbolic combination of the two.

The boost that the Spanish–American War gave in 1898 to film exhibitors was welcome relief after the lull in interest which followed the decline of film's novelty in 1897. War spirit lasted from the explosion of the USS Maine in February 1898 through the brief war. Admiral Dewey scored a great victory over the Spanish naval fleet at Manila in May 1898 and found subsequent success as commander of the navy in the Philippine guerrilla war (1898–1902) and in the troubles with China and Venezuela (1900–8). He remained an important cultural symbol of patriotism and military might to an American public excited about its growing empire and international muscle. Especially in New York State, Admiral Dewey was lauded and long remembered by hero-worshipping citizens, who held a parade and erected a triumphal arch in his honour in New York City in September 1899. The celebrations, captured on film, were the most popular films in Lyman Howe's programmes in October 1899.[29] Cook showed those films in December 1899 and still featured Dewey on his courier cover as late as November 1900.

It seems unlikely that Cook and his partners randomly chose the illustrations for their couriers. Cook probably selected his cover image with consideration of what might have long-lasting appeal. Printing costs were often the largest expense (along with train tickets) for a travelling show, and had to be paid for up-front, so the advertisements had to be good, and also had to last as long as possible. Cook and his partners had chosen the Dewey and warship image when it was prevalent and relatively fresh. The steaming warship image not only associated them in the minds of village audiences with the practices of such larger competitors as Lyman Howe, but it still effectively merged patriotism with the shock and thrill of the 'cinema of attractions'. Even after Cook excised the admiral's head from the advertisement, his trademark warship image might not have seemed entirely outmoded to all his audience members in late 1906. Cinema's evolution from brief scenes of display to one-reel story-telling films in this period was striking, but Cook represented his show as remaining essentially the same over time, despite the fact that his courier resolutely announced each year: 'Everything New!'[30]

Cook was apparently aware of his competitors' advertising. He especially modelled his early couriers on those of Lyman Howe, whom he optimistically considered his closest rival (even if Cook's ambitions and receipts were far more modest, and five or six other small-scale competitors also worked the region). Like Howe, Cook aimed to attract a respectable middle-class audience. Even if Cook did not produce his own films, as Howe did, he could nevertheless represent his show as holding to the same standards of propriety and excellence. On occasions, when his wife and partner, Fannie Cook, was home in Cooperstown when Howe's troupe came through, such as in September 1905, she would be sure to update Cook on their rival's newest advertising:

> Howe's moving pictures are in Fireman's Hall Wednesday night and they will no doubt have a good house, as there were several women around all of last week selling tickets. I will enclose for you one of the [hand]bills they threw around today.

Howe's advertising may have changed significantly by 1900, and continued evolving through the decade as he focused on genteel lectures and travel scenes but, curiously, Cook's advertising remained exactly the same even as he focused on popular entertainment films, which were undergoing many changes.[31]

By 1901, the 'cinema of attractions' had begun to evolve to include narratives of continuity. The one-shot narratives ended by 1903, the simplest chases by 1904. At the time Cook began to travel with his own Cook and Harris High-Class Moving Picture Company in late 1903, dream films and chase films were at their height of popularity. By the time Art Richardson criticised Cook's advertising in late 1906, attractions were being superseded by what Gunning calls 'narratives of discontinuity', with parallel editing and last-minute rescues. These visually complex films were a far cry from one-shot scenes of Dewey's ship. Cook did not see these genres as quite so distinctly separate, however, because he advertised them all in the same way. Cook's advertising practices lend credence to Gunning's argument that some elements of the 'cinema of attractions' lingered until 1910.[32] In an extreme example of representing his show as being the same over time, Cook recycled newspaper reviews of the show from the 1899–1900 season, reprinting them verbatim in 1905 programmes with merely the dates, towns and film titles changed. A review of a Pearce Company performance from the *Williamsport Gazette* dated 28 September 1900, reported:

> A noticeable feature of the entertainment, and one that is especially creditable to the manager, is that the audience does not only see the moving picture, but hears some natural noise accompanying it. For instance, when a train approaches a station, he sees if far in the distance, and as it comes into view he hears the rumble, which gradually becomes louder as the train nears its destination, and diminishes by degrees as it slows up and comes to a standstill. The same detail was noticed while the war pictures were on for when a gun was discharged the audience saw the puff of smoke and simultaneously heard the report. Some of last night's pictures were quite thrilling, especially the naval battles, which were reproduced with remarkable faithfulness to the real thing, and they in consequence were warmly received.

A review of a Cook and Harris programme, purportedly published in the *Albany Journal* on 27 October 1904 and reprinted in Cook's 1905 courier, commented:

> A noticeable feature of the entertainment, and one that is especially creditable to the manager, is that the audience does not only see the moving picture, but hears some natural noise accompanying it. For instance, when a train approaches a station, he sees it far in the distance, and as it comes into view he hears the rumble, which gets louder and louder as the train nears its destination, and diminishes by degrees as it slows up and comes to a standstill. The same detail was noticed while the 'Indians and Cowboys' pictures were on, for when a gun was discharged the audience saw the puff of smoke and simultaneously heard the report.[33]

Were small-town audiences still so impressionable in 1904/5, that the combination of film and sound would be the major attraction of the show? The advertising text describing the novelty of a train roaring across the screen, without a complex plot or sophisticated camerawork, stayed the same over five years. Fascination with the reality of war pictures became, in Cook's later advertisement, delight in the excitement enhancing sounds of *Indians and Cowboys* (a narrative film advertised as 'dramatic and spectacular scene in six parts'.) Either small-town folk were easily amused, or they had not become as bored with the appeal of the 'cinema of attractions' as had sophisticated urban spectators. Perhaps Cook's audiences enjoyed getting that jolt of reaction over and over again. Only the names and descriptions of the programme's feature films varied in Cook and Harris Company couriers over seven years, and Cook even reused some films, such as *The Lost Child* and a hand-tinted fireworks finale, several years in a row. The reprinted early reviews in Cook's courier, although falsified, must have characterised the Cook and Harris show well enough to have been used for so long without too much criticism from audiences, advance agents or opera house managers. The Cooks did a great deal of repeat business during their semi-annual tours of the same circuit of small towns in upstate New York. They could not have survived very many seasons if their show did not deliver full value for the price of admission.

Although advance agent Art Richardson disparaged the Cook and Harris Company advertising and film programme in the fall of 1906, other public reactions that September were more generous. Cook's advertising for the first show of the season, to be held in Cooperstown, promised 'New Moving Pictures, New Illustrated Songs. Everything New and even better than before'. Cook's feature attraction was footage of the San Francisco Fire which followed the earthquake in May 1906. (It was not exactly breaking news by September, however.) After the show, Fannie Cook reported to her husband that 'everybody spoke well of the entertainment, and said it was far above Howe's, or any that the city people had seen in the cities'.[34] A review in the always sympathetic Cooperstown *Freeman's Journal*, noted that 'a large audience was present, including many of our summer population, who pronounced it the best show of moving pictures they had seen. Especially interesting were the scenes of the San Francisco Fire'.[35] Bert Cook received an endorsement from an Odd Fellows Lodge member, whose chapter had sponsored a Cook and Harris performance, that enthused: 'people who have seen Moving Pictures in New York, Buffalo and Rochester say that your entertainment is as good if not better than anything they have ever saw [sic]'.[36] Nevertheless, Cook finally bowed to Richardson's pressure and changed his advertising illustrations. The enthralled audience was gone from Cook's courier, but his 1910 programme gave plenty of hints that the 'cinema of attractions' spirit lingered still. Cook's trademark phrase, 'There are many Imitators, but only One Genuine', was highlighted on covers in 1900, 1905 and 1910. The 1910 cover featured Bert Cook's photograph, surrounded by simple graphics – reminiscent of a projector's beam of light – forming his portrait on the screen. In a symbolic way, Cook's advertising (similar to Lyman Howe's post-1899 handbills) signalled to his audience that he, the exhibitor, still held the dominant role in presenting the movie show to his audiences. Cook also re-employed year after year the same advertising text on the back of his programme.[37] Of nine textual elements on the 1910 courier back cover, six advertising lines were carried over from 1905, and two had been on Cook's couriers since 1900: 'The Highest grade exhibition of Moving Pictures in America, Comprising the Most wonderful Depicture of Living Beings and Objects in Motion Ever Attained by Mechanical Means' and 'No Waits of Delays! This is an advantage we have over nearly all other Moving Picture exhibitors. All our Pictures are accompanied by Realistic Sounds'. That audiences in 1910 would be impressed by the lifelike nature of film images or the use of splices and a film reel to link individual scenes together was unlikely, but Cook was sentimentally attached to the ideas they conveyed. New text on the inside page pleaded: 'Do not compare this exhibition with any five or ten cent small shows; The Cook and Harris Programs are above comparison.' In 1910, Cook was forced to acknowledge both the changing times and the deadly competition itinerants faced from the rapidly proliferating small-town nickelodeons.

In a phrase twice as curious as its inclusion had been in his 1905 courier, Cook persisted in admonishing his 1910 audiences: 'Remember – This is not a Stereopticon or Magic Lantern Exhibition, but the Very Latest Marvel in the World's Famous Moving Pictures'. Was this an intentional reference back to cinema's very beginnings? Both Howe's Animotiscope and Edison's Vitascope had been termed 'the very latest marvel' in 1896. Was this an example of Bert Cook's laziness, or his naïvety, or a lingering affection for the excitement of film's discovery, or a perceptive knowledge of what kind of movie-going experience his particular audiences desired? In the absence of more direct documentation in letters or journal entries, Cook's advertising handbills and couriers leave us many clues but also many mysteries. My own assessment of Cook has moved through a number of stages, from scoffing disbelief to understanding through contextualisation, to admiration of Cook's abilities, his desire to please his customers, and his determination to succeed on his own terms.[38]

In conclusion, continuities in Bert Cook's advertising between 1897 and 1910 far outweighed the differences. His courier illustrations and ideas remained the same even as the typefaces, personnel, performance dates and seat prices changed. When more than half a dozen competing exhibitors played each village, small-town audiences must have tolerated or enjoyed a significant amount of ritual repetition of these at-one-point 'novel' film attractions. If these early actuality, humourous and trick films were pleasurable mainly for their novelty and ability to shock or enthral, why did Cook advertise them (and audience reaction to them) for so long, and why did the same audiences continue to attend his shows twice a year? The same audiences (and their parents and grandparents) throughout the nineteenth century had watched travelling theatrical companies present *Uncle Tom's Cabin*, *Hamlet* and *The Two Orphans* year after year on their opera house stages and had relished both the well-known plots and the surprises each performance offered. Not that much differed in the new century. Novelty and familiar rituals, attractions and films that stressed narrative over display appeared to co-exist in exhibitors' and audiences' experiences.[39]

Once film was no longer a novelty, most exhibitors (Bert Cook was an exception) did not feel the imperative to use audience images in their advertising. They could dwell on the on-screen images, advertising their shows more like theatrical, vaudeville and circus companies which focused on the action on stage or in the ring. By 1900, circus and theatrical printers, notably Hennegan and Donaldson in Cincinnati, Ohio, had moved to service this new market. They designed lines of stock posters for movie shows illustrated with typical representations of scenes from films (cowboys and Indians, melodramatic action, illustrations similar to those used in stock theatrical posters). By 1908, the growing film studios had awoken to the fact that they needed to provide advertising material for their film releases. Several studies approached theatrical printers to develop posters for each upcoming release. The movie poster as we know it today was born.[40]

Notes

1 An initial draft of this essay was presented at the Society for Cinema Studies Conference, Ottawa, April 1997. I wish to thank Robert C. Allen, Richard Abel, Q. David Bowers and George Potamianos for their generous comments, criticisms and suggestions.

2 Cook and Harris Company, 1905 programme, Cook and Harris Papers, New York State Historical Association, Cooperstown, New York. On itinerant film exhibition in the early silent film era, see Kathryn H. Fuller, *At the Picture Show: Small Town Audiences and the Creation of Movie Fan Culture* (Washington, DC: Smithsonian Press, 1996); Douglas Gomery, *Shared Pleasures: A History of Movie Presentation in the US* (Madison: University of Wisconsin Press, 1992); Charles Musser, *Before the Nickelodeon: Edwin S. Porter and the Edison Manufacturing Company* (Berkeley: University of California Press, 1991); Musser, *The Emergence of Cinema: The American Screen to 1907* (New York: Scribner's Sons, 1991); Charles Musser with Carol Nelson, *High-Class Moving Pictures: Lyman H. Howe and the Forgotten Era of Itinerant Exhibition* (Princeton: Princeton University Press, 1991); Calvin Pryluck, 'The Itinerant Movie Show and the Development of the Film Industry', *Journal of the University Film and Video Association* vol. 25 no. 4 (Autumn 1983), pp. 11–22; Gregory Waller, *Main Street Amusements: Movies and Commercial Entertainment in a Southern City* (Washington, DC: Smithsonian Press, 1995).

3 E. A. Richardson to B. A. Cook, 23 November 1906; Richardson to Cook 17 December 1906, Cook and Harris papers.

4 E. A. Richardson to B. A. Cook, 17 December 1906, Cook and Harris papers.

5 Musser, *The Emergence of Cinema*, pp. 18–19.

6 Emmanuelle Toulet, *Birth of the Motion Picture* (New York: Harry Abrams, 1995), pp. 70–1.

7 *Ibid.*, p. 37; David Robinson, *From Peep Show to Palace: The Birth of American Film* (New York: Columbia University Press, 1996) pp. 49, 57.

8 Robinson, *From Peep Show to Palace*, colour insert 6; Stephen Rebello and Richard Allen, *Reel Art: Great Posters from the Golden Age of the Silver Screen* (New York: Abbeville Press, 1988), p. 16.

9 Rebello and Allen, *Reel Art*, p. 16.

10 Robinson, *From Peep Show to Palace*, colour insert 7.

11 Terry Ramsaye, *A Million and One Nights* (NY: Simon and Schuster, 1926; republished, Touchstone, 1986), p. 232.

12 Musser, *The Emergence of Cinema*, p. 18.

13 *Ibid.*, p. 4.

14 Colin Harding and Simon Popple, *In the Kingdom of Shadows: A Companion to Early Cinema* (Madison, NJ: Fairleigh Dickinson University Press), p. 2.

15 Musser, *The Emergence of Cinema*, p. 3.

16 *Wilkes Barre Times*, 1 July 1896, p. 8, reprinted in Musser, *High-Class Moving Pictures*, p. 49.

17 Tom Gunning, 'Primitive Cinema', in Thomas Elsaesser (ed.) with Adam Barker *Early Film: Frame, Space, Narrative* (London: BFI Publishing, 1990), p. 101.

18 Gunning, 'The Cinema of Attractions', in Elsaesser, *Early Film*, p. 58; Gunning, 'An Aesthetic of Astonishment', in, Linda Williams (ed.), *Viewing Positions: Ways of Seeing Film* (New Brunswick, NJ: Rutgers University Press, 1995), p. 129.

19 Tom Gunning examines how films focused on 'the direct address of the audience, in which an attraction is offered to the spectator by a cinema showman … its energy moves outward towards an acknowledged spectator rather than inwards towards the character-based situations essential to classical narrative'. Gunning, 'The Cinema of Attractions', p. 58.

20 Sears, Roebuck Company catalogue 107 (Autumn 1897–Spring 1898), p. 195.

21 *Ibid.*, p. 206.

22 *Ibid.*, p. 195.

23 Sears catalogue 107, p. 210. Sears catalogue 109 (Autumn 1899) repeats the small opera house audience shot with the screen image of 'The Kiss'.

24 Musser, *High-Class Moving Pictures*, p. 29.

25 Not every poster from Howe's phonograph or motion picture performances included audiences, but they were very prominent in his advertising. Musser, *High-Class Moving Pictures*, pp. 41, 43, 45, 57, 68, 84.

26 Lyman Howe posters in Prints and Photographs Division, Library of Congress.

27 Musser, *High-Class Moving Pictures*, pp. 98, 124, 158, 182, 241, 244, 250–1.

28 Musser, *The Emergence of Cinema*, p. 6.

29 Musser, *High-Class Moving Pictures*, p. 99.

30 Tom Gunning, 'Primitive Cinema, A Frame Up? The Trick's on Us', in Elsaesser, *Early Film*, p. 101. On show printing, see Richard W. Flint, 'Circus Posters and Show Printers' (MA thesis, SUNY Oneonta, 1979).

31 Fannie Cook to B. Albert Cook, 4 September 1905, Cook–Harris Papers, file September–October 1905; Musser, *High-Class Moving Pictures*, p. 57.

32 Gunning, 'Non-Continuity, Continuity, Discontinuity: A Theory of Genres in Early Films', in Elsaesser, *Early Film*, pp. 89–93.

33 *Williamsport Gazette*, 28 September 1900, quoted in advertisement for Pearce Moving Picture Company performance at First M.E. Church, Pittsfield, MA, 26 November [1900]; *Albany [New York] Journal*, 27 October 1904, quoted in advertisement for Cook and Harris performance at MP Church, Columbia Centre [New York?] Thursday, 20 April [1905], located in Cook–Harris Papers. Musser, *High-Class Moving Pictures*, pp. 104–9.

34 F. Cook to B. A. Cook, 6 September 1906, Cook and Harris papers.

35 [Cooperstown, NY] *Freeman's Journal*, 6 September 1906, p. 5.

36 F. J. Mitchell to B. A. Cook, 22 October 1906, Cook–Harris papers.

37 Cook and Harris programme, 10 March 1910 at the ME church in Unadilla, NY, Cook–Harris papers.

38 Musser, *High-Class Moving Pictures*, p. 57.

39 On nineteenth-century theatrical audiences, see Lawrence Levine, *Highbrow/Lowbrow: The Emergence of Cultural Hierarchy in America* (Cambridge, MA: Harvard University Press, 1988); Benjamin McArthur, *Actors and American Culture, 1880–1920* (Philadelphia: Temple University Press, 1984); Harlowe Hoyt, *Town Hall Tonight* (New York: Bramhall House, 1955).

40 Janice Steinberg, 'Showmanship in Printing: A Centennial History of the Hennegan Company, 1886–1986', Hennegan papers, Cincinnati Historical Society; Hennegan Printers, 'Condensed Catalogue No. 16' (*c.*1914), Hennegan papers; Alden N. Monroe, 'Bigtop to Bijou: The Golden Age of the Show Poster', *Queen City Heritaage*, 42, no. 2 (Summer 1984), pp. 3–14.

8 Reminiscences of the Past, Conditions of the Present: At the Movies in Milwaukee in 1918

Leslie Midkiff DeBauche

Accounting for the conditions affecting reception of movies exhibited eighty years ago in a particular place also requires excavating salient historical events. Much was going on in Milwaukee in April 1918 to create the social, political, economic – in short, the historical – context for movie-going. This chapter takes its title from one response to the sequence of events most evidently shaping that content: the United States' entry into the First World War. In that month, the Milwaukee Deutscher Club decided, at the instigation of the club's 'younger' members, to change its name to the Wisconsin Club. Arguing against the change, F. C. Winkler, , a founding member of the club, maintained that its German name 'rests in the reminiscences of the past and not in the conditions of the present'. Present conditions were, however, an immensely powerful influence on the social and political life of Milwaukee in the spring of 1918, including its habits of movie-going.

Movie-going in Milwaukee was part of the leisure routine of many of its citizens. The *Milwaukee Journal's* film writer calculated her city's share of the $3,988,860 that the government earned from its war tax on theatre admissions. 'The average per month', she wrote, 'for the district since the tax became effective has been 50,000 of which the city of Milwaukee had considerably over half is attributable to motion pictures'.[1] Her statistics suggest that at least 750,000 tickets were sold in Milwaukee each month. The population of Milwaukee in 1920 was 459,147. Clearly, movie-going was a popular pastime. One way of learning which films were playing at the theatres downtown and in Milwaukee's neighbourhoods was to read the newspapers. But, before reaching the movie advertisements, readers turned the first page with its international, national and state news, and flipped through the inside pages telling of social events, local scandals, editorial positions and advertisements for sales in city stores. The movie notices were embedded in the news of the country and the particular events taking place in Milwaukee. In April 1918, people were making political decisions and voting for state and local officials; they were preparing and conducting the Third Liberty Loan; and, because of the particular demographic characteristics of the area, they were dealing with their German heritage in a variety of ways, including Americanising their surnames and the names of their social clubs. Milwaukee's theatre managers used the opportunities provided by current events to woo customers into their movie houses. They were, however, faced with certain demographic challenges to their jobs as showmen.

Within its city limits, Milwaukee housed citizens professing a full range of reasons for opposing participation in the war. First, being situated in the Middle West, it joined neighbouring farm states in its isolationist attitude to any involvement in a conflict so far away.[2] Second, while Milwaukee was an urban rather than a rural centre, its population, as determined by the 1910 census, was 53.5 per cent ethnic German. The city boasted a vibrant Germanic culture, including a German-language newspaper, social clubs and a brewing industry. Third, socialists, who traditionally opposed participation in war, were elected to the Milwaukee city council, the mayor's office and the House of Representatives in 1916 and 1918. Milwaukee also supported a socialist newspaper, the *Milwaukee Leader*. Finally, Wisconsin was represented in the Senate by the Progressive politician Robert LaFollette Snr, one of only six senators who voted against President Wilson's request for a declaration of war on Germany in April 1917. In the House of Representatives, nine of the fifty members who voted against the war were from Wisconsin. This combination of geographical, ethnic and political characteristics dealt Wisconsin's, and especially Milwaukee's, public image a severe blow, and created a potentially hostile audience for war-related films and programming at the movies.

Still, demographics do not tell the whole story. Milwaukee, like Wisconsin, did its civic duty in public, newsworthy ways. Once the United States entered the war, most socialists in the city worked for the war effort.[3] Mayor Daniel Hoan helped organise the Milwaukee County Council of Defence on 30 April 1917. He served as the chairman of the Council until the end of 1918. A. M. Simons, a journalist for the *Milwaukee Leader*, resigned his position on the paper and was expelled from the party for his pro-government activities. He took a salaried position with the Wisconsin Defence League and directed the Speaker's Bureau that supervised the activities of the Four-Minute Men. Socialists were not alone in putting government needs first. Germans in Milwaukee also demonstrated their allegiance in public ways. The Germania Building was renamed the Brumder Building and the statue of Germania standing in front of it was removed. Two banks – the Germania Bank and the German American Bank – became the National Bank of Commerce and the American National Bank, respectively. Several hundred Milwaukeeans with German surnames had them 'Americanised'.[4] Milwaukee's theatre managers, at once part of a national industry and a local constituency, participated in this civic public relations campaign for their city.

Theatre managers in Milwaukee, together with their colleagues around the country, enlisted in the effort to win the war on the homefront. Even though Milwaukee's unique demographic profile provided an opportunity for exhibitors to act idiosyncratically, as they programmed and promoted their houses, they fell into line with practices standardised and disseminated through such trade journals as *Moving Picture World* and *Motion Picture News*. In fact, I can document few instances of theatre programming or film promotion alluding to the ethnicity of 53 per cent of Milwaukee's population. One occurred soon after America's entrance into the war. On 5 May 1917, the Paradise Theatre showed *Our Allies in Action* and advertised: 'See for yourself the battlefields where the stars and stripes will soon be planted ... [See] German prisoners of war. Some may be friends or acquaintances'.[5]

Theatre managers operated under their industry's mandate to fit their theatre so far as possible into the local community. In Milwaukee, this meant following the lead of business and civic leaders to try to foster a public image of one hundred per cent Americanism.[6] In addition to lending financial support to the war effort through the purchase of Liberty Bonds, Milwaukee film-goers also contributed as they paid a war tax levied on movie tickets. Such 'Hate the Hun' movies as *The Claws of the Hun*, *To Hell with the Kaiser* and *The Kaiser, Beast of Berlin*, played in Milwaukee over the course of the war as they did in other cities and towns in the United States. Elmer Axel Beck's memories of going to see *To Hell with the Kaiser* as a junior high-school student during the war, clearly shows the importance of exploitation tactics in influencing public opinion:

> One Sunday afternoon I went to the Greenfield Theater, a neighborhood movie house and saw on the silver screen *To Hell with the Kaiser*. I don't remember anything from the film except that it portrayed the enemy. But I do remember two things. One was that the title started up the circulation of this advice on word usage: 'Don't say "the hell with the Kaiser", that means you don't care what happens to him. Say "to hell with the Kaiser", because that's where we want him to go'. My second thing I remembered is that everyone who attended was handed a leaflet with a picture of 'Kaiser Bill'. His face, mustache with upturned ends, spiked helmet, was the bulls-eye of a target, concentric circles around it. Directions on the leaflet were to tack the target on your backyard fence and shoot 'Kaiser Bill'. If you didn't have a gun or even a BB rifle, you were expected to throw stones at him.[7]

Beck also remembered winning the Junior Four-Minute Man speech contest at his school: his topic was 'Why Liberty Bonds Are a Good Investment'. His family made 'trench candles' by rolling up the daily newspaper, either the *Journal* or the socialist *Milwaukee Leader*, dipping the cylinder in wax and taking it to school for shipment overseas. For Beck, going to the movies was part of life on the homefront, of a piece with tilling a victory garden, eating Liberty sandwiches (hamburgers), buying Thrift Stamps and throwing rocks at Kaiser Bill's image.

The manager of the Greenfield Theater was not alone in promoting his theatre by 'present[ing] a little something of special effectiveness ... bearing on the war'. In July 1918, *Variety* reported that 'A Milwaukee theater is admitting free any patron who presents a letter from a soldier who is overseas'.[8] Milwaukee also instituted the practice of singing patriotic – as well as other contemporary – songs before feature-film screenings. An advertisement for the Alhambra Theatre boasted: 'We started Community Singing as an experiment. Now it's an assured success. We yield to the public demand and will continue it one more week with Frederick Carberry directing'.[9]

Timeliness was invoked through the choice of a feature film as well as a speaker when the Strand Theatre commemorated the sinking of the *Lusitania*, with *Lusitania* Week in May 1918. *Lest We Forget*, a movie about the sinking starring Rita Jolivet, one of the survivors, was shown. Jolivet also appeared in person at the theatre.[10] In July, a different speaker appeared on the stage of the Alhambra. An advertisement in the 21 July 1918 issue of the *Milwaukee Journal* advised readers that they could come to the Alhambra Theatre to see William S. Hart as 'Shark

Monroe, the savage master of a sealing schooner ... and also hear Lieut. John Hewitt who had just spent thirty-one months at the Front'.[11] Milwaukee theatre managers offered newsreels of interest to their clientele. On 28 October 1917, the Butterfly Theatre offered 'Local Boys at Camp McArthur' programmed with *The Pricemark*.[12]

Milwaukee – like other big cities across the US – hosted the roadshow *Hearts of the World*. Fannie Gordon, the movie critic for the *Milwaukee Journal*, described the superlative qualities of D. W. Griffith's film, which included its very arrival in the city:

> Who of us who, in *autrefois*, endured the flickerings of the 'nickel show' in the cause of cinema art, dreamed in that period only a dozen or so years gone by, that the day would come when a motion picture production would come to Milwaukee in a sixty-foot baggage car? Who, even the king of optimists himself, would have dreamed then of a motion picture accompanied by its own thirty-piece symphony orchestra.[13]

Hearts of the World ran an unprecedented six weeks at the Davidson, a legitimate theatre, opening 29 July 1918 and closing 7 September 1918. It played only twice daily, with ticket prices ranging from twenty-five cents to one dollar and fifty cents in the evenings, and from twenty-five cents to one dollar for matinées. Its longevity at the Davidson resulted from popular demand. An advertisement in the *Milwaukee Journal* noted:

> *The Hearts of the World* has set a record for a waiting line of ticket buyers at the Davidson Theatre. Tuesday night the line extended from the box office for ½ block down 3rd Street and in many places it was doubled or tripled by the ones who were accompanying the actual buyer of the ticket.[14]

This same advertisement explained that seats were available two weeks in advance. An editorial in the *Journal* also urged readers to see the film:

> The Journal commends the play first of all to those loyal Americans whose love of democracy and fair play has kept them on the path of right from the very beginning of the world war. Such will find the film a confirmation and an inspiration. The Journal's appeal does not stop with them. It would urge to see the play all those who grumble about the petty difficulties which the war has brought.[15]

Such ballyhoo was justified, for the presentation of *Hearts of the World* was spectacular. Gordon described the light and sound effects that accompanied the film: an 'electric storm' was created with 'lightning flashes, thunder and wailing winds. ... Hundreds of gallons of water are forced against a concave surface under high pressure and add to the realism of the scene'.[16]

Hearts of the World was not the first war movie to be presented in such a grand style. *The Unbeliever*, the last film produced by the Edison Company, played Milwaukee in late May and early June 1918. Its advertisement in the *Milwaukee Journal* of 2 June noted:

> Eighth Tremendous Day of the picture that has broken all Strand records. The greatest war story the war has produced.... Notice to the Public. Almost 30,000 people have seen 'The Unbeliever' at this theater during the past week. We are firmly of the opinion

that fully that many more loyal Milwaukeeans wish to view this thrillingly appealing patriotic spectacle. It carries the message direct to every American heart that the world must be made safe for democracy mainly through the efforts of this nation.

'The Unbeliever' was made in cooperation with the United States Marines and officially sanctioned by attaches of the government. We are in receipt of countless letters from representative citizens endorsing it as the most timely drama of the present war. Therefore we are holding 'The Unbeliever' for the coming week so that all who wish may see. Charles C. Perry [manager] Special: Journal-Pathe Pictures of Milwaukee's own regiment – the Boys from Camp Custer – and the Memorial Day Parade.[17]

The rhetoric of this advertisement reveals the tensions and the pressures forming the context for the reception of movies in Milwaukee in 1917 and 1918. German cultural heritage, ethnicity and socialism to the contrary, Milwaukeeans – in large numbers – were 'loyal' and possessed of 'American' hearts. No wayward nephew, Milwaukee was, rather, integral to the national family making the world safe for democracy. Charles Perry was providing a service to his community by allowing the film to be held over for an additional week so more people could publicly attest to their patriotism by attending his theatre. He also presumably would continue the record-breaking business he had enjoyed in the preceding eight days *The Unbeliever* had played The Strand. Programming the nationally distributed feature with newsreels of local folks – soldiers and civilians – further helped to integrate Milwaukee into the national homefront and battlefront. Footage of the Memorial Day Parade allowed the audience to participate in an event, a commemoration of the Civil War, in which they had been, unequivocally, on the 'right' side.

Since this advertisement was prominently displayed on the movie page of the most widely read local newspaper, Milwaukeeans had access to the identity which it offered them whether they attended movies or not. The pressures of the times, exercised socially and politically, encouraged its adoption. Many of the tensions evident in the early days of April 1917 were still causing civic strain one year later. The movies, what was showing on the screen, what was happening at the theatre and what was being reported in the papers, reveal the contradictions, competing beliefs and accommodations to the war made by the film exhibitors and moviegoers of Milwaukee.

In the first two weeks of April 1918, newspapers including the Republican *Milwaukee Journal*, which would win a Pulitzer Prize for its war reporting in 1919, the socialist *Milwaukee Leader*, the *Evening Wisconsin Newspaper*, the *Milwaukee Daily News* and the *Milwaukee Free Press* were filled with a variety of international, national and local news stories. Through these stories, we may gain a purchase on film reception. They suggest the topics of conversation for customers waiting for the curtain to rise at the Alhambra in April 1918. They cue a set of referential meanings an audience might glean from film and non-filmic programming at the Orpheum. They offer a set of possibilities – tools a film historian or social historian can use to try and comprehend what the experience of moviegoing meant at this time and in this place, and what difference it made to citizens of Milwaukee. Looking at the news also reveals different ways the movie theatres were used by their managers as they did their job providing entertainment while fulfilling industry-inspired mandates to be prominent citizens in their community.

The leading stories in April 1918 included local and state elections, the start of the Third Liberty Loan Drive and the progress of the war. Among the candidates running for the Senate, Victor Berger, a socialist, promised: 'If elected I shall work for the withdrawal of the American soldier boys from the invasion of Europe'.[18] Although Berger carried the city of Milwaukee, he came third in the state as a whole, winning seven counties. Joseph Davies, the Democratic candidate, came second. (The Orpheum Theatre was the site for a political rally for Davies on the night before the 2 April election.) The Senate seat was won by the Republican candidate, Irvine Lenroot. Vaudeville theatres, including the Miller and the Gayety, the Davidson (a legitimate theatre) and the Alhambra movie theatre advertised that they would announce the election results from the stage.

Socialists fared well in the city elections in Milwaukee. Daniel Webster Hoan was elected to a second term as mayor, and nine socialist ward aldermen joined the city council. The socialist plan to revamp the city council also won despite the opposition of the *Journal*, the *Sentinel* and 'other capitalistic papers'.[19]

Some Milwaukee socialists, and some Milwaukee citizens voting for socialists, may have felt they were protesting against national policy as they voted. And, as we shall see, super-patriotism was also an issue within the city limits. Still, others voting socialist in Milwaukee in 1918 had different reasons. Daniel Hoan's opponents had called him a 'sewer socialist' in the 1916 election. While the intention was to cast aspersions, the name also foregrounded an important part of the socialist political agenda in Milwaukee: the party did advocate public ownership of utilities. In fact, the war created a major rift in American socialism. Milwaukee's socialists, including Daniel Hoan, A. M. Simons and Elmer Axel Beck, who remembered throwing darts at Kaiser Bill and making trench candles, supported the war effort after American entry in the conflict. On election day, the socialist *Milwaukee Leader* borrowed battlefield rhetoric to urge its readers to 'Go Over the Top' and vote in large numbers. The next day, 3 April, it described election results this way: 'Vote Is Slap at Accusation of Disloyalty'.[20] Hoan was quoted as claiming:

> My record as a mayor, as a socialist and as an American has been approved by our citizenship.... This is the most lawabiding and peaceful city in the United States. It is time for all to join hands and boost Milwaukee.[21]

In his inaugural speech later that month, Hoan asserted that:

> Our nation is involved in the greatest war of all history.... Since our participation in that struggle, the citizens of Milwaukee have worked with an admirable spirit to meet every need of the government and the community growing out of the war. They have done this without regard to their opinion of war or their views as to peace.[22]

Readers of the *Milwaukee Leader* were treated to an advertisement for one of the movies in town that election day, *The Little American*, a war film starring Mary Pickford, first released in July 1917: 'Not a war play in the old sense of the word, but dealing with live war issues. Socialists are recommended to see the other fellow's viewpoint in this picture'.[23] 'But we were all patriots', Beck recalled years later.[24]

The Third Liberty Loan Drive was launched on 13 April with a huge parade in downtown Milwaukee, comprising 15,000 marchers walking – to the music of bells, factory whistles and military and high-school bands – down Grand Avenue, Wisconsin Street and Van Buren. The next day, a Sunday, pastors were to preach 'Liberty Loan' sermons. Federal, state and local governmental officials, regardless of party affiliation, worked together on this event that ate up more column inches in local newspapers than war coverage.

Theatres, movie stars and movies were also an important part of the promotional strategy. The Alhambra Theatre promoted a contest for Milwaukee's favourite war song in its movie ads the week before the Bond Drive started. Each day, along with advertising its feature film, Elsie Ferguson in *The Lie*, the Alhambra would provide an update on the relative status of the songs. The top three 'What Are You Doing to Help the Boys?', 'Just Like Washington Crossed the Delaware, General Pershing Will Cross the Rhine' and 'We're All Out of Step but Jim', captured the lead early in this race to win a silver loving-cup, which would be presented to the song's publisher. 'What Are You Doing to Help the Boys?', the theme song of the Third Liberty Loan, won on Saturday 13 April. Workers conducting the Liberty Loan Drive met at the Strand Theatre on 12 April, one day before the kickoff parade, to rally and 'get the details'. These workers would begin door-to-door soliciting on Monday, the day Douglas Fairbanks was to appear at the Butterfly Theatre.

Fairbanks, in company with Charlie Chaplin and Mary Pickford, was travelling across the country 'boosting' Bond sales for the US Treasury Department. He was scheduled to speak on behalf of the Bonds on Monday evening, 15 April, at the Butterfly after a noontime speech to workers at the Allis Chalmers plant just outside Milwaukee, and an afternoon rally – with music provided by the Gimbels Liberty Loan Band – and reception at Gimbels Department Store. At 6.30 p.m. he was scheduled to speak at a one-dollar-a-plate benefit for French War Orphans in Gimbel's Tea Room. The week before, advertisements for the Toy Theatre, which was screening his feature *Wild and Woolly*, announced that 'Mr. Fairbanks will be in

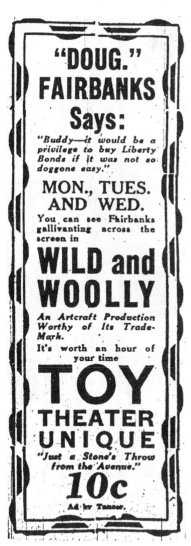

Milwaukee Journal, *15 April 1918.*

135

Mr. Douglas Fairbanks

Coming to Gimbels

In the Interest of

The Third Liberty Loan

MILWAUKEE is to be honored on Monday with a visit from this Popular Favorite of the Movie Stars — Mr. Douglas Fairbanks.

He will arrive in the forenoon from Chicago, Kenosha and Racine and will speak at noon at the Allis-Chalmers plant in West Allis and later in other manufacturing plants.

ABOUT 2:30 P. M. MR. FAIRBANKS and party will be met by Gimbels Liberty Loan Band and escorted directly to the GIMBEL STORE.

He will sell LIBERTY BONDS during the afternoon and at 5:30 will address the 1,300 Gimbel Employes and sell them Liberty Bonds.

AT 6:30 P. M. Monday	Special Liberty Loan Banquet
	Benefit French Orphans' Fund.
	In the GIMBEL TEA ROOM—at 6:30—$1 Per Plate.
	Mr. Douglas Fairbanks Will Speak.

TICKETS ON SALE AT GIMBELS POSTOFFICE

Hear Fairbanks at Gimbels

Milwaukee Journal, *14 April 1918.*

Milwaukee next week to boost the sale of Liberty Bonds – He Himself; meanwhile you can see him [here on film].' In the ad, he bursts through the frame saying, 'Buddy it would be a privilege to buy Liberty Bonds if it was not so doggone easy'.[25] Fairbanks also starred in a short sales film, made for the Treasury Department's Bond Drive, called 'Swat the Kaiser'. This was shown at the Butterfly Theatre in the days before Fairbanks's scheduled visit. On Sunday 14 April, it was paired with motion pictures of the previous day's Liberty Loan parade. Sadly, on Monday 15 April, Milwaukee newspapers announced that 'Due to a Severe cold Contracted in the East . . . He Has Gone to French Lick Springs to Rest . . . But His Latest Photoplay Is Here TODAY'.[26]

In cooperating in this civic effort to sell war bonds (and in allowing political rallies in their auditoriums and announcing election results from their stages), Milwaukee's theatre managers were following trade paper advice to weave their theatre into their local community. Other businesses in Milwaukee joined Gimbels in supporting the Liberty Loan in their advertising. It was also the case that this sort of local tie-in was a time-honoured method espoused by the trade press to create good will for the theatre. Finally, listing these sorts of non-filmic activities reminds us that the movie theatre did more than show movies and that people went to the movie theatre for a variety of reasons.

The Bond Drive was a financial success – Milwaukee exceeded its quota of $14,880,000 by $8,120,350. This was the largest oversubscription to date. Such excess is tempered and, at least in part, explained by another story appearing in the *Milwaukee Journal*. On 16 April, on the *Journal*'s front page, an article told how a worker at the Power and Mining Machinery Company in Cudahy, near Milwaukee, was forced to kneel and kiss the American flag because he refused to buy a bond, 'saying he would not help the government'. After this happened, the paper reported, the night crew of twenty-five men sold him a one-hundred-dollar bond.[27] This humiliating example of super-patriotism occurred ten days after Milwaukee's newspaper readers learned of the lynching of Robert Prager, a German-American suspected of planning to sabotage a mine, by a mob in Collinsville, Illinois.

More examples of the pressures faced by 'hyphenated-Americans' who were also, almost certainly, movie-goers filled the papers in early spring 1918. On 12 April, the Milwaukee Branch of the Wisconsin Staatsverband passed a resolution that, henceforth, the minutes of its meetings would be written in English.[28] Then the Wisconsin Branch of the National German–American Alliance learned that its organisation had decided to dissolve.[29] On 15 April, the *Journal* reported that the German Protestant Methodist Church was planning to hold a patriotic rally at the Second German Methodist Church on 19 May.[30] On 16 April, the *Journal* noted that the twenty-seven-year-old Deutscher Club would now be known as the Wisconsin Club.

Milwaukee Leader, *2 April 1918.*

In April 1918, some citizens of Milwaukee went to movie theatres and rallied for a senatorial candidate, heard – in the most timely fashion – election results and prepared to canvass their neighbours for the Liberty Bond Drive. They also went to watch movies. Still, before the feature film started, they might participate in the war song contest at the Alhambra, or watch newsreels of the Liberty Loan's 'Big Parade' at the Butterfly. The Toy Theatre encouraged patrons in their newspaper advertising to contribute to the Liberty Loan – *and*, had illness not intervened, Milwaukeeans could also have seen Douglas Fairbanks in person at the Butterfly and the Alhambra. Prior to his expected arrival, they might have read about Fairbanks in the Milwaukee newspapers. On 30 March, the socialist *Milwaukee Leader* reported that 'Movie Stars Will Pay Millions in War Taxes'. 'Figures gathered from the stars themselves', the paper observed, 'showed a total running into 9 figures. Leading the list is Douglas Fairbanks, whose income and excess profit tax, together with other taxes levied by the government is $459,000'.[31] On 11 April, Milwaukeeans learned 'Douglas Fairbanks and Wife Agree to Disagree'. In fact, they had agreed to separate.[32]

Exhibitors in Milwaukee joined their colleagues around the country and enlisted in the war effort on the homefront. Their behaviour illustrated the degree to which exhibition was standardised across the United States. Despite trade press advice to blend the theatre into its local venue, exhibitors used ideas derived from nationally-circulated motion picture press books and columns in national trade newspapers as they sold their entertainment to Milwaukeeans. Within the city limits, exhibitors, like their colleagues in the chamber of commerce, worked to foster a patriotic public image for Milwaukee.

Movie-goers in Milwaukee could not escape either the suspicion of the nation or the boosterism of local politicians and merchants by going to the movies. Looking closely at the events covered in the papers in Milwaukee in early April 1918 shows how strong the pressures to conform to national definitions of Americanism and patriotism were. The most prominent movie stars, like Douglas Fairbanks, were not only in the news because of the quirks and foibles of their private and professional lives, they were newsworthy as the government's spokes-people travelling the country hawking Liberty Bonds. In the spring of 1918, Fairbanks made movies and he made speeches. By the autumn, he had also published two books which continued to espouse his prescription for 'making life worthwhile'. Still, in the face of concerted efforts to act one hundred per cent American (which, incidentally, was the title of Mary Pickford's Liberty Loan film), Milwaukeeans negotiated the terrain of ethnicity, socialism and patriotism. They found ways to balance the 'reminiscences of the past' with the 'conditions of the present', when they went to the movies.

Notes

1 Fannie Gordon, 'Happenings on Stage and Screen', *Milwaukee Journal*, 11 August 1918, section IV, p. 2.
2 Ora Ida Hilton, 'Control of Public Opinion During the World War', Ph.D. dissertation, University of Wisconsin, p. 2.
3 Elmer Axel Beck, *Sewer Socialists: A History of the Socialist Party of Wisconsin, 1897–1940*, I, p. 185.
4 *Ibid.*, p. 196.
5 Advertisement, *Milwaukee Leader*, 5 May 1917.
6 '100 percent Americanism' grew out of the nativist movement soon after the First World War began in Europe. In his history of the homefront, David M. Kennedy notes: 'That kind of rank nativism, tinged often with anti-radicalism, seeped deeper and deeper into the American mind as the war progressed, carried by the current of a newly fashioned phrase: "100 percent Americanism". The 100 percenters aimed to stamp out all traces of Old World identity among immigrants. They visited their worst excesses on German-Americans, which at first glance was scarcely surprising'. Kennedy, *Over Here: The First World War and American Society* (New York: Oxford University Press, 1980), p. xxx. See also, John Higham, *Strangers in the Land: Patterns of American Nativism, 1860–1925* (New York: Atheneum, 1963).
7 Beck, *Sewer Socialists*, p. 186.
8 'Envelope Admission', *Variety*, 12 July 1918, p. 42.
9 Advertisement, *Milwaukee Journal*, 14 July 1918, section II, p. 10.
10 Advertisement, *Milwaukee Journal*, 12 May 1918, section II, p. 11.
11 Advertisement, *Milwaukee Journal*, 21 July 1918, section IV, p. 9.
12 Advertisement, *Milwaukee Journal*, 28 October 1917, section IV, p. 4.
13 Fannie Gordon, 'Hearts of the World', *Milwaukee Journal*, 28 July 1918, section IV, p. 2.

14 Advertisement, *Milwaukee Journal*, 31 July 1918, p. 7.

15 Editorial, *Milwaukee Journal*, 1 August 1918, p. 6. 'Every Milwaukeean should see [*Hearts of the World*]', the editorial continued, 'partly because it is great Art, but even more because its plot is such as will uncover a deeper vein of patriotism in every man, woman and child with eyes to see and a heart to feel'.

16 Gordon, 'Hearts of the World'.

17 Advertisement, *Milwaukee Journal*, 2 June 1918, section II, p. 11.

18 'Chicago Tribune Thinks Berger's Victory Possible, Davies Called Friend of Profiteers – Lenroot Branded as "Lukewarm"', *Milwaukee Journal*, 28 March 1918, p. 2.

19 'Vote for 25 Ward Aldermen in Change, Voters Indorse Change by Socialists and Opposed by Capitalists', *Milwaukee Leader*, 10 April 1918, p. 1.

20 'Go Over the Top!', *Milwaukee Leader*, 2 April 1918, p. 1; 'Vote Is Slap at Accusation of Disloyalty', *Milwaukee Leader*, 3 April 1918, p. 1.

21 'Vote Is Slap at Accusation of Disloyalty', *Milwaukee Leader*, 3 April 1918, p. 1.

22 Beck, *Sewer Socialists*, quoting Daniel Hoan, p. 196.

23 Advertisement, *Milwaukee Leader*, 2 April, 1918, p. 3.

24 Beck, *Sewer Socialists*, p. 187.

25 Advertisement for *Wild and Woolly* at the Toy Theatre, *Milwaukee Leader*, 13 April 1918, p. 3.

26 Advertisement for *Swat the Kaiser*, at the Butterfly Theatre, *Milwaukee Journal*, 15 April 1918, p. 6.

27 'Force Man to Kiss Flag and Buy Bond', *Milwaukee Journal*, 16 April 1918, p. 1.

28 'Staatsverband Members Expressed Loyalty', *Milwaukee Journal*, 13 April 1918, p. 2.

29 'To Report On Alliance Conference', *Milwaukee Journal*, 13 April 1918, p. 2.

30 'Patriotic Rally of German Methodists', *Milwaukee Journal*, 15 April 1918, p. 6.

31 'Movie Stars Will Pay Millions in War Taxes', *Milwaukee Leader*, 30 March 1918, p. 2.

32 'Douglas Fairbanks and Wife Also "Agree to Disagree"', *Milwaukee Journal*, 11 April 1918 p. 11.

PART THREE
Audiences and the Coming of Sound

9 This Is Where We Came In: The Audible Screen and the Voluble Audience of Early Sound Cinema

Thomas Doherty

Following the folkways of motion picture spectatorship – what it was like to go to the movies and watch celluloid projected in a theatre in the early 1930s – calls for examining screen memoirs, dredging up reports in the trade press and jogging the memories of ageing movie-goers. On balance, on-site reports attest to a warm, convivial atmosphere in the theatrical space of the motion picture theatre, a movie-going experience qualitatively richer than the jaded aura of today's multiplex maze with minuscule screens and sparse attendance. Congregated together in crowds of hundreds, and sometimes thousands, audiences reacted in a group unity that was garrulous and demonstrative, sometimes boorish and unruly, often communal and choral. More akin to today's response to live theatre than to film screenings, crowd reactions presupposed that the two-dimensional images on screen, no less than flesh-and-blood performers, deserved audible expressions of approval and reproach.[1]

The deportment of motion picture audiences was a behavioural by-product of theatrical experiences that both pre-dated and overlapped with the movies and, above all, of the raucous atmosphere nurtured in the vaudeville hall. In the earliest days of American cinema, live pageants, musical numbers, magic shows and comedy acts preceded, interrupted and concluded motion picture exhibitions.[2] With theatrical performances and film presentations sharing the same bill, the customary reactions of audiences to live performers – catcalls and applause, hisses and cheers – carried over into the motion picture portion of the programme. Though the 1930s witnessed the gradual elimination of live acts from the standard motion picture programme, many first-run venues continued to showcase performers as a featured item on the bill. Similarly, although sound had forced the eviction of pianists and other musicians as screen accompanists, live organists lingered on to play overtures, intermissions and incidental music in many first-class venues. The more communal and less self-conscious participatory rites of movie-going found rousing expression in the songfests led by the organists or prompted by lyrical singalongs from the screen ('follow the bouncing ball!').

The films themselves incorporated a variety of cues to encourage audible audience participation. A typical screen convention of the early 1930s was the opening curtain call which showcased featured players with a close-up and a superimposed credit. Usually in a series of cinematic 'wipes' moving from one player to the next,

143

the curtain call introduced the actors and their parts (full-screen shots for the stars, split-screen shots for the supporting players), awarded a theatrical bow, and gave audiences a chance to applaud favoured players. Studio scouts spotted up-and-coming talent by monitoring audience reaction, treating it as an index of popularity as reliable as fan mail: MGM press agents were first alerted to the magnetism of Clark Gable when females sighed and swooned over his supporting role as a gangster in *Dance, Fools, Dance* (1931).[3] Similarly, in the wake of scandalous tabloid headlines in 1930–1 chronicling the prodigious sex life of Clara Bow, executives at Fox took solace when her first appearance in *Call Her Savage* (1932) sparked several minutes of applause that drowned out the opening dialogue.[4]

In the middle of the diegesis, too, audiences might applaud a performance, particularly if a monologue delivered a moralistic declamation or an all-American screed that invited audible enthusiasm. The rabble-rousing speechifying in social consciousness 'preachment yarns' met with cheers from many Depression-weary movie-goers. During a preview screening of Cecil B. DeMille's vigilante teen-pic, *This Day and Age* (1933), the *Hollywood Reporter* heard 'cheers, and the final long burst of applause' marking a reaction 'tempered by a touch of mob hysteria'. *Gabriel Over the White House* (1933), a hallucinatory tract about a demagogic president who assumes dictatorial powers to solve the problems of Depression America, incited enthusiastic 'applause all through the picture and at the end there is cheering' during its run at New York's Capitol Theatre.[5]

Wise actors paused a beat at the end of a ringing declaration, both to signal an outburst of supportive applause and to prevent the next line of dialogue from being smothered. In *The Mouthpiece* (1932), when a naïve young country girl rebuffs her predatory employer (Warren William, wearing a silk robe over his tuxedo), her virtuous outrage concludes with a dramatic exclamation ('I despise you!'), followed by a measured pause for audiences to register their righteous approval. Stunning photography and elaborate montage sequences were also warmly greeted. Beholding a fabulous shot of a full-antlered moose caught in a perfect pose on top of an Alaskan ridge in the expeditionary film *Explorers of the World* (1931), the audience at the Criterion in New York burst delightedly into applause.[6] Likewise, at the opening and end credits, favoured short subjects and cartoons inspired whistles, cheers and foot stomping by children.

More worrisome to theatre owners and civil authorities were other kinds of partisan expression incited by the screen, especially by the newsreel, the designated site for news and information in the motion picture programme. Looking at the newsreel images of politicians, businessmen, experts and evangelists, movie-goers registered support or contempt much as they cheered on the cavalry in a western or hissed the cad in a melodrama. From many a disgruntled Depression crowd, the reaction to the rosy scenarios and disengaged personalities was rancorous and sarcastic. Bouncy economic forecasts and chirpy commentary in the newsreels inspired snorts of disbelief and muttered expletives. Laughter and hissing greeted the pronouncements of more than one national leader, up to and including President Hoover. Throughout the Great Depression, *Variety* reporter Tom Waller, the trade paper's man at the Embassy Newsreel Theatre in New York, heard 'a riot of catcalls and wails which drowned out most of the dialogue' when one or another self-righteous face spoke up for a discredited dogma.[7] One reason the newsreel shied away from politically charged material was because audiences were not shy about responding to it loudly, passionately, and sometimes, violently.

If audience reactions to characters on screen might blur the lines between the decorum of the theatre and the movie house, motion picture attendance was emphatically unlike theatre attendance in one important way. Whereas theatre-goers rushed to meet the opening curtain, movie-goers came and went as they pleased. For approximately the first half-century of film spectatorship, neither exhibitors nor movie-goers were bound by strict starting times for shows. Throughout the 1930s, newspaper advertisements for motion pictures tended to omit scheduling information about the exact time the show began. The venue, the feature presentation and sometimes the short subjects were listed, but unless an unusual event was scheduled, no firm starting time for the programme was indicated. A personal appearance by a featured player might be in boldface type ('**Douglas Fairbanks, Jr. at 8.00 p.m. sharp**'), but punctuality was ordinarily not a spectatorial virtue. Typically, movie-goers called the management to inquire about starting times and the manager personally replied. ('The cartoon starts at 7.50 p.m. and *Grand Hotel* begins at 8.15'.) On arrival, patrons might loiter outside the theatre or in the lobby until informed that the main attraction was to begin by an announcement from the manager or a placard in the box office window.[8] However, 'hard ticket' screenings (that is, tickets indicating assigned seating) and shows at first-run theatres (where going out for the evening meant dressing up) were more formal and regimented. Ushers cleared patrons out of theatres after each programme and movie-goers waited in the lobby before the next screening began.

If sound synchronisation meant that motion picture exhibition could run like clockwork, the audiences still did not. The compulsion for seeing a motion picture from beginning to end, on time and uninterrupted, was a gradual evolution in motion picture spectatorship, a learned behaviour that is a legacy of the strict screening times of the post-classic era, itself a by-product of the precision timing of radio and television scheduling. Today's 'fill and spill' policies of multiplex mall exhibition ('move 'em in, move 'em out') would in the 1930s have been a breach of accepted decorum and customer relations.

With starting times ever-changing and unpublicised, movies were a sort of moveable feast or a pick-and-choose buffet. Spectators came and went from the theatre in mid-programme, wandering in at any time during the show, even midway or three-quarters of the way into the feature presentation, watching the remainder of the programme, and then completing the cycle by staying until the point of entry. On recognition of the familiar scene ('this is where we came in'), they might then leave or watch the rest of the programme a second time.

Some directors fretted that such casual habits of attendance insulted their creative efforts. Mid-entry movie-going was 'not only a strain on the audiences, but it is also uncomplimentary to the producers and artists', complained Cecil B. DeMille in 1934. 'Energy and talent is expended in the build up of situations and characters toward a climax. The entire object of each motion picture is to hold interest through cumulative effect.' DeMille capped his objections with a tasteful analogy. 'Indigestion is bound to follow if the public ate its meals in the same manner [as it went to movies], starting out with the dessert, coffee, and cheese, and then progressing to the oysters before topping it all off with the roast beef or steak.'[9]

Yet despite efforts by theatre managers and complaints from film-makers, audiences remained determinedly non-linear. 'The majority of the patrons do not desire to be in the theatre on the starting times, but seem to come in during the program', a perplexed usher reported in 1934. 'Many times you will tell persons that the feature will be over in five or ten minutes and that they can rest in a comfortable lounge for that short time, but most of the patrons will pass you up as if you had never mentioned this fact.'[10] Directors and exhibitors might have taken solace from the fact that movie-goers found the pleasures of the screen too irresistible to be deferred.

For audiences throughout the 1930s, the critical time to watch out for was the moment when theatre admissions switched over from matinée to evening prices. Unlike the starting time of the feature itself, matinee and evening starting times, printed in newspapers and handbills, were avidly noted. Frugal movie-goers purchased their tickets moments before 5.00 p.m. at cheaper matinée rates and sat through the end of the last matinee programme before catching the complete evening bill, then leaving where they came in. During the Depression, for the first and last time in motion picture history, lower matinée prices and hordes of unemployed men with time on their hands skewed the prime hours of motion picture attendance from evening to afternoon in some locales. One day in 1932 the Washington Heights Theatre in New York took in $225 in the afternoon and a mere $37 at night.[11]

The savings were worth the time. Ticket prices at regular admission theatres ranged from 10 cents to 75 cents, with a 1932 survey calculating the nationwide average at 18 cents.[12] However, theatre owners slashed prices repeatedly as the Depression wore on. In 1933, most first-run metropolitan theatres had lowered minimum and maximum scales from 30–65 cents to 25–50 cents. Further down the line, frantic exhibitors were 'running on a dime' or returning to the prices of the nickelodeon era with 'nickel matinees'.[13]

These diminishing expectations were reflected in the decline of the architecture housing the motion picture screen and the décor surrounding it. No less than the studios, the great movie palaces constructed in the boom times of the 1920s fell victim in the early 1930s to a combination of sound technology and an unsound economy. Why pay to sit in a plush, 5000-seat venue when a full orchestra played on the sound system of any small-town theatre? Hard times forced many moviegoers to surrender the romance of a night in the city, a better theatrical experience and first look at first-run features. The expense of going out to an elaborate first-run house and paying 'top dollar' (or even 75 cents) for a new feature and a stage show was an indulgence no longer affordable. Better to wait two months and catch the feature at a second-run neighbourhood theatre ('now playing at popular prices at a theater near you!').[14] In 1932, MPPDA counsel Charles C. Pettijohn made a virtue out of necessity when he boasted that 'the humblest theater in the land can show the same production with the same 40 piece symphony orchestra accompaniment that is shown at the Roxy Theater in New York'.[15] MGM's Fred Quimby agreed: 'Ordinary, and in many instances, unattractive theatres presenting outstanding programs are doing a successful business, while beautiful theatre palaces with elaborate surroundings, but presenting weak shows, are starving'.[16] The big theatres that survived did so by lowering prices and changing features more regularly: that is, by becoming more like the neighbourhood theatres.

On 27 December 1932, the opening of Radio City at Rockefeller Centre in New York beckoned to revive the days of the glorious motion picture palace. Though financed by the Rockefellers, Radio City was the brainchild of the legendary show-man and theatre manager Samuel L. Rothafel, who as 'Roxy' saw his name in lights more often than any Hollywood star. Roxy conceived Radio City as a Depression-busting 'cathedral of the motion picture', a monument to faith in the future with its foundation in the past. The huge complex housed two separate venues, the 6200-seat Music Hall, earmarked for elaborate stage entertainment, and the 3700-seat RKO Roxy, designed for prestigious 'A' feature films. Ornate and exorbitant, Radio City was a throwback to boom times and 1920s excess. Adopting the plush-est of exhibition practices, the opening night programme at the RKO Roxy con-sisted of an overture by the house orchestra, an elaborate stage tableaux, a newsreel chosen specially by the Roxy management, a live musical number, a per-formance by the Roxy Ballet Corps, a cartoon, two musical vaudeville acts and finally the featured film attraction, RKO's *The Animal Kingdom* (1932).[17]

The première was grand, glamorous, and disastrous, an occasion that put Roxy in the hospital with a nervous breakdown. Quickly shifting exhibition tactics, both venues scaled down the big variety shows for stage and screen shows at popular prices.[18] Samuel Goldwyn, who epitomised classy productions but never extravagant spending, refused to mourn the passing of the palaces. 'Those theatres throughout the country which were built as monuments in memory of somebody or other must be closed down', he asserted in a not so oblique swipe at Roxy. 'They're not good for talkers anyway – not intimate enough.'[19] Fortunately for Roxy, the man and the venue, *King Kong* (1933) came to New York and helped res-cue the palace from insolvency.

Prior to 1929, the boom in theatre construction had persuaded many exhibitors to spend money on deluxe interior designs for their theatres. It also persuaded them to adopt another totem of upscale privilege, an all-white attendance policy. In the Deep South, of course, segregated movie houses were mandated by law and validated by custom. In the North and elsewhere, however, admission policies for African-Americans varied from region to region, and sometimes from house to house. Though one common practice was to relegate them to 'Jim Crow roosts' in balconies, African-American movie-goers were increasingly pushed out into the separate and unequal 'race houses' during the flush times of the 1920s. By the early 1930s, however, those self-same theatre owners could no longer afford to be so particular about whom they sold tickets to. *Variety* explained how, with merce-nary egalitarianism, showmen 'anxious for the extra revenue from the dusky sec-tion of America's melting pot' now wanted back the 'extra shekels' from an audience they had earlier scorned. Seeing a profit margin in marginal integration, 'those that have balconies are dusting 'em off and them that hasn't are turning to midnight matinees, giving the cottongrabbers the whole house'.[20]

As the venues became less ornate, and the cinematic experience less theatrical, another kind of consumer consumption emerged: the concession business. Although the well-stocked concession stand brimming with candy, popcorn, sodas and junk food blossomed only in the post-war era, low maintenance gum and candy machines first became widespread in the early 1930s. Still, carpeted floors and lush upholstery made management leery of permitting sticky food and liquid refreshments into theatre interiors. The lingering ambience of live theatre surrounding motion picture exhibition also discouraged eating in public space: one does not eat in front of other people. 'A man goes to the [motion picture] theater to see a show', *Variety* wrote in 1931. 'If he wants a cup of coffee or a sandwich, he seeks the nearest drug store.'[21]

However, another kind of oral fixation was brazenly satisfied in many theatres. In their long march to cultural saturation, cigarettes consolidated the social gains of the 1920s and conquered new territory in the 1930s. In 1933, Radio City Music Hall and the RKO Roxy made an official policy of what was already unofficial in many venues by permitting smoking in the mezzanines and balconies. Seizing the opening, the *United States Tobacco Journal* urged cigarette sellers to 'act jointly in forcing upon operators of competitive New York houses recognition of the Roxy's aggressive policy' and to 'take similar action in every community throughout the country'.[22] Tobacco companies and exhibitors also cooperated for mutual advantage by giving away free cigarettes to movie-goers before shows. In accord with cultural norms and lax fire code enforcement, the nicotine-stained atmosphere on the Hollywood screen was inhaled for real in the off-screen space of most theatres.[23]

In fact, ventilation was becoming a crucial component of motion picture exhibition. During the Depression, air conditioning was one of the few reliably cost-efficient investments in theatre refurbishment. Although some motion picture theatres had installed air-cooling systems as early as 1922, true air conditioning was still limited to luxury theatres in the early 1930s, only gradually moving into the small neighbourhood venues as the decade went on. For theatres cooled only by aerial fans, attendance fell off markedly in the summer months. With few homes and almost no workplaces equipped with air-conditioning, the climate-controlled motion picture theatre sold the interior temperatures as zealously as the show. 'Come Inside – Where It's Cool', sighed icicle-covered lettering on marquees, in type sizes larger than the film title. In 1934, when John Dillinger exited the air-conditioned comfort of the Biograph Theatre to meet his death on the streets of Chicago, he had walked in to seek relief from a sweltering summer night.

Motion picture attendance was also influenced by factors unique to the era and long since forgotten. Local outbreaks of infantile paralysis kept mothers and children away from the movies. Every spring, too, box-office revenues fell off sharply during Lent when Catholic mendicants gave up, or tried to give up, the pleasures of Hollywood. What exhibitors dubbed the 'Lenten slump' was a yearly reminder of the impact of Catholics on the box office. On the other hand, theatre attendance might be too devoted and long-staying. Since neighbourhood theatre owners tended not to clear out the house after each programme, one featured attraction of the motion picture theatre during the Depression was shelter. For 15 cents, an afternoon of climate-controlled comfort, a cosy seat and big-screen entertainment was a bargain.

Selected Short Subjects: The Perfection of the Balanced Programme

With *The Birth of a Nation* (1915), the flagship product of the American motion picture industry became the narrative feature film, the 'A' picture which today remains Hollywood's public face. Yet just as motion pictures first appeared as one item on a play-list of varied theatrical acts, the 'A' feature never stood alone. It served as the main attraction in what was termed 'the balanced programme' (or 'the diversified bill' or 'the staple programme') that comprised the format for motion picture entertainment throughout the classic Hollywood era.

The wraparound material for the 'A' picture was the short subject, a one- or two-reel film ranging anywhere from five to twenty-five minutes in length, the subject matter of which included, but was never limited to, travel, sports, history, musical presentations, singalongs, vaudeville performances, dance acts, magic shows, personality portraits, nature studies, fashion parades, Technicolor novelties, serialised adventure, newsreel specials and animated cartoons. Two-thirds of the shorts fell readily into the category of comedy and the balance of the rest (travelogues, sports, beauty pageants and the like) contained comic elements in wisecracking commentary, zany stunts and trick photography. So prolific was short-subject production that in 1931 the Academy of Motion Picture Arts and Sciences could give only the roughest of estimates for yearly output, somewhere between 1,000 to 1,500 shorts per year, excluding the five separate twice-weekly newsreels.[24]

Though collections of shorts had either comprised or accompanied 'an evening's entertainment' since the silent era, the Depression caused exhibitors to pay closer attention to a balanced and consistent programme. 'In the past, the feature buy has received the exhibitors' whole consideration, with little or practically no thought about the importance of the type or quality of the short features to be used in completing the program', declared Fred Quimby, general manager of MGM's short division in 1932. 'This may have worked during boom days, but right now there is very little booming.'[25] Even the big downtown houses, formerly insensitive to short subjects, began to attend carefully to the balanced programme. Informal reports from exhibitors indicated that some shorts 'were drawing more paying patrons than the features'.[26] The new element of sound was credited with giving the shorts added appeal. 'The difference between the old silent shorts and the present-day talking shorts is almost like night and day', showman Charles E. Lewis declared. 'Previous to the sound era, shorts were better known as program fillers. Today, they are granted the more appropriate title of program builders.'[27]

The incessant metaphor used to describe the function of short subjects in the balanced programme was culinary. If the featured attraction was the main course, the selected shorts were side dishes, appetisers, desserts or cocktails prepared to supplement the 'A' feature and make it go down easier. The comedy short is 'the appetizer that whets the taste for the entree of the film menu, or the tasty dessert which tops off the entertainment feast', enthused Lew Lipton, head of RKO–Pathé's comedy unit. 'Sitting through two feature pictures, even good ones, is like eating a heavy meal comprised entirely of meat. Balance is just as important in entertainment fare as it is in food.'[28] The short-subject specialists at Educational

VARIETY KEEPS EVERYBODY HAPPY

WHEN YOU DRAG THE WHOLE FAMILY
IN WITH A "BARGAIN OFFER". . .

AND HALF OF THEM GO TO SLEEP. .
THEY CAN'T CONSIDER THAT A "GOOD BUY"

BUT A GOOD VARIETY PROGRAM
PROMISES AMUSEMENT FOR ALL . .

AND KEEPS ITS PROMISE . .
MAKING EVERYBODY HAPPY. .

You're not in a "one sale" business. You have to keep your customers coming back if you want to succeed. And the way to do that is to keep everybody happy . . . . with a good balanced show . . . . one fine Feature . . . . and plenty of variety . . . . with selections from *Educational Pictures'* great short feature program. Try it out through May and watch it click . . . . the public demands comedy and variety, with quality . . . . and *Educational Pictures* satisfy that demand.

Advertisement in exhibitor's trade journal, 1930s.

Pictures (company motto: 'the spice of the program') drew voraciously on dietary analogies. 'Even the cheapest hash-house knows better than to list "Monday: Steak. Tuesday: Hash. Wednesday: Pork Chops"', read advertisements. 'Whether folks want dinner or entertainment, they want a complete and balanced menu – and they want every dish appetizing.'

As the head cook, the individual theatre manager exercised a good deal of personal judgement over the composition and arrangement of the balanced programme. Depending on whether a venue was urban or rural, first- or third-run, exhibitors built a programme suited to local tastes and idiosyncrasies. With films no longer measured by the number of reels, the rough estimate from the silent era, but now timed down to the second, exhibitors could synchronise their programmes for quick turnaround and additional screenings, adding and subtracting short subjects depending on the running time of the feature and the day-to-day reaction of movie-goers.

To help the selection process, exhibitors in large metropolitan houses handed out questionnaires to gauge audience preferences, while small-town theatre managers canvassed customer opinion in the lobby after the show. In 1934, an extensive survey by the *Film Daily* ranked audience preferences in short-subject fare along the following lines:

1. animated cartoons
2. newsreels
3. comedy shorts
4. travelogues.[29]

Calibrating the selection and sequencing of shorts to the tastes of his special clientele, one theatre manager constructed a balanced programme comprised of the following play-list, with the approximate running time of each item:

1. Fox Movietone Newsreel (eight minutes)
2. Universal Newspaper Newsreel (eight minutes)
3. cartoon (seven minutes)
4. live musical interlude on organ (five minutes)
5. comedy short (ten minutes)
6. feature presentation (70–90 minutes)
7. comedy short (ten minutes)
8. trailers (ten minutes)

– a motion picture diet with seven varied side dishes, one main course, and a sit-down time of roughly two hours.[30] Both the placement of the newsreels at the top of the bill and their back-to-back programming was atypical, but exhibitors often varied the sequencing or experimented with different items, depending on the peculiar tastes of the community. Usually, the newsreel played further 'down on the bill' and immediately preceded the feature, indicating its privileged status as information. Within the balanced programme, however, there existed a variety of options and exhibitor strategies.[31]

Juggling the short and feature material called for agile sleight of hand. For 'exclusive run' theatres playing a single popular feature for weeks (the so-called grind houses), a judicious selection of new shorts might lure repeat viewers to the main feature. For non-exclusive theatres, where the turnover of films was rapid, the multiplication of shorts was often large. Depending on product flow and profitability, a small-town theatre changed features two or three times a week, with a yearly turnover of between 100 and 150 feature films.[32]

Resembling the pacing of a five or six-act vaudeville bill, the arc of the balanced programme was monitored to avoid clashes between segments, mixing and matching the line-up of supportive shorts and 'A' feature anchor as subject matter dictated. Downbeat features required lightweight shorts, effervescent features warranted the heft of more solid stuff. When *An American Tragedy* (1931) lived up to its title all too well, exhibitors were well advised to serve up more palatable morsels with the hard-to-swallow main attraction. 'It is cold, dreary entertain-

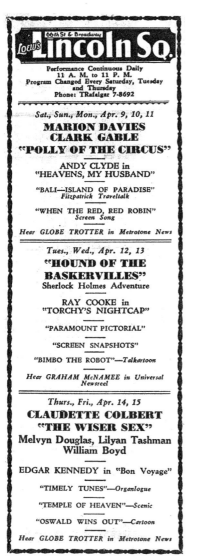

Motion Picture Herald, *April 1932.*

ment, especially these days when laughs are so essential. Not a single giggle in the entire picture ... so surround it with "extra good" shorts full of plenty of hearty laughs', counselled *Motion Picture Herald*. Conversely, because *A Connecticut Yankee* (1931) was a 'great comedy', the wise programmer should 'play dramatic shorts and musicals on the bill to balance the heavy laugh feature'.[33]

Like the rationale for the Production Code, the strategy for balancing the bill presumed a motion picture audience made up of the great family of man, a mass audience of all ages, both genders and indeterminate class. Though every item on the bill should possess broad crossover appeal, individual segments targeted an ideal demographic slice of the movie-going public. Serious Dad kept abreast of world affairs in the newsreels, Mom and Sis checked out the latest make-up tips in biweekly Technicolor shorts like *Beauty Secrets from Hollywood* (1931), and the kids sat still for the cartoons. But each item on the bill also needed to be tolerably entertaining to the non-targeted member too. When Mom and Sis checked out the fashions, Dad and Junior checked out the girls.

Though *Variety* claimed in 1931 that children from ages five to sixteen comprised a mere 8 per cent of film audiences, they were valued by exhibitors as 'hidden persuaders' in the family's movie-going decisions.[34] Having deserted the movies with the coming of sound – too much talk, not enough action – the children's trade came back gradually, coaxed with animation, serial adventure and madcap physical (as opposed to wisecracking verbal) comedy shorts.[35] Their attention spans and material preferences were considered an appropriate match for the running times and subject matter of the shorts. The popularity of Saturday afternoon 'kiddie matinees', made up entirely of comedy shorts, cartoons and serials, confirms the link between the short subject and the juvenile audience. 'We cannot make comedies that the children frown upon while the grown ups laugh', declared Universal producer Stanley Bergerman in 1931. 'That has been one of the great evils of the talking picture, and we must see that there are no more long-faced kids curled up in theatre chairs while some sophisticated two-reeler or other is being projected in front of their fathers and mothers.'[36] Thus Educational Pictures promised 'comedies, cartoons, and novelties [that] bring in the children as well as the adults, send them home happy, and bring them back for more'. Taking a pedagogical cue from his Jesuit educators, *Motion Picture Herald* publisher Martin Quigley urged that the ritual of movie-going be inculcated early in the young. 'Neglecting the child audience means, in a very definite sense, endangering the future of the business, because the child patron of today is the adult patron of tomorrow, provided a love of pictures is instilled at an early age.'[37]

All the major studios produced shorts to limit overhead costs, to keep the production machine greased and to occupy salaried employees. MGM's slate for the 1931–2 season gives a fair sampling of the range of short subject matter and the resources devoted to their production and distribution:

8 Pitts and Todd Comedies (2 reels)
6 Dogville Comedies (2 reels)
8 Boy Friend Comedies (2 reels)
8 Our Gang Comedies (2 reels)
8 Charley Chase Comedies (2 reels)
8 Laurel and Hardy Comedies (2 reels)
4 Harry Lauder Comedies (1 reel)
13 Fitzpatrick Travelogues (1 reel)
12 Flip the Frog Cartoons (1 reel)
12 Sport Champions (1 reel)
6 Fisherman's Paradise (1 reel)

Weighted heavily towards comedy, the MGM line-up offers a full catalogue of short-subject staples (cartoons, sports and travel), for a product run of 93 items in all, not counting the 104 issues per year of the Hearst Movietone newsreel, distributed through MGM. Theoretically, the short subject also served as a proving ground for talent being groomed for better-paid and higher-status work in feature films. Yet both behind and in front of the camera, short-subject workers tended to get the short end of a motion picture career, pigeonholed as second-raters never to get a shot at the big time. Appropriately, child stars graduated more easily from the diminutive shorts to the adult 'A' feature, as if growing up from a ten-minute to a ninety-minute screen format. Shirley Temple was first schooled in Educational's *Baby Burlesks* shorts and Jackie Cooper in Hal Roach's *Our Gang* comedies.

One short subject that was incorporated for a time in the balanced programme was the paid advertisement in the guise of entertainment. In 1930–1, under pressure to generate income and cut production costs, the studios entered into agreements with corporate entities to distribute what today might be termed 'infomercials' filmed advertisements for corporations and brand-name products with the production values and style of short subjects. They were sent out to theatres through the normal lines of distribution and inserted unannounced into the motion picture programme. Movie-goers rebelled. Patrons who paid money for tickets vehemently opposed sitting through screen advertisements (radio advertisements were tolerable because radio entertainment was considered free). 'Screen advertising may be a source of revenue to the theatre – but it is a dangerous one', Fox warned its house managers. 'Every dollar that it earns is but an

Motion Picture Herald, *October 1932.*

advance drain on future income of your house' because annoyed patrons 'wisely choose to voice their disapproval by staying away from your theatre'. Paramount and Warner Bros joined Fox in a blanket policy forbidding the practice. 'Do away with whatever screen advertising you are now using, and turn down any that may appear in the future', Fox ordered in 1931.[38]

So severe was the resentment to 'unpopular and cheapening' screen advertising that even glimpses of authentic brand-name products in entertainments were perceived as surreptitious advertising. When an identifiable brand of insecticide was spotted in a Hal Roach short, the producer indignantly denied commercial subvention. 'I have never accepted one cent from an advertising company for any advertising that ever appeared in a Hal Roach comedy', he declared.[39] In 1931, fearful of running afoul of the Federal Trade Commission, the major studios agreed not to plug products in their entertainment films.[40] The antipathy to brand names abetted the monopolistic ubiquity of the generic 'Acme Company' as the exclusive supplier of consumer items to the kitchens and grocery stores of Hollywood cinema, a conceit later satirised explosively in the malfunctioning arsenal of Wile E. Coyote in Chuck Jones's *Road Runner* cartoons.

For many exhibitors, the debate over appropriate short-subject material was academic. Studio-owned theatres played the studio-produced shorts, period. Likewise, since the practice of block booking extended to the shorts, exhibitors who coveted the new MGM feature with Garbo or Gable booked the MGM slate of accompanying shorts, whether they wanted them or not. The truly lame short subjects would be left in film cans, unopened and unplayed, written off as the price of doing business with a major studio.

Calculating the commercial appeal of shorts was difficult because, with the exception of children's matinées and the few speciality theatres devoted exclusively to short subjects, they never played independently on the bill. Trade estimates placed the total market for short subjects at $30–$40 million a year.[41] Typically, however, exhibitors classified shorts as 'clinchers' – that is, if a potential moviegoer called the box office to inquire about the main attraction and seemed lukewarm when told the title, the tactical mention of a popular short closed the sale.

Shorts served as the main line of defence against a programming practice that the studios vehemently opposed: the double bill. Seen as tarnishing the lustre of the main feature, the double bill squeezed profit margins and, more ominously, left openings for independent productions and Poverty Row studios to muscle in on the territory of the majors. The big studios simply couldn't supply enough movies for twin bills; they needed to control the distribution pipeline to maintain the value of the product and the exclusivity of the supply. Conversely, Poverty Row productions of the sort typified by Monogram Pictures drew best when linked to a major studio feature film.

To heighten the profile of shorts as a counterbalance to the double bill, screen teasers, lobby space and newspaper ads accentuated their attraction and denigrated the penny-wise, pound-foolish practice of twin-feature movie-going. An aggressive promotional campaign for short subjects was official policy throughout the Fox chain, where each theatre manager was told 'to possess an intimate knowledge of certain short subjects of special value to his theater or neighborhood and arrange his displays and advertising accordingly'.[42] 'Double-featuritis is doomed!', proclaimed Educational Pictures. 'Balanced programs are the order of the day. Wide awake exhibitors now show ONE feature – and balance the programs perfectly with short subjects from Educational's great series of one and two reelers.' In 1931, MGM led the movement to defeat the double-bill 'evil' by inserting a clause into exhibition contracts forbidding the double-featuring of any MGM picture.[43] Despite the coercive efforts by the majors, however, double bills proliferated during the Depression in second- and third-tier theatres that kept solvent, barely, with the exhibition equivalent of two-for-one sales.

Although sound technology provided greater expressive range to all kinds of shorts, the animated cartoon was the main beneficiary. In demonstrating the allure of sound on film, Walt Disney's *Steamboat Willie* (1928), the first synchronised cartoon, was nearly as powerful a shock wave as *The Jazz Singer* (1927). In surveys, some patrons dutifully designated the newsreels as their favourite shorts, but the animated cartoon ranked as the universal favourite with young and old, male and female. 'Animated cartoons are the most popular subjects on the screen', the manager of Trans Lux's Short Subject Theatre stated in 1932. 'The synchronization is a never ending wonder to patrons who marvel at the exact timing of the action with the talk and sound.'[44] Referring to the attractions of one of the most fetching of the animated stars, a colleague agreed: 'Betty Boop stands number one with our patrons over all others'.[45]

A privileged site for subversive shenanigans, cartoons and shorts often came in below the radar of official notice.[46] The cartoonish dimensions of the animated world made a biting remark or a nasty gesture less incendiary. Even censors felt ridiculous bowdlerising cartoons. When they did – as when Ohio censors banned a Mickey Mouse cartoon because it showed a cow reading Elinor Glynn's scandalous novel, *Three Weeks* – they were objects of ridicule.[47] Under less scrutiny than feature-length, straight-faced cinema, the cartoon content is often cheekier, sexier and nastier than the feature film, particularly during the freewheeling pre-Code era from 1930 to 1934.

For sheer animated eroticism, Max Fleischer's Betty Boop reigned supreme as a flesh and blood temptress. Shimmying her way through twelve episodes a year, she

IT SOUNDS LIKE A BARGAIN ONCE...BUT..

FIRST TIME
TWO LONG FEATURES

A DOUBLE FEATURE PROGRAM SOUNDS
LIKE A BARGAIN. . . THE FIRST TIME

3 MONTHS LATER
TWO LONG FEATURES

BUT IT'S QUALITY, NOT QUANTITY THAT COUNTS,
AND THE DOUBLE BILL SOON BECOMES TIRESOME

TODAY
BIG FEATURE
COMEDY NEWSREEL NOVELTIES

THE DIVERSIFIED, BALANCED PROGRAM
APPEALS TO EVERYONE . . . . . .

3 MONTHS LATER
BIG FEATURE
COMEDY NEWSREEL NOVELTIES

AND ATTRACTS A CROWD THAT HAS
A NORMAL AND STEADY GROWTH

You can't keep up interest in bargain sales if you try to hold one every day. The only program that will build business *consistently* is the variety-quality program . . one good feature and a balanced show of such quality short subjects as *Educational Pictures* bring you week in and week out . . **Mack Sennett** **Comedies, Torchy Comedies, Ideal Comedies, Terry-toons,** Mack Sennett's Cannibals of the Deep . . these and many other short features that have proven their worth on the screen and at the box-office.

Advertisement in exhibitor's trade journal, 1930s.

was a 1920s throwback, the last of the good-time party girls to became a star in the early 1930s. Every four weeks, she repelled and reciprocated the sexual overtures of pirates, ghosts, employers, animals and the co-stars she soon supplanted, Bimbo and Koko. 'Please don't take my boop-oop-e-doop away', she pleads musically to a sexually rapacious boss.

The most culturally resonant – and politically charged – cartoon of the early 1930s came from the unlikely drawing boards of the Walt Disney studio. First screened at Radio City Music Hall during the week of 25 May 1933, *The Three Little Pigs*, a Walt Disney Silly Symphony, built slowly in popularity to became a national sensation. Playing multiple dates and return engagements throughout summer and into fall 1933, it was probably the most widely seen cartoon of the 1930s.[48] A record 350 prints circulated constantly and exhibitors ballyhooed the cartoon with more fervour than the accompanying feature. 'Standing room only' crowds comprised mainly of adults with children 'brought just to see the cute short subject' flocked to theatres. The theme song 'Who's Afraid of the Big, Bad Wolf?' permeated the air via radio, phonographs and street-corner singalongs.[49] The animated fable took hold as a double-edged metaphor: the fear of life being blown away by the cold winds of the Great Depression and the hope that, with sound reconstruction policies and honest statecraft, the wolf could be kept outside the door.

In 1934, animator U. B. Iwerks argued that animated cartoons were 'as necessary to any well-balanced program as the feature itself'. Though not exactly a disinterested observer, Iwerks asserted that 'since their inception, the animated cartoons have done more to promote healthy box office receipts than any other type of screen fare.'[50] An exceptional cartoon attraction might outshine the top of the bill. Marvelling over the protracted appeal of *The Three Little Pigs*, the *Hollywood Reporter* asserted: 'There is not a feature attraction today that will outdraw that cartoon masterpiece and there are few multiple-reel attractions that will outdraw ANY Disney picture.'[51] Disney's *The Big Bad Wolf* (1934), the eagerly anticipated follow-up to *The Three Little Pigs*, deserved dominant marquee space, feature notwithstanding. 'Give it top billing', *Motion Picture Herald* urged exhibitors; 'It is worth it'.[52] The platonic ideal for the running time of a cartoon was 600 feet of film, or about seven minutes. 'It is my firm belief that the brevity in cartoons is what has kept them alive on the screen today', opined Leon Schlesinger, who decreed that the length of the average cartoon be exactly 600 feet and 'during that 600 feet enough action takes place which would ordinarily be sufficient for the usual two-reel comedy'.[53]

Besides further animating the cartoons, sound recording inspired one of the most popular conceits for the short subject: the talking animal as featured player. Waddling through miniature sets and decked out in human clothing, creatures great and small were filmed in dramatic situations with human voices dubbing in badly synched, pun-laden wisecracks. Billed not as 'talkies' but as 'barkies', sold to exhibitors as the 'bow-wow-wow in your program', the Dogville Comedies, a series of MGM shorts initiated in 1930, became instant hits due to the visual/verbal incongruity of dogs walking and talking their way through human scenarios. No fewer than two competing ensembles of trained simians practiced the art of human impersonation, with Educational's Tiffany Chimps dressed in prison stripes for *The Little Big House* (1930) and Columbia's Monkey Shine mimics in blackface for *The Jazzbo Singer* (1932). Both troupes performed in Spanish and French versions for overseas distribution. The casting call for animal talent extended to things with feathers in *A Fowl Affair* (1931), a novelty short made up of a cast of articulate chickens, ducks and turkeys.

The shorts not only served as side dishes supplementing the main feature: they fed off them. To shift and mix metaphors: like pilot fish in the wake of the 'A' feature leviathan, the shorts devoured material from the main part of the bill. Almost as if resentful that the 'A' feature should get the lion's share of attention, the choice marquee space and the biggest budgets, the subaltern material tweaked and mocked its betters. Virtually every 'A' feature that captured the public's attention got some kind of come-uppance in the shorts in the form of animated satires, animal parodies, slapstick re-enactments and sundry desecrations of genre. MGM's *Trader Horn* (1930), for instance, inspired *Trader Hound* (1930), a cartoon version featuring a Great White (Dog) Hunter, and *Trader Ginzberg* (1931), a live action takeoff in which a zealous Jewish radio salesman pursues his clients into the African jungle to make the sale. Perhaps the weirdest example of the parodic impulse was Educational Pictures' *Baby Burlesks*, a short subject produced between 1931–2. The series featured toddlers in nappies in satiric send-ups of popular film genres, the attraction being the darling cuteness of near babies acting as gangsters and molls, starlets and directors. Since parody demands an intimate acquaintance with the tropes of the original, the satiric shorts confirm the acquisition of a shared motion picture background among the American public. The short relied not only on general knowledge of a popular genre, but a detailed familiarity with the specific source of inspiration. Again and again, the parodic short subjects replay dialogue exchanges and whole scenes with precise fidelity to the original. The Dogville Comedies mocked not just a genre, or a sequence, but duplicated, shot for shot, line for line, the filmic grammar of the bipedal source material. For example, the one must-see film of 1930 was Lewis Milestone's *All Quiet on the Western Front*. By January 1931, MGM had concocted its third Dogville Comedy, *So Quiet on the Canine Front*, a shaggy-dog deconstruction of the anti-war epic which also incorporates visual and generic elements from deep background Great War films such as *The Big Parade* (1925) and *What Price Glory?* (1928). Its opening scene is a detailed re-enactment of the opening scene of the (human) *All Quiet*, in which the German schoolboys leap to the defence of the Fatherland at the urging of their high-school teacher. With the dogs positioned to sit upright at school desks, the (canine) *All Quiet* replays Milestone's dynamic montage of fresh-faced puppies volunteering for service as cannon fodder. Later, in No Man's Land with the dogs of war, the Huns are played by dachshunds.

Elocution Lessons

If the transition to sound was a technological and economic revolution for the studios, it was an aesthetic and experiential challenge for movie-goers. Attending to silent cinema, the modern spectator feels an absence; the original spectator felt only wholeness. In memoirs and interviews, silent film movie-goers recollect a rapture of almost religious dimensions before the motion picture screen. Being 'spellbound in darkness' meant a mystical union of image and spectator, the intensity of total immersion in narrative and selfless surrender to emotion: sobbing at melodrama, gasping at thrills, hissing at villains and rolling in the aisles in spasms of laughter. It was a world spectators did not eavesdrop in on but glimpsed from afar, the distance enhancing the sense of wonder and desire for involvement.

The larger-than-life stature of the stars and the transcendent quality of silent-era spectatorship is evoked by the celestial vocabulary invented to describe it, such coinages as 'stars', 'goddesses' and 'movie palaces'. To the silent screen aficionado, actors were beatific visions, movies a firmament unto themselves. Film historian James Card recalled how he and his group of stubborn cineastes held out for years against the dialogue picture before finally capitulating in 1930 to *All Quiet on the*

Western Front. Looking back in 1949, film critic James Agee counted himself fortunate to be among 'those happy atavists who remember silent comedy' and claimed that 'the only thing wrong with screen comedy today is that it takes place on a screen that talks'.[54] Against the halcyon age of star worship and screen raptures, the entry of sound heralds a fall from grace. Spectators are cast out of a prelapsarian landscape into an unbidden encounter with the photographic reproduction and audiographic record of reality.

Contrary to popular belief, it was not Al Jolson's prophetic ad lib ('You ain't heard nothin' yet!') that tolled the death knell for the silent screen, nor the isolated musical sequences and spoken utterances. It was the stark juxtaposition of the sound world against the silent world, the placement of the alternative diegetic universes side by side, that forever smothered the old art. In *The Jazz Singer*, Broadway star Jack Robin (Jolson) pauses to coo a few affectionate lines to his mother before resuming 'Blue Skies' at the piano. Robin's disapproving father barges in and shouts 'STOP!' Extinguishing the magic of sound, the word plunges the diegesis back to silence, linking the old-world patriarch with the now outmoded medium. For the first time, spectators experienced silent film as the absence of synchronous sound and what was once self-sufficient would henceforth be lacking.[55]

Although by the early 1930s talk was no longer a magical incantation, the grammar of motion picture sound was still being invented and learned. For example, the technique of voice-over narration was not introduced formally until 1933, and six years after the birth of the talkies, spectators still required blatant visual cues to comprehend the linkage between voice-over and image. Although the true première of the flashback voiceover is probably lost in the archives (*The Widow from Chicago* (1930) cuts to a flashback with voice-over narration in typical Warner Bros style, no fuss and no bother), the technique was introduced as 'narratage' by Fox in *The Power and the Glory* (1933), directed by William K. Howard from a screenplay by Preston Sturges. The studio's publicity department hyped it as 'the first major experiment in sound dramatics'. According to Sturges, 'it embodied the visual action of the silent picture, the sound of the narrator's voice, and the storytelling economy and the richness of a novel'.[56]

The voice-over narration is cued with a remedial lesson in film grammar. As the narrator Henry (Ralph Morgan) begins to recall his lifelong friendship with Garner (Spencer Tracy), the camera moves in on Henry's face, tracks right, and dissolves into his recollection, a group of boys frolicking in a swimming hole. The three-step series of visual cues makes the logical connection between the disembodied off-screen voice and the images on screen. An alternative visual cue deploys a tinted curtain wiping diagonally down from upper screen right to lower screen left when Henry's voice-over initiates a flashback.

Even so, *The Power and the Glory* befuddled more movie-goers than it impressed. One amateur critic wrote to the *Hollywood Reporter* to offer a 'paid admission perspective' on the narratage innovation. Though 'progressive' movie-goers 'knew that the producer and director were leaving the groove, selling the story of unusual lives in a new way for talkies', he reported that 'some in the audience were not ready for the jar'.[57] Before the medium acquired fluency and its auditors a sharp ear for meaning, Hollywood's tentative stumbles and stutters taxed the patience of spectators. The technical problems in retooling motion picture production and the aesthetic shifts in motion picture form could make movie-going a dissonant and unsettling experience.

Whilst directors and actors were forced to master a new craft and unlearn the old one, theatre owners undertook the sorrowful task of firing loyal house musicians and the costly chore of wiring their venues for sound, and spectators were alternately thrilled and disconcerted by the intimacy of dialogue.[58] Technical troubles bedevilled exhibition as much as production: rewired motion picture theatres were prone to faulty electrical systems and bad acoustics, and theatrical amplification remained primitive and unreliable. Buzzing and humming on the soundtrack, volume levels too loud or too soft, and tinny music and indecipherable conversations gave patrons headaches and had some yearning for the serene days of intertitles. 'Do you want an evening of soothing recreation? Do you want to rest your nerves?' asked a silent film exhibitor in an attempt to counter-programme against the talkies. 'No squawking! No vibrations!' – just the 'perfect music' of a live piano and xylophone.[59]

As silent actors made the transition to sound and the seen became the heard, fans and critics listened carefully to evaluate the timbre and tone of each fresh entry into the realm of the audible. A voice shattered the illusion of private imaginations. As each silent face spoke, auditor–spectators judged them anew, measuring the sound against the visage and their own preconceptions. While Garbo talking was a triumph, and Joan Crawford passed muster, others were less fortunate. Clara Bow expressed the frustration of a generation of silent film stars whose box-office stock had 'dropped faster than Wall Street'.[60] 'The talkies contain no action and no close-ups, and pretty soon they'll have no stars', she grumbled. 'The things are so stilted they kill a star's personality.'[61] 'Dialogue retards tempo', asserted Douglas Fairbanks, the icon of swashbuckling mobility in the silent screen. 'This is the tragic phase of the talkies.'[62]

Not one of the great action stars or silent clowns of comedy's greatest era weathered the transition to sound: after the initial success of *City Lights*, even Chaplin's box-office revenues fell off steeply.[63] The skills of the silent comedians – acrobatics, pantomime, gesture, expression and agility – were visual not verbal. Typical was the unwelcome debut of Harold Lloyd in his first talkie, *Welcome Danger* (1929). 'No gags of tongue and brain can elicit such audience response as has been elicited in the past by Mr. Lloyd's gags of grit and brawn', observed a prophetic reviewer.[64] Supplanting the comedic ballet of the silent clowns were the wisecracks of Mae West, the backtalk byplay of Laurel and Hardy and the cacophony from a quartet of babel, the Marx Brothers.

Silent films recycled for the sound era fared little better than the silent stars. Despite the economic advantages of remaking projects already owned and tested, the box-office verdict on early sound versions of silent scenarios was decidedly 'negative for substantial results'.[65] The sensibility gap between the last decade and the present one was painfully evident in pallid remakes of *Tol'able David* (1921) and *What Price Glory* (1926) in 1930, and *The Squaw Man* (1915) in 1931, the last a work of self-plagiarism by Cecil B. DeMille. With advertisements highlighting the new technology, several classics of the silent era were re-released with synchronised soundtracks: *The Birth of a Nation* (1915) in 1930 (with a special sound prologue featuring a priggish D. W. Griffith chatting with a reverent Walter Houston) and *The Big Parade* (1925) and *Ben-Hur* (1926), both in 1931. ('*Ben-Hur* – at last in sound – the roar of the mobs! – the hoofbeats of the chariot race! – what a difference!') Mangling rather than enhancing the original films, the injection of blaring musical scores and clanging sound effects into beloved silent classics repelled the old fans and failed to attract new customers.

The audible screen rewrote the terms of motion picture spectatorship and recast the experience of movie-going. A poignant bell-wether of how quickly the change occurred, and how radical the sensibility shifted, is a popular series of short subjects released by Paramount in 1932. *Screen Souvenirs* was a compilation of silent era clips accompanied by voice-over wisecracks, a comedy which invited spectators to laugh in ridicule at the films that once held them spellbound in darkness.

Notes

1 The reconstruction of audience responses and behaviour in this section is culled mainly from the pages of the exhibitors' trade journal, *Motion Picture Herald*. Its weekly feature, 'What This Picture Did For Me', in which exhibitors from around the nation commented on box-office returns and in-house reactions to specific films, is an especially rich source of movie-going lore.
2 On silent film exhibition strategies, see Richard Koszarski, *An Evening's Entertainment: The Age of the Silent Feature Picture* (New York: Charles Scribner's and Sons, 1990).
3 See 'Star Names Get No Applause in Short', *Variety*, 20 August 1930, p. 3.
4 'Clara Bow's OK Film Comeback', *Variety*, 15 November 1932, p. 3.
5 'Audiences Cheer Gabriel in NY', *The Hollywood Reporter*, 5 April 1933, p. 1; '*This Day and Age*', *The Hollywood Reporter*, 18 July 1933, p. 3.
6 '*Explorers of the World*', *Motion Picture Herald*, 19 December 1931, p. 49.
7 'Newsreels', *Variety*, 20 December 1932, p. 12.
8 'The End Was Not Yet', *Motion Picture Herald*, 23 January 1932, p. 26.
9 'That Continuous Programming', *Motion Picture Herald*, 19 May 1934, p. 25.
10 'Seeing Film From Start Important', *Motion Picture Herald*, 25 August 1934, p. 57.
11 'N.Y. Grosses Do Flops', *The Hollywood Reporter*, 3 March 1932, pp. 1, 2.
12 James Cunningham, 'Asides and Interludes', *Motion Picture Herald*, 2 January 1932, p. 21.
13 'Admissions Slashed an Average of 25% in Current Move', *Motion Picture Herald*, 28 January 1933, p. 18.
14 See 'Inside Stuff – Pictures', *Variety*, 16 April 1930, p. 31; 'Depresh Public Waits Until Price Is Right; 10c Houses' Competish Socking First Runs, Chains Complain', *Variety*, 5 July 1932, p. 4; and W. R. Wilkerson, 'What is Happening to Downtown Theaters?' *The Hollywood Reporter*, 3 April 1931, pp. 1, 2.
15 'Pettijohn Opposes Exclusive Dating for Class "A" Films', *Motion Picture Herald*, 2 July 1932, p. 36.
16 'MGM Completes Line Up of 89 Short Subjects', *Motion Picture Herald*, 9 July 1932, p. 30.
17 Terry Ramsaye, 'RKO Roxy Opens and Closes, As Music Hall Goes to Film Policy', *Motion Picture Herald*, 7 January 1933, p. 11.
18 Terry Ramsaye, 'Static in Radio City', and 'Music Hall Starts Combination Policy as RKO Roxy Continues', *Motion Picture Herald*, 14 January 1933, p. 25.
19 'Production Costs Not Cut, Must Be Halved, Says Samuel Goldwyn', *Motion Picture Herald*, 25 February 1933, p. 12.
20 'Colored Screen Players in Person for Builder Uppers for Balcony Biz', *Variety*, 28 June 1932, pp. 1, 30.

21 'Inside Stuff – Pictures', *Variety*, 27 October 1931, p. 21.

22 'Cigarette Campaign', *Motion Picture Herald*, 14 January 1933, p. 14.

23 'See Liberal Smoking Policy as Stimulus to Cinema Attendance', *Variety*, 19 January 1931, p. 31; 'Smoking Now General on B'way', *Variety*, 17 January 1933, p. 12.

24 'Great Popularity of Comic Cartoon Shorts', *The Hollywood Reporter*, 6 April 1931, p. 2.

25 'MGM Completes Line Up of 89 Short Subjects', *Motion Picture Herald*, 9 July 1932, p. 30.

26 'Shorts in Big Demand', *The Hollywood Reporter*, 5 February 1931, pp. 1, 2.

27 Charles E. Lewis, 'Program Fillers or Program Builders', *Motion Picture Herald*, 14 March 1931, p. 7.

28 'Shorts Audience Appetizer', *The Hollywood Reporter*, 27 July 1931, p. 15.

29 'Critics Forum', *The Film Daily*, 7 May 1934, p. 1.

30 'Two Newsreels Shown as Unit', *Exhibitors Herald-World*, 10 May 1930, p. 10.

31 'Pick Your Shorts with Care', *Motion Picture Herald*, 23 April 1932, p. 62.

32 Philip Reid, 'An Answer to Samuel Goldwyn', *Motion Picture Herald*, 9 January 1932, p. 12. Complaining about the dearth of quality product, this small-town exhibitor reported showing 156 pictures in 1931, while in 1932 he was only showing them at a rate of 104 for the year.

33 'A Connecticut Yankee', *Motion Picture Herald*, 21 March 1931, p. 39; Charles E. Lewis, 'Passing in Review', *Motion Picture Herald*, 3 October 1931, p. 29.

34 'Children from 5 to 16 Form 8% of America's Film Audiences', *Variety*, 17 November 1931, p. 4.

35 'The talker emphasis on sophisticated dialogue is said to have had an effect on kid patronage throughout the country', noted 'Inside Stuff – Pictures', *Variety*, 4 June 1930, p. 66.

36 'Featurize Your Shorts', *The Hollywood Reporter*, 27 July 1931, p. 7.

37 'Serials Bring the Kids', *Motion Picture Herald*, 28 March 1931, p. 36.

38 'Fox Orders All Ad Reels Out of Circuits', *Motion Picture Herald*, 6 June 1931, p. 19. See also Terry Ramsaye, 'Sponsored Film Does Fadeout with Leading Film Companies', *Motion Picture Herald*, 30 May 1931, p. 9.

39 'Roach Denies Use of Paid Advertising', *Motion Picture Herald*, 16 May 1931, p. 42.

40 'Accused of Dog Ads', *Variety*, 3 November 1931, p. 5.

41 Fred Quimby, 'Don't Waste Short Product', *The Hollywood Reporter*, 27 July 1931, p. 4.

42 'Double Bill Fight to Boost Shorts', *Motion Picture Herald*, 9 May 1931, p. 45.

43 'No MGM Dual Features', *The Hollywood Reporter*, 29 April 1931, pp. 1, 2.

44 Bernie Rybach, 'Animated Cartoons!', *Motion Picture Herald*, 23 April 1932, p. 64. See also 'Wholesale Demand for Cartoon Shorts – Nearly All Cos. Listening', *Variety*, 28 May 1930, p. 13.

45 'What This Picture Did for Me', *Motion Picture Herald*, 25 March 1933, p. 40.

46 'Chicago Censors Now Threaten All Shorts', *Variety*, 12 February 1930, pp. 1, 8.

47 'Those Ohio Censors', *Variety*, 19 November 1930, p. 11.

48 'Top Spot in Shorts is "Silly Symphony"', *Variety*, 8 August 1933, p. 4.

49 'Newsreels', *Variety*, 26 September 1933, p. 12; '3 Little Pigs', *Variety*, 10 October 1933, p. 5.

50 U. B. Iwerks, 'Cartoons Becoming Increasingly Important', *The Film Daily*, 14 May 1934, p. 4.

51 W. R. Wilkerson?, 'Tradeviews', *The Hollywood Reporter*, 18 September 1933, p. 1.

52 'The Big Bad Wolf', *Motion Picture Herald*, 28 April 1934, p. 40.

53 Norman Klein, *Seven Minutes: The Life and Death of the American Animated Cartoon* (New York: Verso, 1993), pp. 87–8.

54 James Agee, 'Comedy's Greatest Era', [1949] reprinted in *Agee On Film, Volume One* (New York: Grossett & Dunlap, 1969), pp. 2, 4.

55 See R. E. Sherwood, 'The Silent Drama', 27 October 1927, reprinted in George C. Pratt, *Spellbound in Darkness: A History of the Silent Film* (Greenwich, CT: New York Graphic Society, Ltd., 1966), pp. 463–4.

56 Preston Sturges, *Preston Sturges* (New York: Simon and Schuster, 1990), p. 272.

57 ' "The Power and the Glory" from Viewpoint of a Fan', *The Hollywood Reporter*, 20 June 1933, p. 3.

58 In both popular and scholarly writing, the early sound era, however defined, is well-travelled territory. One of the best general guidebooks is Scott Eyman, *The Speed of Sound: Hollywood and the Talkie Revolution, 1926–1930* (New York: Simon and Schuster, 1997).

59 ' "No Squawking", He Advertises; And Makes Silent House Pay Big', *Exhibitors Herald-World*, 19 April 1930, p. 41.

60 'Inside Stuff – Pictures', *Variety*, 25 June 1930, p. 126.

61 ' "100% Too Much" Says Clara Bow', *Exhibitors Herald-World*, 21 June 1930, p. 73.

62 'Dialog Must Meet Action, Says Fairbanks', *Motion Picture Herald*, 16 May 1931, p. 23.

63 ' "City Lights" Under Gross Rental Forecast, but Still May Be Record', *Variety*, 8 April 1931, p. 4.

64 '*Welcome Danger*', *Exhibitors Herald-World*, 18 January 1930, p. 41.

65 'Inside Stuff – Pictures', *Variety*, 24 September 1930, p. 56. See also, 'Annual Story Panic at Studios; Floppo Remakes and Play Shortage', *Variety*, 8 April 1931, p. 5.

10 Hillbilly Music and Will Rogers: Small-town Picture Shows in the 1930s

Gregory A. Waller

In his 1928 instructional handbook, *Motion Picture Theater Management*, Harold B. Franklin insists that 'a theater, like a man, is a personality – for better or worse – by itself; and each one defines itself to the locality in its own way'.[1] If this might have been in some measure true in 1928, how true was it several years later, after the conversion to sound had helped to regulate and perhaps standardise the exhibition and hence affect the reception of the movies in the United States? To what extent does it make sense to pay attention to locality and region as relevant factors in the cultural history of American film during the Depression?

The principal representation of American regionalism in the movies is to be found in westerns, particularly in the low-budget variety that were a mainstay Hollywood product during the 1930s. While there are many films set in the mountains of Tennessee, in ante-bellum plantation days, in the bayou or the swamp, the 'Southern' does not exist in the same way that the western does. In his book *Hillbillyland*, J. W. Williamson set out to analyse 'what the movies did to the mountains and what the mountains did to the movies'. His discussion of the Depression focuses on the stereotype of the hillbilly fool, as most influentially found not in the movies, but in *Esquire* magazine cartoons and Al Capp's *L'il Abner*.[2] There's also a take on Hollywood going hillbilly (via Broadway in this case) that Williamson somehow missed, an elaborately absurd production number from Fox's New Deal musical, *Stand Up and Cheer* (1934). 'The country's crying for hillbilly tunes', declares the head of the newly created federal Department of Entertainment, and since 'the public must be pleased', he concocts – or perhaps simply imagines – a song-and-dance extravaganza called 'Broadway Goes Hillbilly'. With 'mountain music' the latest object of fickle, ever-shifting consumer taste, Broadway – and, by implication, Hollywood – must deliver the goods, which in this case results in a surreal re-combination and re-staging of already-known cowboy and hillbilly music and iconography: poverty becomes opulence, urban turns rural and back again, as chorus girls swap slinky satin gowns for gingham and straw hats and then for satin overalls and lariats. By the logic of *Stand Up and Cheer*, the regional is a conventionalised style – easily incorporated, readily exploited, ripe for parody and jazzy updating. By bringing together Broadway and Hillbilly (and the western), the Department of Entertainment stands up for and so reconstitutes Depression-era America, creating a producer-driven, topically minded, metropolitan-based national culture capable of performing regionality.

```
┌─────────────────────────────────────────────────────────────┐
│                                                               │
│         RIALTO THEATRE                                        │
│              Columbia, Kentucky                               │
│        Tuesday,  March  16th                                  │
│   Uncle Abner's Radio Artist Stage Show                       │
│              (POPEYE IN PERSON.)                              │
│   Featuring the Farm Boys and Girls' Hill Billy Band.         │
│   Students from both schools will be admitted to the          │
│   matinee for only 10c.  Others for 16c.  Don't miss this     │
│   matinee—Tuesday at 3:30.   The stage show only at           │
│   the matinee.  No picture.                                   │
│   The picture, "DEVIL'S PLAYGROUND," and the                  │
│   stage show at the two night shows.                          │
│            Regular admission 10 and 27c.                      │
│                                                               │
└─────────────────────────────────────────────────────────────┘
```

Stand Up and Cheer reminds us that by 1934 (at least) mountain music and the rural, white South could no longer be taken *only* as sites of authentic, deeply rooted Anglo-American folkways.[3]

We cannot now know what audiences in Appalachia or the Ozarks did with 'Broadway Goes Hillbilly', but certain aspects of the local or regional movie-going experience are somewhat more accessible to the film historian. There is, to use Harold Franklin's word, the 'personality' of the movie theatre itself, which I take to include management style, architectural design, interior décor, booking policies and promotional strategies, as well as the theatre's civic and social role, or what we might call its public persona in the community or neighbourhood. Douglas Gomery and others have written on the practices and policies of first-run picture palaces and studio-owned theatre chains during the 1930s.[4] By way of contrast, the theatres I use as my examples in this chapter were small-town (or very small city) venues located in the agricultural region of south-central Kentucky, a state that had not enjoyed the economic prosperity of the 1920s before things got much worse during the Depression. My study focuses on the theatres listed below, which also details seating capacity, if known, and the size of the local population according to the 1930 Census. All these theatres, however, drew their patrons from well beyond narrowly defined town or city limits.

Campbellsville (population: 1,923)	Alhambra (500 seats)	Cozy (200 seats)
Clay City (population: 1,551)	Ace	
Columbia (population: 1,195)	Paramount	Rialto (300 seats)

Glasgow (population: 5,042)	Trigg	Plaza (1700 seats)	
Greensburg (population: 770)	Bowen	New Mossland (700 seats)	Fort Airdrome
Jamestown (population: 410)	Mary Agnes		

By way of comparison, I also examined the motion picture business in the Appalachian coal-country of eastern Kentucky, using as a test case the Family (200 seat) and Virginia (600 seat) theatres, both of which were located at Hazard, which had a population of 7,085 in 1930.

SPECIAL FEATURE

BOB and BILL SANDERS

----IN A----

Musical Program

These Boys not only entertain you with music on various instruments but will also sing

"Old Time Hill Billy and Mountaineer Songs"

They need no introduction to the people of Campbellsville as they have appeared at this Theatre before.

Those who attend will enjoy a real treat by these two Boys!

--Additional Feature--

Buck Jones

In His Latest Picture

"WHITE EAGLE"

Also A 2-Reel Comedy "JUST A BEAR"

Friday and Saturday, November 4 and 5

Alhambra Theatre

10ᶜ   ADMISSION   **25ᶜ**
Matinee: Saturday 2:30 P. M.

Local newspapers, oral-history interviews, antiquarian collections and paper ephemera reveal much about these theatres as examples of small-town film exhibition in the United States during the Depression. Needless to say, such sources are not absolutely reliable nor even remotely comprehensive. But they offer a body of information often unavailable elsewhere concerning theatre design, advertising, viewing habits and promotional activity. For example, even the relatively small collection of flyers and posters kept by the daughter of a theatre owner in Campbellsville, and now housed in the University of Kentucky Special Collections Library, vividly demonstrates this exhibitor's reliance on contests, ticket giveaways and promotional tie-ins to local merchants, and – more importantly – it helps to explain how segregation operated in terms of special 'coloured' screenings. This sort of material, particularly newspapers and oral histories, also offers crucial information about three specific areas: the civic role of the theatre, the exhibitor's booking patterns and the performance of live music in these movie theatres during the 1930s.[5]

First, there is a marked emphasis in the local press and in anecdotal accounts on the entrepreneurial acumen, initiative and sense of civic responsibility shown by hometown exhibitors. All of the Kentucky theatres I examined were independently owned and operated by local residents. Some of these venues had been open since the early 1920s, others were newly constructed in the midst of the Depression. For the most part, they were near the tail-end of the run-zone-clearance distribution system, but that fact hardly seemed to have registered with local residents, who were more inclined to admire the way their hometown exhibitors had managed to thrive in the midst of hard economic times.[6] When one theatre owner undertook a major redecoration of his venue in 1931, the town newspaper praised him for his 'brave move in the face of all the moaning and groaning. It is an expression of faith in the community'.[7] Indeed, each new theatre or costly updating was likely to be perceived as a 'distinct contribution to a bigger and better' hometown.[8]

The exhibitor's commitment to place and his standing as praiseworthy civic booster extended well beyond his 'brave' investment in the economy of Main Street. For example, in 1936 Bruce Aspley, owner of the two theatres in Glasgow, received the American Legion award for 'fine and upstanding citizenship'. Aspley, the local newspaper effused, 'is very public spirited – no call has ever been made upon him for any civic, benevolent or religious cause but he has responded willingly and cheerfully. He has thrown open the doors of his theatres for religious meetings, for the use of the city schools, for public gatherings, and even for charitable entertainments'.[9] For theatre owner Paul Saunders of Campbellsville, this sense of 'public spirit' (and good public relations) meant screening special motion-picture programmes for groups like the Parent–Teachers Association and the American Legion. Saunders also allowed his theatre to be used for meetings of the Rotary Club and the Sportsmen's League and arranged benefits for the Cancer Prevention Drive, the Red Cross European Relief Fund, the high-school band and local flood victims.[10]

During the 1930s, this type of civic activism directed towards such non-controversial goals was itself, of course, a political position as well as a way of demonstrating that the movie theatre was committed to the community at large. These uses suggest that the small-town movie theatre (which likely occupied a central spot on Main Street) carried on the work and took over the civic role filled by the multi-purpose opera house earlier in the century. 'Make the [movie] theatre a community center', declared a 1926 advertisement for the Paramount Theatre in Columbia, and this advice seems to have been followed in all the localities that I examined.[11] The ready availability of picture shows for meetings, benefits and sponsored screenings also underscores the working relationship between the exhibitor and certain primary institutions of the small town: churches, schools and service organisations. In more rural, predominantly Baptist areas, there was still substantial opposition not only to specific films and Sunday screenings, but to picture shows in general. Not surprisingly, there are also many examples of small-town Kentucky exhibitors adjusting their schedules with local churches in mind. The Rialto, for instance, made clear in its advertisement for *Snow White* (1937) that, although its contract with the distributor called for a Sunday screening, 'the time has been arranged so that it will not conflict with any of the church services'.[12]

There seems to be no question that theatre owners like Aspley and Saunders were highly responsive to the civic and charitable concerns of their communities. To what extent did the booking policies of small-town exhibitors also reflect a sense of specific locality or what could be seen as a regional orientation and affiliation? One especially striking example in this regard was the use of locally produced newsreels or slides, though it is impossible to tell just how widespread this practice was in the 1930s. The first instalment of the Plaza Theatre's in-house newsreel in 1938, for example, offered footage of the arrival of mail at the local airport, as well as pictures of 'well-known professional or business men', and 'candid camera shots'.[13] A decade earlier, L. O. Davis had begun screening his own motion pictures of area festivities and news at his Virginia Theatre in Hazard.[14] In addition, advertisement slides for local merchants and brand-name products were apparently standard components of the movie show, and, on at least one occasion, theatres in Campbellsville and Greensburg screened slides of townspeople (mostly children) and Main Street stores, in all likelihood shot by an itinerant photographer.[15]

Such instances suggest that exhibitors could quite literally localise their programming, but slides and in-house newsreels accounted at best for but a fraction of what was screened in small-town picture shows. The question remains: how much choice was available to an exhibitor in Columbia

---

Sunday, Monday, Tuesday
April 10, 11, 12

Walt Disney's First Full-Length Feature Picture!

"Snow White and the Seven Dwarfs"

Sunday matinee at 2:30

Sunday night at 9

(After the Revival Services at the Methodist Church.)

Mon. & Tues., matinees at 3:30
Mon. & Tues., nights at 7:45

Adm.—Children 16; Adults 27c.

(The terms of the contract for "SNOW WHITE AND THE SEVEN DWARFS" made it necessary to have this Sunday showing, but the time has been arranged so that it will not conflict with any of the church services.)

or Hazard in terms of selecting, arranging and programming Hollywood product?[16] I have yet to find business records for any of these theatres, but anecdotal evidence suggests that Saunders, for one, dealt directly with regional booking agents, at least until about 1940, and thus, in principle, he was able to gear his offerings to local tastes, assuming that there were movies pitched towards such tastes. Judging from his advertisements for the Alhambra, this meant three things: holding over certain films for longer than usual runs, as was the case, for example, with almost all Will Rogers films; occasionally bringing back a title, for example *It Happened One Night* (1934) or *Jesse James* (1939), for a return engagement; and arranging weekly schedules so that, at least two-thirds of the time, westerns filled the prime Friday and Saturday slots, when downtown was crowded with rural folk. In the rare instances when a movie had something of an explicit Kentucky connection, it might be held over, as when the Rialto scheduled several extra (sold-out) performances of *In Old Kentucky* (1935) with Will Rogers. Or the film might be re-booked, as was the case with *The Trail of the Lonesome Pine* (1936) – based on the bestselling 1908 novel set in Kentucky by John Fox – in January and March 1937.

For a sense of one theatre's bookings for an entire year, consider the Rialto's 1935 schedule, which included some 150 movies designed to fill three changes of programme. There were matinées on Saturday and sometimes on Thursday, but no screenings on Sunday. During 1935, the Rialto's bookings included *The Thin Man* (1934), *The Bride of Frankenstein* (1935), *The Devil is a Woman* (1935), *It Happened One Night* (1934) and *Black Fury* (1935), though the schedule was dominated by musicals, comedies, college pictures and B-westerns. The only films accorded return engagements were *Imitation of Life* (1934) and Shirley Temple's *Curly Top* (1935), together with Will Rogers's *Judge Priest* (1934) and *Life Begins at 40* (1935). This schedule seems relatively typical of the theatres under consideration here, though it is possible that there was more variation and programming 'control' in terms of which shorts (particularly serial episodes, cartoons and newsreels) were on the bill at each theatre. Judging from the bookings at the Rialto and these other small-town Kentucky theatres, it is difficult to see any striking regional or local patterns at work, beyond the appeal of the folksy humour of Will Rogers, the drawing power of patently Kentucky-related movies, and the prominence of certain genres, notably westerns. These trends are surely worth noting, though the major impression left by a survey of advertised playdates is that the film-booking practices at the Rialto and the Alhambra are best understood not in terms of a particular region or locality but in terms of their status as small-town, provincial theatres far removed from first-run venues.

In fact, more than any of the specific films shown, what stands out in the 1935 schedule at the 300-seat Rialto is that it included seven live performances, each co-billed with a regular film programme. All but one of these shows featured what was advertised as 'hillbilly' or 'mountain' or 'cowboy' music by the likes of Fiddlin' Abner Smith, the Georgia Wildcats, and the Northwest Mounted Police Company. These live shows typically had nothing much to do with the co-billed feature film. On 21–2 January 1935, for instance, the Rialto paired the costume drama, *Marie Gallante* (1934), starring Spencer Tracy, with the string band tunes and rural clowning of Uncle Henry and His Original Kentucky Mountaineers, who had also

RIALTO THEATRE
Tuesday, July 9

GEORGIA WILDCATS'
Cottonfield Jubilee
14 PEOPLE IN THIS SHOW
TUESDAY, JULY 9th
There Will Be Two Shows!
First Show Starts At 8:00 P.M.
—ADMISSION—
Children   15c   Adults   30c
(TAX INCLUDED)

appeared at the theatre two months earlier on the same bill as *Strange Wives* (1934). And, conversely, none of the material I have examined indicates that any Kentucky exhibitors tried to package hillbilly music with a seemingly more 'appropriate' movie, like a Will Rogers vehicle or the Wheeler and Wolsey comedy, *Kentucky Kernels* (1934).

There was, however, considerable variety among the theatres surveyed in how often and what type of live performances were booked as the 1930s progressed. Somewhat surprisingly, however, I found no direct correlation between the size and standing of the movie house and the reliance on amateur as opposed to professional talent. For example, soon after the New Mossland Theatre opened in Greensburg in 1937, it tried to outdo its competition in the surrounding counties by bringing in well-known country music performers almost every other week, including fiddler extraordinaire Curly Fox and Grand Ole Opry regular Uncle Dave Macon.[17] In contrast, Glasgow's Plaza Theatre – by far the largest and most palatial of the venues surveyed – favoured local performers for its elaborate amateur talent contest, which lasted for six consecutive weeks in 1936 (and was held again in 1938). This contest drew a range of different entrants: tap dancers, singers, acrobats, tuba soloists and Hawaiian guitar players, as well as more recognisably regional acts, including the prize-winning Kentucky Ramblers, a string band decked out in overalls, blue shirts and red bandannas.[18]

In the early 1930s, patrons at the Rialto could sometimes see a small-time touring vaudeville troupe or a group of local white citizens don blackface for a benefit minstrel show, and, on occasion, a theatre might book a ventriloquist or hypnotist or some other novelty act. But for all purposes, as the Depression continued, live professional entertainment in these venues meant hillbilly/mountain/country-and-western music, which was likely to be already familiar to anyone with a radio in Kentucky in the 1930s. What exactly was this music? How did it figure in the ongoing relationship between commercial culture and regionalism in the United States? And did booking these musicians somehow mark the theatre as 'regional' or complement the role of the picture show as 'community center?'

According to Bill C. Malone, the most prominent and influential historian of country music, the 1930s marked a crucial transition in this genre. What began as devalued, regionally circumscribed 'hillbilly' music became something called 'country-and-western', a legitimated, marketable quantity for the commercial music industry at large. Several factors figured in this transformation: the immense popularity of singing cowboys like Gene Autry and Tex Ritter; the new electrified hybrid style of Texas musicians like Bob Wills and Ernest Tubbs; the influence of mass-marketed catalogue stores like Sears–Roebuck (which sold sheet music, recordings and inexpensive instruments); the revival of the recording industry after 1934, with the introduction of low-priced records and the spread of the jukebox; and, above all, the immense popularity of radio.[19] During the Depression, the appeal of country music increasingly stretched well beyond its origins in the south-eastern United States; something resembling a full-blown country music industry began to take shape; and hillbilly music, in Malone's phrase, 'took great strides toward national dissemination and eventual national homogenization'.[20]

My point is not to argue with this master narrative (one that is familiar enough in the historiography of other popular musical genres and, indeed, of Hollywood) – a story of consolidation and standardisation which seems inevitably to call forth a compensatory or corrective celebration of heterogeneity and difference, as Malone's own richly detailed work demonstrates. Yet any claims for the 'regionalising' or 'localising' significance of live country music in small-town movie theatres in the 1930s must acknowledge that these very musicians participated in a commercial entertainment form then in the process of going national, borne on radio's airwaves.

For it is via radio that movie theatres enter the hillbilly picture, which should remind us that the relations across and between media and entertainment forms are crucial in understanding the cultural history of film in the United States. By 1931, 40 per cent of American homes had radios; by 1938 that percentage had doubled. The airwaves were a prime commodity, and radio became the dominant medium for music during the period, broadcasting recordings, live in-studio or remote performances and 'transcriptions' of live shows.[21] The effect on regional music was quite varied. In the Northeast and upper Midwest, for example, ethnic programming flourished, helping to promote the popularity of both polka bands and also hybrid outfits like the Minneapolis-based Skarning and His Norwegian Hillbillies.[22] Elsewhere in the Midwest and throughout the South, and eventually across the United States and into Canada, radio proved to be essential in what Malone calls 'the discovery, refinement, modification, and eventual standardization of southern country music'.[23]

Soon after the Sears–Roebuck-owned station, WLS, began operation in Chicago in 1924, it premièred its National Barn Dance, a blend of down-home music, humour and advertisements that soon became a nationally available Saturday evening mainstay for the NBC network and a programming model followed by countless other stations large and small.[24] One such imitator was WSM in Nashville, which renamed its own barn-dance show the Grand Ole Opry in 1927. By the early 1930s country musicians – not only singing, but also telling jokes, performing skits and hawking their own songbooks and personal appearances – were regularly featured on a range of Saturday night barn dances as well as early morning and noontime shows, mostly sponsored by flour, drug or laxative companies.

WSM and WLS gained particular prominence because they offered strong broadcast signals, up to 50,000 watts, as did WWVA from West Virginia, whose own barn-dance show – the World's Original Jamboree – could be received all over the north-eastern United States and parts of Canada.[25] So-called X-stations, broadcasting from just across the Mexican border, transmitted with even greater power, enough to cover almost the entire US with programming that included evangelists' exhortations, patent medicine advertisements and live (via transcription) country music by, among others, the Carter Family, who performed twice daily in 1938–40 from a station near San Antonio.[26] The growth and influence of these powerful stations – not to mention the spread of national networks – emphasise commercial radio's capacity to transcend locality and regionality as defined by, say, Campbellsville, Kentucky, Appalachia or the South. Yet, at the other extreme (and loosely analogous to the small-town picture show), limited-market radio stations featuring country music also thrived. These included, for example, WLAP in Lexington, Kentucky, which by 1938 was daily offering live shows with Uncle Henry and His Kentucky Mountaineers at 7.00 a.m. and the Bar X Boys at 4.30 p.m. All told, one estimate has it that, by the late 1930s, 'there were approximately 5000 radio shows in the United States using live country music', including about 500 'large-cast barn dances', at least ten of which were aired on national networks.[27]

Regular radio airplay meant that country musicians had a large potential audience for live performances, which usually took the form of one-night stands, always advertised with the imprimatur of the home station's call letters. According to Bill Bolick, who with his brother made up the Blue Sky Boys (one of the major influences on what would later be called bluegrass music), personal appearances were crucial sources of livelihood for country musicians, since only the very largest radio stations paid their performers a regular salary. Bolick recorded for RCA's Bluebird label and had much success in the later 1930s at small radio stations in North Carolina and Georgia. This led to to countless live shows, usually staged at rural or small-town schools, courthouses or churches. The Blue Sky Boys occasionally also played movie theatres, which required more time on their part, since the musicians did a half-hour show before each screening of the feature film. For these movie theatre bookings the brothers received 50 per cent of the total box office, after the $12 or $15 for the film rental fee had been taken off the top.[28]

The Blue Sky Boys' shows were prime examples of what Richard A. Peterson calls the 'barnstorming' practices that lasted through the Second World War. Such acts commonly performed on small, independent radio stations supported by local sponsors, and worked as many one-night stands as possible in the listening area before moving on to another station. These working conditions favoured small ensembles, often what Peterson calls 'multi-talented and sober sibling groups' like the Blue Sky Boys, Bill and Charlie Monroe, and the Girls of the Golden West.[29] In the Kentucky theatres I surveyed, however, the live country music performance almost always involved a larger group or a multi-artist entourage, which turned the show into more of a special event. This is significant since 'sibling groups' were also likely to specialise in 'traditional' (read: hillbilly or mountain or folk-rooted) music. Perhaps more important, the booking of larger shows underscored a theatre's status as the multi-functional centrepiece of Main Street, capable of meeting civic needs as well as fulfilling the demand for big-time, if not necessarily big-city, entertainment.

As was apparently the case further south, live country music performances in Kentucky during the 1930s were held at a number of different venues in addition to movie theatres: county fairs, schools, armory halls, even at courthouses or public squares. Sometimes the chief drawing card would be an 'old-time fiddle contest', which might include local talent. More frequently, these well-publicised performances relied on the standardised format of the radio barn dance, which, as Peterson notes, was quite similar to vaudeville 'because of the fast-paced sequence of diverse acts' providing an eclectic mix of musical styles and comedy turns.[30] For example, publicity photos (circa 1938) for a Columbus, Ohio show by the touring Renfro Valley Barn Dance suggest something of the range of talent involved, which included: Dolly, a 'real cowgirl' in leather skirt, fancy boots, and cowboy hat; comedians Little Clifford and the Duke of Paducah, whose outfits call to mind silent-film comedians; Aunt Idy and the Coon Creek Girls in bows and gingham; and the Callahan Brothers and Fiddlin' Slim Miller in more stock male hillbilly attire.[31]

The Renfro Valley Barn Dance merits special attention here because it was an extremely successful Kentucky-based operation that made much of its rural, regional identity. The guiding force behind Renfro Valley was native Kentuckian John Lair, who left the insurance business to work at WLS developing what was at first called 'hill-billy' talent. This included the Cumberland Ridge Runners, a group he created and managed. Lair thus knew first-hand what Mary A. Bufwack and Robert K. Oermann call the 'acute image consciousness and superb publicity machinery' of WLS.[32] Lair relied on this experience when he began his own radio barn dance, the Renfro Valley Folks show, at WLW in Cincinnati in 1937. Two years later, the show moved to a site in Renfro Valley, Kentucky, where Lair constructed a self-styled 'pioneer settlement', complete with a 1,000-seat barn auditorium, country store, lodge, ample space for displaying sponsors' products and twelve log cabins fitted with indoor plumbing and heating, soon to be followed by a small museum, stables, craft shops and more parking lots and tourist accommodations. All-in-all, the new Renfro Valley was a sort of proto-theme park with live radio shows as its principal draw. While within easy driving distance of Ohio and Indiana, it was figuratively situated deep in what the entrepreneurial Lair called the 'Valley Where Time Stands Still'.[33] Unlike other barn dance programmes, Lair told prospective advertisers in 1939, the Renfro Valley Barn Dance offered performers 'actually living the parts they play on the program', and thus audiences 'will be convinced of the sincerity and truthfulness of the entire performance, and will be apt to give additional credit to any statement made in behalf of the sponsor'.[34] Advertisers like Bugler Tobacco and the Allis-Chambers Company, manufacturers of farm machinery, stood to benefit from the radio broadcasts, the live shows at the Renfro Valley site, and the personal appearances that Lair booked for his barn-dance performers at small towns and cities throughout the region. Particularly in the late 1930s and early 1940s, moving picture theatres like the Alhambra in Campbellsville provided a prime venue for the travelling Renfro Valley Barn Dance.

Headlining these shows were the Coon Creek Girls, one of several popular groups frequently booked at Kentucky movie theatres during the 1930s that looked – and may have sounded – the part of 'authentic' regional talent. Acts like Sunshine Sue and Her Rock Creek Rangers, Uncle Henry and His Kentucky Mountaineers, Uncle Abner's Radio Stars, the Kentucky Ridge Runners, and the Tennessee Ramblers exemplify one variation on what Peterson calls 'the theme of rustic authenticity' that was formative in the history of country music from the

CAPITOL FRI. FEB. 11th

ON THE STAGE!   HERE IN PERSON!
RENFRO VALLEY BARN DANCE
STARS IN PERSON
A'NT IDY AND "LITTLE" CLIFFORD
NEW RADIO COMEDY SENSATION

COON CREEK GIRLS BAND
RADIO'S ONLY GIRL HILLBILLY BAND, SINGERS
INSTRUMENTALISTS AND COMEDIANS

| WHITEY FORD | • | THE DUKE OF PADUCAH |

JUST AS YOU HEAR THEM OVER WLW EVERY SATURDAY

| ON THE SCREEN | RICARDO CORTEZ - PHYLLIS BROOKS IN "CITY GIRL" |

| ADMISSION PRICES | MATINEE TILL 5 P.M. ADULTS 27c - CHILD 10c | EVENING ADULTS - - - 38c CHILDREN - - 10c |

1920s into the 1950s.[35] In *Creating Country Music*, Peterson argues that authenticity was imaged in three sometimes overlapping constructions in the 1930s: as the old-timer, the hillbilly, and the cowboy with a hybrid combination of hillbilly music and the visual image of the cowboy emerging as dominant by the end of the decade. (Compare the more 'unstable' and patently fabricated images of chorines becoming mountain gals becoming cowgirls in the song-and-dance number from *Stand Up and Cheer* mentioned earlier.) Impresarios, performers, audiences and media industries all participated to different degrees in the ongoing joint process of 'fabricating authenticity' and institutionalising this commercially successful genre of popular music.[36]

We can readily find this process of fabrication at work in terms of the musicians who played Kentucky movie theatres. For example, Lily Mae Ledford of the Coon Creek Girls admitted that John Lair 'discouraged my buying clothes, curling my hair, going in for make-up, or improving my English. "Stay a mountain girl ... plain and simple at all times," he said'.[37] And, as early WLS star Bradley Kincaid, renowned as the 'singer of mountain ballads', explained to a fan who was upset that Kincaid wore a hillbilly get-up for his live shows: 'the theatre people everywhere demand that you wear the costume in keeping with the type of program you give. The costume that I wore is their conception of what the average mountain boy would look like. Personally, I would have preferred to come out on the stage in a nice new suit'.[38]

Peterson is correct in emphasising that 'mountain' authenticity was but one marketable performance style available to radio musicians. In fact, the country

GENE AUTRY

MOVIE AND RADIO STAR PERSONAL APPEARANCE

And Company of Cowboy Entertainers with "CHAMPION" The Wonder Horse

ONE DAY ONLY **SAT. JAN. 15**

PLAZA Theatre
Glasgow, Kentucky

SPECIAL MORNING SHOW 10:30. Continuous Show 10:30 a. m. to 10:30 p. m.
Avoid the Crowd—Attend the Morning or Matinee Shows. NO ADVANCE IN PRICES.

performer who appeared most frequently at the theatres under consideration, fiddler Clayton McMichen, did not enact this form of rustic regionality. While appearing regularly on WHAS in Louisville, Kentucky, McMichen brought his Georgia Wildcats to, among other venues, the Rialto Theatre in Columbia in 1933, twice in 1934, and again in 1937 and 1938, playing jazz-inflected country swing music.[39] Would small-town theatre audiences in the 1930s have taken McMichen to be a regionally rooted performer because of (or in spite of) his particular brand of country music or because of his ties to a Kentucky-based radio station? Here, again, it seems to me that we need both to note the importance of live, radio-driven, country-music performance in small-town movie theatres and to acknowledge that such music in all likelihood did not always signify a certain construction of regionalism or a localised alternative to mass commercial entertainment.

This point becomes still clearer when we realise that – in addition to Clayton McMichen and the Coon Creek Girls – screen cowboys and other 'Western' acts also performed live in Kentucky movie theatres. For example, Tom Keene, the Sons of the Pioneers, and Tex Ritter and his Musical Tornadoes appeared at the Virginia Theatre in Hazard.[40] The dean of singing cowboys, Gene Autry, played a well-publicised one-night stand at the Plaza Theatre in Glasgow in 1938.[41] Making available these touring shows reaffirmed the movie theatre's prominent role in the community, a role here measured not by the strength of hometown ties, but by what looked to be a direct, privileged link to Hollywood. This connection to the far-distant mythicised centre of national entertainment had always been a major selling-point for the small-town exhibitor, who could promise his customers the best and most popular films even as he sought to mollify local ministers, shoulder his civic duties, make the most of Will Rogers and B-Westerns, and prove that there was money to be made in the midst of the Depression.

It is precisely the contradictory, or at least multiple, functions and roles of the small-town movie theatre in the 1930s that are its most telling characteristic. In Hazard and Columbia and Campbellsville, the picture show occupied a central place on Main Street (symbolically, perhaps, it *was* Main Street) as entrepreneurial business, public meeting place and community benefactor, as target of sermons and source of civic pride, and as provider of Hollywood product that was sometimes and in some ways tailored for local consumption. This picture show entered into the community's daily life to a degree that would not have been likely in the metropolis, even for the grandest picture palace. Although we will never know precisely how exhibition affected reception, I am convinced that the Plaza and the Alhambra significantly informed and authorised what their regular patrons made of the movies. And, on the basis of reminiscences and oral-history interviews, I cannot but believe that the pictures and the picture show meant something different for the teenager, the old timer, the farmer, the housewife and the African-American citizen.

As well as what these particular theatres suggest about the role and place of the small-town picture show in its home community, what may be most intriguing about these Kentucky venues in terms of film history is that they frequently served as sites for live musical performance – well after the introduction of the sound film and well into what Giuliana Muscio, among others, has argued was the continuing trend during the Depression towards the 'nationalization and homogenization of the American experience'.[42] That the performers were by and large professional entertainers, barnstorming or on radio-sponsored tours, does suggest some degree of homogenisation across these theatres (in contrast to, for example, the local musician playing daily at the same picture show during the 1910s or 1920s). That these travelling entertainers were offering some type of hillbilly/country-and-western music, which had already proved commercially viable, further complicates the issue.

Most obviously, appearances by the likes of the Golden West Cowboys and the Georgia Wildcats at small-town Kentucky movie theatres attest to the interaction between the film and radio industries, broadly understood, and to the sheer cultural power of radio during the 1930s. We might consider the independent exhibitor who booked such acts as simply one part of a radio-driven loop, who thereby promoted the standardisation of entertainment. (Such a claim is persuasive, however, only if we downplay what could have been significant differences between live musical performance on the radio and in the movie theatre and if we reject the possibility that performances in movie theatres could reinforce or evoke the various roles music had traditionally played in small-town life.) This explanation fits well with the argument, offered by Susan Smulyan in *Selling Radio*, that by the early 1930s, radio had become a commercialised, advertiser-driven, truly *national* medium controlled by a few all-powerful networks.[43] Yet, as noted earlier, while Depression-era country music radio was nationally available, it was also diverse and varied in terms of the power of individual stations, the music featured, and even the barn dance format it preferred. If the booking of the Renfro Valley Barn Dance or Uncle Henry and His Kentucky Mountaineers by a small-town exhibitor was a smart way to make the most of commercial radio's growing presence, it was, at the same time, a means of reaffirming the movie theatre's local status and even claiming – if indirectly – some sort of regional affiliation.

What has come to seem most problematic and intriguing to me in the course of investigating the ties between pictures shows, radio stations and country music is the notion of 'region' as a category, as something distinct from but related to the local and the national. Three ways of understanding the fate of the regional in America during this period are particularly germane to my considerations here. First, in assessing the 'commercialization of American broadcasting' between 1920–34, Smulyan notes that a crucial shift in early radio occurred precisely when 'broadcasters began to think of themselves as regional rather than as local outlets'. So began a process that led, she argues, to the hegemony of national networks at the expense of 'regional needs', which for Smulyan are associated with 'ethnic and racial diversity'.[44] Second, focusing more specifically on what he calls 'southern music', Malone argues that the emergence of country and western as an institutionalised form of pop music was a victory for 'deregionalization', that is, for the 'obliteration of regional differences within country music'.[45] Finally, *Stand Up and Cheer*, as suggested earlier, presents what passes for the regional – here 'mountain' and 'hillbilly' – as already merely a style, ripe for plucking and parodying by Broadway and Hollywood, more fodder for the all-consuming Department of Entertainment. Why then even bother with region and, in particular, with the hillbilly or southern mountain region? Because, even after the ostensible silencing of regional voices, the homogenising of regional difference, and the recycling of regional style, the cultural politics of region still mattered in 1930s America – as evidenced in the ongoing construction of region. If the *Glasgow Times,* in a 1940 editorial, could sarcastically declare that 'hillbilly radio stations should be so classified and given time on the programme between 3:00 and 3:01 in the morning',[46] then 'hillbilly' remained something to be reckoned with, as a type of music, a familiar radio programme format, and a category to be marked and banished. I take this also to suggest that communities like Glasgow participated in an ongoing, contested process of self-definition, wherein certain versions of the local, the regional, and the national might be actively resisted or embraced, certain lines of affiliation strengthened or cut, all at the same time. And the picture show could not help but be at the centre of this process, bringing Hollywood to town, taking a highly visible place in local civic and business affairs, and occasionally even letting Main Street go hillbilly or some facsimile thereof.

Notes

Thanks to Brenda Weber for her careful reading of this essay, to Bill C. Malone for his encouragement and concrete suggestions, and to the helpful staff at Berea College Archives.

 1 Harold B. Franklin, *Motion Picture Theater Management* (Garden City, New York: Doubleday, Doran & Company, 1928), p. 29.
 2 J. W. Williamson, *Hillbillyland: What the Movies Did to the Mountains and What the Mountains Did to the Movies* (Chapel Hill: University of North Carolina Press, 1995), pp. 37–50.
 3 For my purposes the key companion text to *Stand Up and Cheer* is David E. Whisnant, *All That Is Native & Fine: The Politics of Culture in an American Region* (Chapel Hill: University of North Carolina Press, 1983).
 4 See, for example, Douglas Gomery, *Shared Pleasures: A History of Movie Presentation in the United States* (Madison: University of Wisconsin Press, 1992), pp. 34–56; Tino Balio, *Grand Design: Hollywood as a Modern Business Enterprise, 1930–1939* (Berkeley: University of California Press, 1993), pp. 26–30.
 5 In particular, I have examined all extant newspapers for this period published in Hazard, Campbellsville, Greensburg, Glasgow, Columbia, and Cave City, Kentucky, as well as any relevant county newspapers. See also the oral history interviews housed in special collections at the University of Kentucky library. I have also relied on interviews that were conducted for my documentary film, *At the Picture Show* (1993), a look at moviegoing and film exhibition in Campbellsville, Kentucky from the 1920s to the 1940s. For information on exhibition in the silent era in Kentucky, particularly in Lexington, Kentucky, see my *Main Street Amusements: Movies and Commercial Entertainment in a Southern City, 1896–1930* (Washington: Smithsonian Institution Press, 1995). Special thanks for the superb work done on Hazard, Kentucky, by my

research assistant, Katherine Ledford, who was funded by a grant from the College of Arts and Sciences at the University of Kentucky.

6 For an overview of the political and economic situation in Kentucky during the Depression, see George T. Blakey, *Hard Times and New Deal in Kentucky, 1929–1939* (Lexington: University Press of Kentucky, 1986).

7 *Campbellsville News-Journal*, 28 May 1931, p. 2.

8 *Adair County News*, 6 January 1931, p. 1.

9 *Glasgow Times*, 4 June 1936, p. 1; 23 January 1936, p. 1.

10 *Campbellsville News-Journal*, 27 April 1927, p. 6; 21 April 1938, p. 1; 2 February 1939, p. 1; 13 June 1940, p. 1.

11 *Adair County News*, 28 September. 1926, p. 1.

12 *Adair County News*, 30 March 1938, p. 5. This sort of accommodation had long been the rule in Columbia. In August 1926, for example, the Paramount Theatre canceled Tuesday, Thursday, and Friday screenings so as not to interfere with a Baptist revival meeting (*Adair County News*, 10 August 1926, p. 1).

13 *Glasgow Times*, 30 June 1938, p. 1.

14 *Hazard Herald*, I June 1928, p. 1.

15 An extensive collection of glass-plate slides that were screened in Campbellsville are now part of the Saunders collection at the University of Kentucky library.

16 Brian Taves, 'The B Film: Hollywood's Other Half' in Balio, *Grand Design*, p. 326, briefly describes the 'states rights' distribution system in the 1930s that served many 'small or rural theaters'.

17 *Adair County News*, 22 December 1937, p. 4.

18 *Glasgow Times*, 5 March 1936, p. 2.

19 Bill C. Malone, *Country Music, U.S.A.*, rev. ed. (Austin: University of Texas Press, 1985), pp. 78–175. See also Malone's *Southern Music American Music* (Lexington: University Press of Kentucky, 1979) and *Singing Cowboys and Musical Mountaineers* (Athens: University of Georgia Press, 1993); Charles K. Wolfe, *Kentucky Country: Folk and Country Music of Kentucky* (Lexington: University Press of Kentucky, 1982), provides invaluable biographical data about performers of the 1930s. For some sense of how the history of early country music – so inevitably bound up with issues of authenticity, origination, and commercialization – is told outside of an academic framework, see Turner Broadcasting's six-hour TV documentary, *America's Music: The Roots of Country* (1996).

20 Malone, *Country Music, U.S.A.*, p. 94. Victor Greene argues in *A Passion for Polka: Old-Time Ethnic Music in America* (Berkeley: University of California Press, 1992), pp. 113–79, that the fate of so-called 'old-time ethnic music' in the United States was very similar to what happened to hillbilly music. During the 1930s, Italian, Czech, Polish, and Finnish musicians, according to Greene, became more commercial-minded and less locally and mono-ethnically oriented. By 1940, this popular 'cross-over' style – dubbed 'international' music by the trade press – had taken its place in the mainstream popular music industry alongside country-and-western.

21 Transcriptions were direct recordings of live radio broadcasts on wax discs, which could be duplicated and rebroadcast. See Susan Smulyan, *Selling Radio: The Commercialization of American Broadcasting, 1920–1934* (Washington: Smithsonian Institution Press, 1994), pp. 122–3.

22 Greene, *A Passion for Polka*, pp. 122, 149–52.

23 Malone, *Country Music, U.S.A.*, p. 32. See also Richard A. Peterson, *Creating Country Music: Fabricating Authenticity* (Chicago: University of Chicago Press, 1997), pp. 97–155.

24 One way to trace the history of WLS as it attempted to find/create a radio audience in the 1920s is through the elaborate ads (complete with photos) it ran in local newspapers. See, for instance, *Adair County News*, 28 April 1925, p. 2; 28 December 1926, p. 3; 4 January 1927, p. 3. On the entire radio barn dance phenomenon, see Peterson, *Creating Country Music*, pp. 97–117, and Mary A. Bufwack and Robert K. Oermann, *Finding Her Voice: The Illustrated History of Women in Country Music* (New York: Henry Holt, 1993), pp. 74–107.

25 Ivan M. Tribe, *Mountaineer Jamboree: Country Music in West Virginia* (Lexington: University Press of Kentucky, 1984), pp. 43–72.

26 John Atkins, 'The Carter Family', in Bill C. Malone and Judith McCulloh, eds., *Stars of Country Music: Uncle Dave Macon to Johnny Rodriguez* (Urbana: University of Illinois Press, 1975), pp. 107–8.

27 Bufwack and Oermann, *Finding Her Voice*, p. 107.

28 Telephone interview with Bill Bolick, 6 January 1998.

29 Peterson, *Creating Country Music*, pp. 130–6.

30 Peterson, *Creating Country Music*, pp. 98–106.

31 *Columbus (Ohio) Star*, 27 March 1938, p. 10, in Berea College, John Lair Collection, Box 59, Promotional Material. Note that this mix of performers was still much less eclectic and 'pop' oriented than what Timothy A. Patterson has found to be case at the WLS *National Barn Dance* and the WHO *Iowa Barn Dance Frolic* earlier in the 1930s ('Hillbilly Music among the Flatlanders: Early Midwestern Radio Barn Dances', *Journal of Country Music*, 6, no. 1 [1975], pp. 12–18). For some sense of the diversity of talent grouped under the 'barn dance' banner later in the decade see, for example, Tribe's encyclopedic survey of the acts booked on West Virginia country radio stations. Even the publicity photographs Tribe includes suggest the wide range of performers who became regulars on such stations in the 1930s and early 1940s, including rustic types, cowboy singers, juvenile and family acts, mountaineers, farmers, Indians, and city slickers (*Mountaineer Jamboree*, pp. 42–109).

32 Bufwack and Oermann, *Finding Her Voice*, p. 96.

33 Malone, *Country Music, U.S.A.*, pp. 96–7; Wolfe, *Kentucky Country*, pp. 76–84; *Renfro Valley 50th Anniversary Keepsake* (Renfro Valley, 1989), pp. 1–12; 'History of the Renfro Valley Barn Dance', in *Renfro Valley Keepsake* (1940), pp. 3–4 (Berea College, John Lair Collection, Box 59).

34 John Lair, 'The Renfro Valley Barn Dance' (Berea College, John Lair Collection, Box 1: Correspondence, Freeman Keyes file). Complicating the notion of fabricated authenticity here is the fact that, as Wolfe notes, the *Renfro Valley Barn Dance* did serve as a 'local clearing house for talented Kentucky musicians' (*Kentucky Country*, p. 84).

35 See Wolfe, *Kentucky Country*, pp. 66–95 for biographical information on these and other Kentucky-based performers.

36 Peterson, *Creating Country Music*, pp. 3–11, 55–94. See also *Readin' Country Music: Steel Guitars, Opry Stars, and Honky Tonk Bars*, ed. Cecelia Tichi (Durham: Duke University Press, 1995).

37 Bufwack and Oermann, *Finding Her Voice*, p. 104.

38 Bradley Kincaid, letter to Emma Riley Akeman (14 April 1931). Berea College, Bradley Kincaid Music Collection II, Box 13–1: Correspondence, personal 1931–1932.

39 On McMichen, see Malone, *Country Music, U.S.A.*, p. 52; Wolfe, *Kentucky Country*, pp. 89–92. A similar point could be made about another group that regularly played Kentucky movie theatres: Milwaukee-born Pee Wee King's Golden West Cowboys, who for a time had a daily 7:00 a.m. show on WAVE in Louisville. King shortly afterwards became a mainstay on the *Grand Ole Opry* (*Adair County News*, 24 March 1937, p. 5).

40 *Hazard Herald*, 13 April 1939, p. 8.

41 Soon after, Autry would be touring extensively over the United States in shows that featured one of his own films and a stage performance based on his nationally available *Melody Ranch* radio show, another step in a remarkable career that, according to historian Douglas B. Green, 'helped to bring hillbilly music out of its backwater, gave it a new life, a deserved and long-needed dignity, and national exposure' ('Gene Autry', in Malone and McCulloh, *Stars of Country Music*, p. 154).

42 Giuliana Muscio, *Hollywood's New Deal* (Philadelphia: Temple University Press, 1996), p. 21.

43 Smulyan, *Selling Radio*, pp. 7–10.

44 Smulyan, *Selling Radio*, pp. 21, 63.

45 Malone, *Southern Music American Music*, p. 85.

46 *Glasgow Times*, 29 August 1940, p. 1.

Index

185